THE POLITICS OF LITERARY THEORY AND REPRESENTATION

The Politics of Literary Theory and Representation

Writings on Activism and Aesthetics

Edited by
PANKAJ K. SINGH

MANOHAR
2003

First published 2003

ISBN 81-7304-454-6

Published by
Ajay Kumar Jain for
Manohar Publishers & Distributors
4753/23 Ansari Road, Daryaganj
New Delhi 110 002

Typeset by
Ajay Art, Delhi 110 085

Printed at
Lordson Publishers Pvt. Ltd.
New Delhi 110 002

To the memory of

Jaidev

1949–2000

Contents

Preface

The occasion that brings together so many celebrated creative writers and critics is a sad one: the tragic and untimely demise of Professor Jaidev. To pay a tribute to this rare mind—one of the brightest in the academic world—and an exceptionally fine human being, this volume has been planned. The essays in the volume including those specifically focusing on Jaidev's critical practice discuss issues central to the contemporary academic debate: issues such as the changing parameters of aesthetics-ideology interface, hegemony of the mainstream or centre and the subaltern voices, narratives of 'nations' in opposition to those of the 'nation', (ir)relevance of modern literary theory, the need to interrogate the Western models and search for alternative models, essentialism and universalism *v.* specificities and diversities, etc.

I am grateful to all the contributors for readily and promptly sending their articles and I extend my apologies to all those friends of Professor Jaidev, including myself, whose papers could not be included in the volume due to constraints of space. I am indeed grateful to Professor Bhim S. Dahiya for his valuable advice, to Dr Naresh K. Jain for painstakingly going through the manuscript and offering crucial advice, and to Professor Vinay K. Khanna for his valuable contribution in the whole editorial exercise. Girija Sharma, Meenakshi F. Paul and Diamond Oberoi helped in proof-reading and, to express his profound respect for Professor Jaidev, Shri Nand Lal Verma typed the manuscript with his characteristic efficiency and promptness.

I also take this opportunity to thank Professor Jaidev's wife Saroj, his daughter Anu and son Atul, since the gain of the academic world was the loss of the family. Dedicated to the pursuit of knowledge with the virtual renunciation of an ascetic he was so little of a family man or a man of the world, and yet a friend to so many!

PANKAJ K. SINGH

October 2001

Is, Is Not

My friend
Death cannot demolish
All those iron bridges
You built so involuntarily
Between yourself
And her . . . and him . . .
Them and
Everyone;

You spill out of
All those cups of tea
You'll never drink;

You emerge from
The cigarettes
You'll never smoke;

You breathe in
Your daughter's poems
You'll never read;

Pulsate in the silence
Worn by your son,
In the reserve
Wrapped around your wife;

My friend,
I saw it, years ago,
When you shed those fulsome tears
Before the fiend struck you
Before it fed on your insides;
It was around you,
Shadowing you
For years

Till it exorcised you
Of reading and writing
Teaching, researching,
Of all memory

Till you looked a hundred

Saw pigeons
Haloed with light,

Saw strangers listening
At the window
Hush . . . sh . . .

Till Amma and Baba
Finally came
To take you back
Into the womb of
Time

SUKRITA

Jaidev

He lies there
like a poem
unfinished, unshared.

The bouquet of earnest lines
on unquenched embers.

Silver oaks have lost a friend,
ferns along bridle path
will miss the gentle steps.

Sunset yellows happen,
so do the sunrise ones—
a chrysanthemum
on his pale yellow shawl
sways in confusion
as a shaft of midday sun
hurts his exposed feet. Now—
someone draws the curtain.

Is life a whisper that passes by?
A far-away smile beckons,
once again.

VEPA RAO

Shimla
29 September 2000

Introduction

PANKAJ K. SINGH

The evolution of Jaidev from a conventional teacher of English literature to a leading literary and cultural critic in the country is broadly indicative of the gradual shift in the location of English studies in India. In the early seventies, when many of us started teaching or pursuing research the colonial legacy was quite intact in the hegemony of the British canon in the syllabi, with only a small space conceded to American literature. With the new English literatures emerging from the erstwhile colonies of the British and the rise of culture studies, in the eighties and more particularly in the nineties the need to reframe English studies in our own cultural context was felt. While continuing to be an avid reader of world literature, Jaidev, from the early nineties, with his book *The Culture of Pastiche*, turned more and more to Indian literature in his critical practice, and insisted on the inclusion of non-Eurocentric literatures, including Indian literature in translation, in the syllabi. His excitement at the discovery of the rich treasure of various Indian literatures, which competed with the best in the world literature and which even anticipated much of the recently hyped 'innovations' in the Western literature and theory, made him give a passionate call for a 'translation renaissance'.

Translation, Jaidev felt, is of great cultural value, as historically right from the classical times to the recent colonial times it alerts us to our plural and composite culture. A creative activity in its own right, he saw translation also 'as the best possible kind of literary criticism' since juxtaposition with other works from different Indian languages truly reveals any text's interrelation with other Indian literary traditions. In the ongoing revolution in translation, Jaidev saw the true postcolonial condition as it 'has made us both self-conscious and self-assertive' since it is 'culture-sensitive and free from the colonial cringe'. Speaking about his translatorial experience while rendering Bhisham Sahni's novel *Basanti* into English, he maintained that his problems would not have been so varied and formidable had he been translating it into any other Indian language rather than English, a language culturally so alien. Translating Hindi literature into English, writing mainly on Indian works, he also simultaneously started writing in Hindi.

This is, however, not to suggest that he was an advocate of Nativism. He was open to all sources of knowledge and was well grounded in Western literary theory as is evident from his numerous articles on self-reflexivity, deconstruction, intertextuality and so on. He was appreciative of the insights offered by the Western theory but he was also quick to perceive its limitations which led him to interrogate various theoretical constructs as in his letter to T.S. Gill wherein he succinctly critiques the concept of intertextuality.

Reading or writing about literature was never a matter of mere aesthetic engagement with Jaidev. He read it and examined it for its larger relevance to the socio-cultural context. Hence his critical writings had a distinct quality where conscience was as strong a motivating force as intellect, as pointed out by Amiya Dev and illustrated by E.V. Ramakrishnan in his article. 'Pure intellect' had no meaning for him, be it in critical theory or in creative writing. It had to be located historically, in its time, in its sociocultural context, in its people. Hence in several reviews published in *Indian Review of Books* his anxiety about nation and its meanings had started surfacing—the irrationality of the gradual erosion of India's secular democratic framework, the gross materialism and 'Americanism' of our 'modernity,' the oppressive nation-state which exploits and then erases its common 'citizens' from its conscience and memory—and he saw literature as 'one of the few conscience-keepers we are left with'. This explains his valuing Mahasweta Devi as among the most important writers in contemporary India because as a creative writer she amply reveals the blending of intellect with conscience, of aesthetics with social activism.

The emphasis on location in the historical context of both the creative writer and the theorist made Jaidev deride the culture of pastiche—both in Indian society and in Indian writing which had technical virtuosity, surface spark and decontextualized importation of existentialism, modernism and aestheticism, etc., from the West, without making any attempt to assimilate or contextualize the received trends which some gifted writers have been able to achieve. His insistence on social and moral significance of theory and literature gave much of his critical writing the tone of a crusader, as E.V. Ramakrishnan also points out.

More recently Jaidev had started looking for the authenticity of 'Indianness' in Indian literatures, not in any essential sense, but in concrete terms, in gross reality of its people, places, cultures, castes and any number of other specific collectivities. In his last paper, on which he had contemplated for several months but which unfortunately could not be written—an abstract of which is presented here—he was attempting to define 'Indianness' as *mamatva*—'a pervasive motif in Indian life and Indian fiction'—not merely as part of ideological position but also as a matter of strategies of narration, controlling reader's sympathy and judgement by positing 'author-reader *rapport*' as characterizing Indian writing as opposed to 'author-character *rapport*' characterizing Western fictional mode. *Mamatva* 'rules out excessive egotism, solipsism, narcissism; it attempts at sharing, community and communication, and involves reaching out to others, usually the less lucky ones', who 'deserve not only the narrator's *mamatva* but also the reader's, particularly at the praxis level'.

It is his (and equally Mahasweta Devi's) *mamatva* for the victims, for the downtrodden, that makes Jaidev read *Doulati* as a national allegory which subjects the nation to merciless scrutiny, 'chargesheets' it, puts it on trial. In fact, it is a nation which is in dire need of redefinition and negotiation at the conceptual level, by its victims, the low caste bonded labourers and bonded prostitutes in this particular case. The realities and the sections of humanity represented in Mahasweta Devi's story are just obverse of the conditions that sustain the current theoretical globalism and hence offer a resistant discourse to counter much of the Western literary theory. For example, as Jaidev puts it, the 'postmodernist globalism' that seeks to render nation irrelevant is too much in complicity with a multinational consumerism where 'consumer' is replacing the citizen.

Jaidev's essay on *Doulati* bears the stamp of a keen analytical mind, rigorous in its intellectual analysis of both the aesthetic and the ideological aspects of the novel, reflecting profound and discriminating scholarship on the one hand and the agony, anger and passionate conviction of a political activist on the other.

II

No wonder Mahasweta Devi prefaces her two stories, specially translated by her for this volume, with the remark 'Jaidev was the only critic who understood me'. Never interested in 'academic discussion of literature' nor 'in any theory' but only in 'life', Mahasweta Devi also sees writing as a potential site of her political activism. While for hegemonic structures, be they of caste, class, gender, race or nation, literary representation has been a potential instrument of manipulating, silencing, or misrepresenting the oppressed, for the dispossessed victims literary representation is the only empowering site to register their protest and contest oppressive hegemonies. With the zeal of a crusader Mahasweta Devi consistently foregrounds the plight of the exploited and exposes the politics of the exploiters, the class-caste-gender nexus with the state, as prevalent in mythical times as in the contemporary context of the post-Independence India. 'Kunti and Nishadin' is an interrogative rewriting of a segment of the *Mahabharata* from the point of view of the Nishadin whose mother-in-law and her five sons were made to die in the fire of Lakshagriha to cover the escape of Kunti and her five sons, and who holds up for interrogation the whole practice of *Rajavritta.* Contemporary India has its own subalterns in the lower castes, the tribals, the landless, the poor and their women whom Mahasweta Devi gives voice in her writing. 'Mahdu: A Fairy Tale' is too true a story of the dispossessed 'citizens' of a 'free' nation. It is a harrowing depiction of the 'hunger', literal starvation of the poor tribals whom the nation has just erased from its memory, except as useful specimens for some, for proving certain theories about starvation and its pattern in certain groups of humans.

In India the tradition of literature engaging with social, moral and political issues is an old one, as Bhisham Sahni points out. From the medieval times, Kabir is a fine example, embodying religious devotion and scathing social comment in sublime poetry, and so are some of his contemporaries. Though in the West sometimes there has been a tendency to make a division between apolitical works depicting the inner individual world and political works about the outer social world, deriving from their larger political systems—the capitalist and the communist—such categorization appears irrelevant to Bhisham Sahni. Himself a socially committed writer, Sahni feels politics is an integral part of life at both individual and collective levels, though primarily it is the *human* aspect of any event and not so much the political that moves or inspires a writer to creativity, of which his own writings are ample evidence. As he observes, fortunately the practice of incorporating larger social and human issues so obvious during the nationalist phase in such first-rate writers as Premchand has continued in the democratic set-up of post-Independence India.

However, as Meenakshi Mukherjee points out, even during the nationalist phase when nation was euologized and idealized, motivated ideological manipulations of the nationalist discourse were not uncommon. Illustrating from some nineteenth century Indian works, she reveals how even then the Hindu upper caste values constituted the discourse of nation leading to curious contradictions in the representation of gender. In addition to the pervasive imaging of woman as mother, detrimental to her autonomy, woman was presented as unambiguously defenceless, in need of protection, serving as a metaphor for the besieged nation. She was also simultaneously the *veerangana*, the empowered woman in the resurrection of such heroic figures as Sanjukta, Rani Padmini and Lakshmi Bai. However, this nationalist project which preferred an ideologically constructed woman to the historical woman subject to pressures of her time and exalted the abstract notion of country over its people and their material context did not go uncontested even in the colonial times.

Literary textuality has always been a site of contest for both hegemonic and resistant voices. To contest the marginalization or erasures of the subaltern in the hegemonic discourse autobiography has emerged as a powerful literary genre to expose the degrading and dehumanizing practices of the establishment and to extend social consciousness of the oppressed to the reader.

Apart from the empathetic depictions by outsiders, the degraded and the despised, both in the East and the West, create their own literature recording the saga of their suffering and of their heroic survival in autobiography or in narratives giving subject positions to the abused and the deprived. Suzette Henke's paper delineates in shocking detail the ordeals of African-American slave women, their sexual abuse and gruelling poverty, in the genre of *testimonio* by ex-slaves in the nineteenth century America, and the plight of the proletariat, the wage slaves of late capitalism and industrial revolution, victims of an economic servitude beyond their comprehension, whose hunger is as mighty as Mahdu's in Mahasweta Devi's story. Harish Narang's paper in equally graphic detail presents the plight of the Dalits who are born prisoners of the caste system in a free democratic nation but who have nothing in common with the upper class, urban, wealthy members of the geopolitical nation India. These narratives interrogate and subvert the claims of the mainstream, be it the great American Dream or the great Indian Meaning, which uses religion to keep the victims in psychological bondage.

In addition to their social function of exposing the social and political injustice of the hegemonic order the reconstruction of their own personal and collective humiliation and of their survival serves a therapeutic function for the individual as well, and aims at creating an aesthetics which challenges the idea of aesthetic detachment and by rousing compassion in the readers aims at including them in the struggle for social and political justice for the abused, dispossessed and dehumanized sections of humanity. The poetics of the literature of the marginalized or the subalterns or the oppressed can never be a matter of pure aesthetics; political stance is an integral part of their literary creativity.

III

In the field of literary theory also an interrogation of hegemonic structures of knowledge, most notably of the Western theoretical constructs has begun, leading to academic activism of the sort which has larger sociopolitical implications. Bhim S. Dahiya raises a valid objection to the evolution of literary criticism towards a 'scientific system' and 'philosophical discourse' rendered in a specialist's idiom accessible only to the initiated and leading to alienation from literature and dehumanization of the human subject. Jasbir Jain and Arun Mukherjee specifically contest the limitations and politics of literary theory in the context of postcolonialism, cautioning against their uncritical acceptance. Illustrating from such widely diverse literary sources as Mahasweta Devi and Amitav Ghosh, Jasbir Jain demonstrates the irrelevance of the terms 'pre-' or 'postcolonial' and such specific constructs as 'postcolony' which bypass indigenous hegemonic structures of nation, state, caste, religion, etc., which have no less ignored or erased the knowledge systems of the powerless and which need to be contested as much as the interventions of the First World. This certainly calls for developing our own resistant and oppositional discourses.

Located in the First World academy, which privileges postcolonial theory but marginalizes postcolonial literatures and their teaching, Arun Mukherjee, with an intensity of conviction, interrogates the assumptions of the postcolonial theory-mill which is churning out 'pure' theory without any reference to literature. Contesting the stance of 'essentialism', formalism, and 'universalism' in Western literary theory in her earlier writings, here she more specifically questions the reductive and homogenizing tendencies of postcolonial theory with its discourse located in abstractions. It is a theory 'which speaks, writes and acts on its own, just like a human subject', and clubs under a smug label 'postcolonial' diverse literatures, erasing the historical and cultural specificities and pluralities of their social contexts. She emphasizes the need to test postcolonial theory in our own local pedagogical sites, in our own institutional places and practices, and to examine the work of dominant theorists in terms of their situatedness.

One way of developing indigenous tools of literary criticism could be by going back to ancient Indian literary theory and re-examining its continued relevance and updating it in the context of cotemporary requirements. In his essay K. Ayyappa Paniker shows at length how classical Indian literary theories are capable of further evolution and can usefully help us read modern literary works even by non-Indian writers such as Shakespeare, Conrad, Eliot and Beckett.

Specifically dwelling on *rasa, dhvani, anumiti, vakrokti, alankār,* etc., from the Sanskrit tradition and *tinai, akam, puram*, etc., from the Dravidian tradition, Paniker illustrates their relevance in the present times even in relation to the recent Western theoretical constructs such as semiotics, reader-response, intertextuality or such postmodernist constructs as self-reflexivity, pastiche, textual subversion or even eco-poetics, etc.

It is useful to remember that the Indian theorists acknowledged the natural limitations of any theoretical formulation and understood theory more as a 'framework for inference' rather than a stranglehold. Hence despite meticulous classifications, categorizations, subcategorizations and sophistication in formulations the classical theory is not mechanical or rigid; it offers enough scope for flexibility and evolution, beyond the core universals in any theoretical construct, in the light of the specificities of individual texts. The direction of course, as Paniker states, should be 'from theory to the works and back to theory'—a tenet all too conveniently forgotten lately by the Western academy and regretted by many critics in this volume.

Though the tendency to uncritically import theory continues in some quarters, a potential area of resistance, relocation and interrogation of hegemonic discourses both in literature and literary theory is also fast emerging. And yet a dilemma remains: the teachers of English are treading two parallel tracks whose paths have yet not converged, an anxiety often expressed by Jaidev also. The individual reading and research of teachers of English remains largely irrelevant to their teaching in the classroom. The institutional academy is still entrenched in the colonial practices of interpretation and examination, making the teachers' departures from dominant practices peripheral to the students' learning process. Does that mean our students will still have to take a similar circuitous path for discovering their own paradigms for reading and interpreting literature and theory, which are increasingly becoming sites of political, nay humanistic and rational academic activism?

PART I

Not by Law Alone: *Douloti* as a National Allegory

JAIDEV

> Law? The law is a strange thing! It stands there, on one side, but the other side shows several ways of bypassing, cheating it. It is not at all possible for the likes of Rajaram to find any relief through the law. In the Bangla countryside, the law, judiciary, religion, ideology—all have long become sellable-buyable items. With the passage of time, their value has declined like that of an aged whore![1]

For its action, *Douloti*[2] (1985), one of Mahasweta Devi's Palamu novellas, keeps itself confined to Palamu district. Most of its chief characters are quite ignorant of India, the nation-state. When one of the *bandhua randis* owned by the brahmin brothel-runner Parmanand Misra returns to the brothel with the news that a conflict has broken out between India and China, not only is she herself at a complete loss regarding the identities or meanings of the antagonists, but the aged bawd Rampiari too dismisses the whole issue, saying that the parties involved must be two rich contractors. In another telling scene, a Gandhian sadhu travels all the way from Delhi to Seora village determined to uplift the harijans. He inaugurates his mission by telling the *bandhua* labourers that since everyone, including them as much as their landlord, is the same mother's offspring, they are all equal. This scandalizes a poor washerwoman. Rajvi retorts that as most of the low-caste kids born in the village do happen to be the landlord Munavar's 'bastards', it is possible only to speak of a common father, not of a common mother. When the Delhi sadhu clarifies that his reference is to Bharat Mata, their common motherland, the villagers' faces go blank. Rajvi voices their confusion:

Oh Sadhuji, my place is Seora village. What do you call a country? I know *tahsil*. . . I know station. I don't know country. India is not the country.

Hey, you are all independent India's free people, do you understand?
No, Sadhuji. *(Imaginary Maps,* 41)

Even those few of the *bandhuas* who do remember 1947 remember it for the freedom it brought to their caste-superiors, who, these *bandhuas* recall, had celebrated the occasion by distributing *puris* and *kachoris*. 'When you people got your independence . . .'—is these slaves' characteristic and indeed most valid response to 1947.

Predictably enough, the upper-caste characters in *Douloti* are fully aware of 1947, the nation, and the new opportunities for profit that exist for them now, in post-1947 India. The novella does not grudge India or her upper castes and classes their independence, but, being about the prevalence of slavery in postcolonial India as it is, it is at pains to demonstrate that both the nation and independence have remained in the service of the likes of Munavar, the rajput landlord-moneylender-*bandhua* owner, Parmanand Misra, the brahmin brothel-owner, and their influential clients and friends. It requires a more charitable reading of the novella to see the nation as being metaphorically imaged as a *bandhua randi*, as the accurate metaphors for it here are the bawd, the brothel, and the brothel-owner.

The only functional use Douloti or her *bandhua* father can find for 1947 is for indicating the year of her birth: she was born the year following your independence'. She was sown in 1947 itself. Without going in for any pet Rushdiean equations, Mahasweta makes Douloti's 27 years a parable of postcolonial India,[3] a parable addressed to whatever/whoever professes to be the nation. The intent becomes utterly clear at the end, where Douloti dies coughing out blood in the night leading on to 15 August 1975.

Though only 27, Douloti already looks a wrinkled, sickly skeleton. Her body has been ploughed most mercilessly, but also most systematically, for nearly 14 years—for the daily yield that has been appropriated by her brahmin owners. She is allowed freedom only because she is now no longer a profit-making machine. Seeing the end, the consumptive, syphilis-ridden girl trudges homeward—only to collapse at what actually happens to be a wayside village school, still far away from Seora, her native village. It is so dark that the girl does not even know that the smooth, soft patch she has sunk upon is actually a map of India expressly drawn in colour by the schoolteacher for the following day. Soon the map turns grotesque with Douloti's blood draining all over:

In the morning at six, Mohan Srivastava, the master at the Basic Primary School in Bira village of Tohri Block, heard an uproar as he was fixing the Indian tricolour on a bamboo pole.
He came out with the flag in his hand.

. . . .

. . . looking front, he closed his eyes. His body jerked again and again, as if his arms and legs were tied and a machine-gun was being emptied into him.

Filling the entire Indian peninsula from the oceans to the Himalayas, here lies bonded labour spreadeagled, kamiya-whore Douloti Nagesia's tormented corpse, putrefied with venereal disease, having vomited up all the blood in its desiccated lungs.

Today, on the fifteenth of August, Douloti has left no room at all in the India of people like Mohan for planting *the Indian flag.* What will Mohan do now? Douloti *lies stretched over the whole of India.* (*Imaginary Maps*, 93-4)

It is from the harrowing perspective offered by the end that one is able to appreciate the point behind such apparently clumsy stylistic eccentricities as the narrator's sudden shift to Doulotis and Ganoris from Douloti and Ganori. The novella is Douloti's story—but its protagonists are innumerable Doulotis spread all over the nation. Again, the end perspective enables us to see why Douloti's story keeps deferring her own arrival into it until about a third of it is over. The reader is not allowed to just 'read off' the girl or her *bandhua* father (the character who is the first to appear in it) at first glance. They are both historically, contextually moulded, and as such intelligible only after their context has been elaborated: 'All these things had to be related to explain how it was that Ganori Nagesia became Tedha Nagesia. These had to be pointed out' (my translation, Part II; in *Imaginary Maps,* 30). Indeed, Douloti is always more important as Doulotis, as how she appears all across the face of India. In this respect, it is instructive to note that while the real-life Douloti came from Uttar Kashi in western U.P., the father Ganori Nagesia was modelled upon a *bandhua* Mahasweta came upon in Palamu.[4] It is its drive towards national allegory that explains the firm, informed authorial intrusion half-way in the narrative:

This bonded labour system prevails all over India. In Andhra the people of Matangi, Jaggali, Malajangam, Mahar and other castes become Gothi. In Bihar Chamar, Nagesia, Parhaiya, Dusad become Kamiya or Seokiya. In Gujarat the Chalwaris, Naliyas, Thoris and others become Halpati. In Karnataka the low of birth become Jeetho, in Madhya Pradesh Haroyaha. In Orissa Gothi and in Rajasthan Sagri.

The Chetty rayats of Tamil Nadu keep Bhumidases. In Uttar Pradesh the Bhumidas is called Maat or Khandit-Mundit or Sanjayat. The Bhumidases of the Laccadive Islands are Nadapu.

> *Bonded labourers are thus known by different names in different regions.*
> The system is slavery, *and the outcastes and harijans happen to he its victims.*
>
> (*Imaginary Maps*, 61-2)

It is therefore hardly surprising that *Douloti,* a collection of Mahasweta's Palamu tales, should be dedicated to the nationwide community of our bonded labourers.

* * *

The facts of Douloti's existence are easy to catalogue, and they speak for themselves. Born in 1948, she is carried away openly from her village home in 1961 or 1962 by a brahmin brothel-owner from a nearby town. Parmanand Misra has reasons to feel proud. A greatly valued client has demanded a harijan teenager who should also be a virgin! The demand is nearly impossible to meet, for all harijan girls are deflowered quite early by the village landlords, even if they are already engaged or married. Parmanand Misra fulfils his fairy-tale task with the timely help of the village priest, who, of course, is very knowledgeable about all harijan girls. On his part, Misra descends on the village claiming to be a latter-day Vishnu, a Sankatnarayan, and as such he demands a Lakshmi for his consort. In his more modern reincarnation, this god says he is against untouchability and bonded labour. Douloti is carried away by him in lieu of the three hundred rupees that he has paid to the village landlord-moneylender Munavar to secure the release of her crippled father from bonded slavery. This suits Munavar, for Ganori Nagesia is no longer worth keeping. When Ganori Nagesia's oversight leads to the death of a bullock, Munavar yokes Ganori himself to the paddy cart. He collapses under the weight, and although he survives the accident, his back is permanently broken. Hence his popular name Tedha Nagesia. Hence also Munavar's ready release of him from bondage for three hundred rupees.

Douloti is promised marriage—an incredible thing, for she is a harijan and Parmanand a brahmin, even though a much-married one—but she is at once offered to the harijan-virginity-obsessed client Latia Sahib, an influential government contractor. Latia is quite a legend in the area for two reasons. He has never constructed a single satisfactory bridge but has nevertheless remained the most favoured government contractor. And he has a seemingly unending sexual urge, thanks to his rich diet and his constant experiments with aphrodisiacs; this urge he spends only on harijan girls. He takes to Douloti and remains her sole user for nearly three years. He operates a fleet of trucks, and treats Douloti as yet another truck: as soon as her body begins to creak, he discards her and gets another harijan virgin.

Douloti is then passed on to another contractor, a Singh Sahib. He keeps her for over two years. Singh's departure coincides with Parmanand Misra's sudden death. The brothel now passes on to his son, who introduces new management policies here. Unlike his father, who showed some concern for the health of the band of prostitutes, the son Baijnath Misra believes in making a fast buck. He compels each girl to take dozens of customers every night—irrespective of what such an overloading would do to them. He is a better economist and sees that it is more profitable to reduce their rates and take more customers than to have fewer customers paying more money. Of course, the girls turn into old, rickety things very fast, but then, thanks to a good drought, the 'old cows' get easily replaced.

It is thus that even though she is only in her mid-twenties, Douloti looks like an emaciated, sick, old creature. She is discharged only when she cannot attract even the one-rupee customers; she is dying, of course.

Douloti was secured for three hundred rupees, the sum which together with some fifty rupees spent on her dress and cosmetics, was actually shown as a loan extended to her. In less than fourteen years, she has earned her two Misra masters as much as forty thousand rupees. When she is shown out of the brothel, the interest on the principal amount has not been paid off yet.

The novella duplicates Ganori Nagesia's career in his daughter. Both are *bandhua* slaves. The father had borrowed two hundred rupees—and as a result had become Munavar's bonded slave. His pointless release—it is not desired by him but forced upon him by Parmanand Misra—turns his daughter into a bonded prostitute. The system is illegal, but is practised in broad daylight. It offers lavish returns to *bandhua* owners. How acceptable, nay how dignified the practice is can be gauged from the fact that the train makes an unscheduled halt for Munavar and state ministers who turn up at Seora to oblige him. Equally revealing is the suggestion that Parmanand Misra, if only he had sincerely desired it, would have got a Padmashree! As for Latia Sahib, he accompanies all kinds of government officials to collect donations during the India-China conflict!

The novella does not permit the reader the consolation that the *bandhua* system is restricted to the countryside only. Bono, a Seora harijan, thinks he is going to be free as a worker in a Dhanbad colliery. But once there, he realizes that he is now the labour-contractor's *bandhua*. He is part of a labour gang who are not allowed to form a union, for they are casual labour. The contract labourers are fleeced by everyone, the shopkeeper, the moneylender, the post office staff, and the contractor's goons. He flees back home after committing a righteous murder. His stay at Dhanbad has not at all been productive: he has not been able to save a single penny. However, when he returns home, he is carrying quite some money. This money belonged to the goon whom he had murdered in his Dhanbad shanty. With this money he raises a *kutcha* hut, thinking that he has escaped slavery. However, Munavar soon deputes his musclemen to raze the hut, fetch Bono like a pig, and give him a sound thrashing. The next morning, Bono is freed but by then he has been forced to mark his thumb on a court paper stating that he has taken a loan from the landlord and in return has become his *bandhua*. He escapes again, but while his escape poses no threat to the system, it turns Munavar all the more repressive. In any case, who can blame Bono if he turns to a Christian missionary for relief.[5]

Relating his experiences at Dhanbad, Bono says, 'Government – unine [union] – contractor – slum landlord – market-trader – shopkeeper – post office, each is the other's friend'[2] (*Imaginary Maps,* 24). This is a neat description of how exploitation creates a whole intricate circuit of vested interests. As a system, exploitation retains some degree of flexibility. The Gandhian missionary from Delhi is an irritant, but is persuaded to preach status-quoism. Rampiari is not supposed to own a brothel of her own, but once she can do that, the system will accommodate her. Father Bomfuller's report can be a threat to the landlords, but then some cooperating officials bury it under a heap of files in New Delhi. The VIP clients apparently pay nothing to Parmanand Misra, but their patronage means safety to him. Indeed, one of Munavar's strengths is that his son occupies a high government position.

The novella shows that money is invariably thicker than blood.

Munavar has been begetting any number of children on harijan women, but these children are born only to become *bandhuas*. Like him, Latia Sahib never wastes a thought or feeling on his children from the prostitutes. On his part, Parmanand Misra condemns all bastards delivered by his Lakshmis to begging; their daily earning is expropriated by him and adjusted against their mothers' debt. There is little to choose between these high mercenaries and the Seora brahmin priests: they too regularly molest the harijan women but prefer the dark—for seeing a harijan face is considered inauspicious!.

Already it should be obvious that to talk of Douloti is also to talk of numerous other characters both high and low. The 75-page long novella contains an almost equal number of identifiable characters, besides many unnamed choral figures, whose narratives intersect Douloti's. Each such character has a narrative of his or her own, and it is a tribute to the author's talent as well as her compassion that each such narrative exists in clear outlines so that the reader can easily fill in the details. There is something truly epic about the novella. For example, Somni, a fellow prostitute, tells Douloti how she was brought to the brothel to repay by her earning the loan her husband had taken in the village.[6] She does not blame the *bandhua* husband for taking another wife, nor this new wife for mistreating her [Somni's] son. Somni, however, is trapped. Here, in the brothel, she has borne Latia Sahib three sons. They are beggars, and she spends out all her secret savings to buy medicines for them. She is allowed to leave the brothel when she is a mere skeleton, and a deranged one at that. By that time she has lost her sons too.

Douloti is certainly important in her own right, important as a tragically wasted, blighted life, but she is even more important as the site on which a whole variety of 'the Great Indian Meaning'—mythological, historical, sociocultural, or of class, caste and gender—converges to get illuminated as a set of operative, oppressive forces even as they establish a real, material relationship with her. It is in their astonishing range that these forces turn *Douloti* into a national allegory, or rather, an elaborate charge sheet against the nation.

Consider the apparently innocuous issue of names in the novella. A number of the high characters openly, brazenly project themselves as affiliated to gods. Parmanand Misra calls himself Sankatnarayan; the priest who sets him after Douloti is Hanuman Misra; Parmanand's assistant is the bawd called Rampiari. Another brothel owner is named

Kishanji. Munavar—which in Persian means the bright, the dazzling—calls himself a cream-white creation of God. This band of predators flaunt their divine connections, projecting the predicament of the *bandhuas* as something divinely ordained right at the moment of their birth. Who can blame the victims if they have got the whole oppressive mythology introjected: many sincerely believe that a tonsured brahmin actually descends all the way from heaven to declare in 'chaste' Hindi that the newly born harijan infant will stay a *bandhua* all its life.

History as memory reinforces this vicious mythology. Prior to Independence, the local prince would force the village harijans to bow down to the great ancestral swords on Diwali and leave offerings before them. The collection would then be used by the prince for gambling! Postcolonial India has seen the abolition of princely regimes but has ironically multiplied the number of unofficial, uncrowned princes. The District Collector receives similar offerings, the local police post receives its cut on the vegetables the poor harijans bring to sell on the market day. Internal colonizers have been flourishing all along.

The characters in *Douloti* are thus of two kinds: high and low. The high are starkly imaged in Munavar, as he yokes Ganori to his cart, cracking the whip. Like Munavar, the Misra brothel owners keep indiscriminately loading customer after customer upon the bodies of their prostitutes until the girls are mere wrecks or until they die. The image they use for the girls is lorries or trucks. They must be loaded to the full, must keep plying non-stop, must ply as fast as they can.

In between the two kinds—high and low—are ranged various characters from the outside. There are some crisply described as the bespectacled researchers and social workers who approach the *bandhuas* not so much for the sake of knowing or communicating with them as for the sake of proving their theories right. Unable to see that the terms *bandhua, kamia, sevak* all denote the same status, they leave the *bandhuas* in disgust at their 'refusal' to classify themselves accurately!

It is not that things have not changed since 1947. Only exploitation as a system has not faced any real, sustained threat. If anything, it has grown more and more sophisticated and repressive. In the 1962 elections, it is enough for Munavar to name his candidate—and the candidate wins. In the next elections, though, he has raised a private army of goons so that his candidate gets elected. In the town during the 1960s Parmanand Misra does not altogether neglect the health of his *bandhua randis*, but his successor during the next decade treats them as trucks deserving no maintenance simply because it is better to discard the creaking ones and obtain new ones. During the 1960s Kishanji is benevolent to his 'fleet' of prostitutes but in the 1970s he takes to selling off women and children in markets far away: the new line involves fewer hassles. In a parallel development, the state-owned collieries stop recruiting regular labour and instead entrust the task of supplying labour to contractors who treat the workers as *bandhuas* and maintain discipline with the help of professional goons. This history is the underbelly of the development story that passes for official postcolonial history.

Munavar, Latia, Kishanji, the Misras, the labour-contractor in Dhanbad, the official machinery, the priests, the Deputy Collector, etc.—all constitute the Great Indian Meaning in practice. This Meaning ropes in all kinds of motifs, ranging from Lord Rama's treatment of Shambhuk to Mahatma Gandhi's 'deservedly' violent end, to legitimize an ideology in which those who are weak or marginal not only have no means of escape but are actually expected to be grateful to their exploiters. This Meaning arguably perverts whatever motifs it picks up from mythology or history, but its perversions are more the norm than aberrations. In any case, they work!

Resistance develops to the Great Indian Meaning but alas, in spite of New Delhi, Patna, or social research centres. It develops, simply because it is in the nature of injustice to give rise to resistance, although side by side the ever more effective means of repression also keep getting fashioned by those who favour the status quo. The arrival of the Naxalites not only brings in a great number of police, para-military and military forces, but the contractors and landlords also raise their private armies.

In a scene far, far superior to the ending of *The Untouchable,* the statements of *bandhua randis* at the Misra brothel are solicited by Father Bomfuller, a missionary collecting facts about bonded labour for submission to the Government of India. The priest is assisted by four persons, each of whom is a significant embodiment of social and political attitudes. Father Bomfuller is anguished by the scale—which is nationwide—of bonded slavery, but does not believe in exceeding his brief: he is only a collector of facts. As the group enter the brothel, the owner Baijnath Misra challenges them. He has nothing to hide, nothing to be embarrassed about. The girls are his *bandhuas* and he is therefore free to use them the way he likes to. The government has no business to interfere, for two clear reasons: most government officers do keep *bandhuas,* and the low-born are allowed by our scriptures to be treated as commodities or chattel. He is convinced that his trade is above board.

Father Bomfuller is appalled to learn how an initial investment of Rs. 350 has generated a profit of over Rs. 40,000 to the Misras without there being any prospect of freedom for Douloti.

Now follow several exchanges between Mohan Srivastava, a well-intentioned Congressite schoolteacher, Prasad Mahato, hitherto a reformist Socialist harijan leader, Puran Chand, a Gandhian, and Bono, the runaway *bandhua* from Dhanbad and Seora, who is now personal assistant to Father Bomfuller.

The Gandhian Puran Chand recommends peaceful fasting to transform the hearts of evil-doers. When Bono asks him if he would have resorted only to such fasting if the honour of his own female relatives had been at stake, Puran Chand dismisses the question saying that the women of his caste are never dishonoured. Puran Chand's response is less Gandhian and more class/caste-based. One cannot expect anything more than moral support from the Gandhian. In times of crisis, he is unlikely to see evil, let alone confront it. Mohan Srivastava on his part cannot shed his faith in constitutionally elected governments.
He hopes that such governments would act and eradicate social evils.

The most crucial characters in the brothel scene are Prasad Mahato and Bono. Prasad Mahato is a harijan himself, and his encounter with Douloti and other *bandhua randis* coincides with his contact with some Naxalites. The result is that he abandons his peaceful, reformist mission, goes underground and forms the Palamu Bonded Labour Liberation Front in 1971. On his part, Bono, now an aged person, joins the group of Prasad Mahato.

All his life, Bono has been a free-floater, an escape artist of sorts, escaping *bandhua* slavery but otherwise not at all able to act except in an improvisatory manner. He kills a goon in his Dhanbad slum not because he thinks he should but rather because his hands turn autonomous and do not rest until they have strangled him. Later, the same hands find themselves tied down at Munavar's place and are utterly helpless. Once again, he escapes and becomes Father Bomfuller's assistant. All along, though, he has been reflecting, learning, and clarifying things to himself. In some ways, he is the true protagonist: for he keeps learning and changing, learning to change and to act. He learns from the outsiders how big the community of *bandhuas* is, and he imparts to them, including Mohan Srivastava the teacher, that while it is true that the harijans do borrow money from moneylending rajputs in times of marriage or other social ceremonies, the reason for their inability to pay back the loan lies in their not having any land of their own. The point is that Bono develops into a thinking being with the help of others to whom, in turn, he imparts several ground lessons.

Something similar can be imagined taking place between the Naxalites and Prasad Mahato, the organic intellectual. Prasad is wanted by the police, and is of course involved in radical activities. Still, he is clear that the battle has to be fought on several fronts. He knows that although nothing can be changed by the laws alone, it is nevertheless important to fight for just laws as well. If the laws are just, then their radical action will be for their implementation, and thus look more credible. If just laws are enacted, then there will also be more Mohan Srivastavas to support the radical groups.

Two details about the brothel scene are worth underlining. The entire scene highlights the distance between Douloti and other prostitutes on the one hand and the rest of those present on the other. The distance is both spatial and vertical, and hence unbridgeable, between the prostitutes and characters like Father Bomfuller the researcher and Puran Chand the Gandhian. It is vertical between the brothel owner and his commodities. The distance here is ideological and interest-bound, and hence there can be no question of any dialogue between them. Bono who most 'feels' Douloti's suffering, understands the language of her fingers as these gently caress his calloused feet. In spite of having lived some thirteen years in this hard place, she behaves towards him as a near kin, and offers him a rupee for tea as he is leaving the brothel. Hardly any words are exchanged between them, but they each understand the other. It is difficult to convey in words the impact of the poignant, mute interaction between Douloti and Bono.

What Mahasweta Devi is at pains to emphasize by focusing on the distance between the characters is the fact that for any resistance to be successful, the initiative has to come from within the oppressed sections. The outsiders, even when they are well-intentioned like Mohan Srivastava, or resolute and trained like the Naxalites, can help but not initiate action by themselves. This fact has another important implication: as Mahasweta Devi categorically states in the 'Preface' to *Agnigarbha,* even though the so-called Naxalite menace was suppressed, 'the reasons that triggered off the Naxalite movement remain'.[7]

Mahasweta knows how limited such moral supporters or facts-collectors usually are, but she does not believe in a rigid, exclusionary agenda according to which one is either totally on one's side or else is an enemy. A seemingly minor detail in the scene deserves attention. In spite of his correct belief that the police and the state government are on his side, Baijnath Misra does feel scared as soon as Father Bomfuller mentions the Government in New Delhi. And he allows them to record statements and also orders tea and snacks for them when Father Bomfuller threatens to forcibly take him to the police station. The moral is that if only they develop a social conscience and resolve to enforce justice, the Government and the police could effectively end so much of oppression. They have the means, only the desire is lacking. Mahasweta Devi does not have any illusions about the nation-state or its so-called democratic apparatus, but she does not wish to carelessly dismiss these.

If one pursues this route a little farther, one comes to understand Mahasweta's appreciation for those who, although they do not directly take to arms, do contribute whatever they can to the just cause, even if they do so largely to preserve or raise their self-esteem.

The above statement should not be interpreted as indicative of condescension on her part. Mohan Srivastava does not join radical politics, but he does risk his security by helping Prasad Mahato rather than the police; and in doing so, he willingly 'loses' the official reward! A tiny act this, but then each tiny act helps. Bono, who offers his services to Prasad, is much too old for any real action. Still Prasad welcomes him. He too will be contributing his tiny share to the movement.

The organic intellectual emerges from within the oppressed group. Like all intellectuals, he is made an intellectual, not born one. He is made one with the help of experience, observation, reflection. Above all, he proves to be as willing to learn from and collaborate with the sympathetic outsiders as he is to impart them his ground-based wisdom.

The most important moral *Douloti,* like several of Mahasweta's tales, holds out is this: all those who fight on behalf of the victims fight equally, if not more, on behalf of their own conscience. There is no attempt in Mahasweta to glorify or idealize the Naxalites as the saviours of the oppressed. They are deservedly the heroes of post-colonial India, but there is no suggestion that they are heroes because they risk their lives for the tribals or harijans. They are heroes of the nation as a human collectivity to which their inner conscience responds. They are heroes because they care for its dictates. Their sacrifices are sacrifices offered in the hope that this nation can be civilized, made to learn the basic lessons in human decency.

* * *

In a strong rejoinder to Fredric Jameson's simplistic thesis about Third World texts all of which he says should be read as national allegories,[8] Aijaz Ahmad has asserted that collectivities in the specific sense of classes and social formations are as relevant categories in the postcolonial societies as they are in the First or the Second World. Ahmad's rejoinder is part of an internal debate within the Marxist camp, and is actually more sharply against the currently dominant postmodernist and post-structuralist positions according to which nation and nationalism are imaginary, obsolete, or irrelevant categories, are 'mere myths of origin and essentialist coercive totalizations' (Ahmad, 12). Ahmad, like Edward Said,[9] does not see the nation as an irrelevant category—but does not allow it to eclipse the more basic categories like class and relations of production, either. Nations have often been coercive but there is nothing to stop them from being progressive or revolutionary (Ahmad, 11).

The term 'national allegory' is not gratuitous, although it makes more sense if we remember the following: (1) it is universal in application rather than restricted only to Third World texts; (2) not all texts are national allegories, although in many texts the nation intrudes through astonishingly transformed motifs and patterns; (3) national allegories are not necessarily xenophobic, chauvinistic or issued as character certificates for the nation; (4) they more often than not do proceed along specific lines of class, caste, gender, and region,[10] and as such can effectively subject the nation to merciless scrutiny, put it on trial or on the operating table, as it were, instead of reifying or fetishizing it as something beyond interrogation; and therefore, (5) it is not at all necessary for national allegories to resort to that kind of rhetoric which takes the form of: 'Ask not what your country can do for you'.

One has to be wary of many an arrogant post-structuralist exercise in debunking the nation aimed at wishing away the Third World nationalism on the ground of its origins or its having been hijacked by the flawed nationalist bourgeoisie. Whenever or however we might have turned into a nation, the nation today is a realized fact, albeit admittedly a badly realized fact acutely in need of redefinition and negotiation right at the conceptual level. The postmodernist globalism that seeks to render nation irrelevant is too much in complicity with a multinational consumerism in which the rights of the consumer are the lone consideration, not those of the citizen.[11] As such, that globalism is utterly unresponsive to all such chunks of humanity as are not market-worthy. Honestly, one sees very little evidence in practice of the First World having truly outgrown its nationalist habits of the heart. Given a crisis, it can anyway always resurrect nationalism if that would help even the so-called multinational corporations. Post-structuralist theory, like any theory for that matter, might be quite out of step with the way things really are. Mahasweta Devi depicts realities which are often the obverse of the conditions that sustain such theoretical globalism. Very comfortably-placed intelligent people can work the nation to their maximum advantage and then 'forget' it for the sake of going global: their preferred range notwithstanding, the nation continues to exist and work for them. Mahasweta's harijans and tribals are often ignorant of India or 1947, but the blows that continue to batter and cripple them generation after generation are administered by the nation: the nation again continues to exist. Theory, to that extent, is no magic wand with which historically generated realities can be exorcised.

In any case, our national victims can hardly appeal to global corporations or agencies to protect them. Their local communities are of no help to them either, as seen from their treatment by the landlord, the police, the forest officers, the priests, and so on. They get no justice from Patna. Even New Delhi sides with the oppressors. Still, all these oppressors are specific, concrete enough to protest against, to wage a struggle against. Most specifically, how many countries beyond India would be able to even comprehend the concept or mechanism involved in the practice of owning *bandhua randis?* Even if these are explained to them, how many multinational corporations would oppose the practice when such people have no status whatsoever as consumers? Even if some international groups decide to take up their cause, the remedies still have to be routed through the nation. Mahasweta Devi is realistic enough to concentrate on the concrete, instead of generalizing the issue to such an extent that its hard outlines get all but totally blurred. She always prefers to start by 'concretising the specific milieu' and then to suggest 'an entire web of social-economic relationships'.[12] The fact that *Douloti* ends with its focus on the Indian map should be enough to prove how important as well as how terrible and specific India remains for her Doulotis and her Ganori Nagesias.

Mahasweta Devi sees no practical use in abandoning national terms of discourse. She is insistent that her tales are parables of India, national allegories along the collective lines of class, caste, gender and tribe. Aijaz Ahmad is right in arguing that there is nothing unusual, or exclusively Third Worldist, about such a procedure. We all know about the 'condition-of-England' novel which continued well into the second half of the twentieth century. We also know how effectively Faulkner made his Compson family a metaphor of the American Deep South. Realism, critical realism, as Ahmad notes, has always tended to extend the meaning of the personal and individual to the public and social. There is no contradiction between the impulse towards national allegory and that towards class or caste realism.

This explains Mahasweta's fierce objection to being termed either merely a Bengali writer or a writer of subaltern fiction. She insists that she is an Indian writer.[13]

Douloti also allows us to infer another strong logic behind Mahasweta's 'obsession' with the nation. This reason is of a different order. The novella can be read as a plea for the nation to be defined by the victims rather than by the ruling, parasitic groups. The nation as a concept is not to be dumped, it is only to be saved from the self-styled Bharat Bhagya Vidhatas. There is no doubt that much vision, much imagination and intelligence, much overdetermination have made the nation as we have it today: after all, all kinds of significances from Lord Ram down to Mahatma Gandhi, from predestination to efficient management policies, from fear of hell to fear of the police have contributed to the vicious, repressive entity that the nation is today. Let the victims' alternative vision, imagination, intelligence, and culture—all their resources and potential energy which are not allowed expression or realization—be given a try. To put it more correctly, the novella is a plea for a radical change at the structural level so that the alternative vision is able to fashion a more decent, less asymmetrical India.

Let me refer in brief to two core motifs present throughout the novella.

One pushes *Douloti* towards a fairy tale. It comprises extraordinary events like a brahmin claiming to be Lord Vishnu but seeking a harijan girl for his consort, a merciless landlord experiencing a sudden change of heart, and an injured *bandhua* being served meals in hospital that are beyond his wildest dreams and being offered miraculous, gleaming pots, alas, for relieving himself! *Douloti* is no fairy tale, of course—the fairy tale effects are generated from above. So that the narrator finds it necessary to disabuse the reader of any fairy tale expectations: 'This incredible event might well have led to a fairy tale, but it was to climax in life, in a blood-stained, painful life' (my translation, Section III). In subverting the fairy tale motifs by pointing towards life, *Douloti* proves to be superior to Garcia Marquez's *Innocent Erendira.* For the fairy tale motifs are not just fantasy or even magical realism: they point, on the one hand, to a situation in which those above overawe the harijan villagers by their seemingly miraculous acts and in which, on the other hand, the helpless, bewildered harijans have no alternative but to accept the incredible disasters as part of their fate. Subversions of such motifs are absolutely in harmony with the novelist's concern for the lowly, her hard intervention in the narrative being an example of her pedagogical solicitude for them. By contrast, *Innocent Erendira* hardly subverts the fairy tale motifs, and indeed keeps turning more and more extravagant until the end.

The other pervasive motif in the novella is *mamatva*, maternal, protective regard. This motif is invariably associated with the victims, both male and female. Bono's hands kill the rapist-goon in Dhanbad, because the goon arouses no *mamatva* in him, because he does not appear to be any mother's son. Later, as Bono the captive looks at the ruthless landlord Munavar, he finds that Munavar arouses no soft feelings in him, that Munavar, too, does not strike him as any mother's son. Latia Sahib rapes Douloti repeatedly every night, and while the girl faints, he keeps devouring her, grunting like a pig. A fellow prostitute refers to Latia Sahib's orders that Douloti is to remain his exclusive possession, and concludes that she, Douloti, has secured the man's heart. This astounds Douloti: has the man a heart at all? In contrast, she goes very maternal while caressing Bono's calloused feet, in the brothel scene. It is her unrealized maternal affection that similarly makes her donate part of her secret savings so that Somni can buy some food for her beggar-children. In an indescribably beautiful, tender scene, Bono the runaway *bandhua's* life story is transformed into a folk song by the female harijan farm workers: this song has for its protagonist a lovely yellow bird that descends to the farm to pick up with its red, red beak some scattered grains behind the women; the song quietly fades into a detail about the women's children picking up grains quite like the lovely bird from above. Bono is the bird, Bono is the children. Bono, who is capable of *mamatva*, is also the recipient of *mamatva.* One has only to contrast such characters with the landlord Munavar's enormous wife, who quite candidly says that she cannot identify with anyone except herself, anyone in this case including her son and his wife. *Mamatva* is a value, although in the given order it doesn't have any; this is Mahasweta's way of reinforcing her call for an alternative structure, a structure in which *mamatva,* together with the tender poetry it generates, would have value!

* * *

This is not exactly the occasion to discuss the literary features of *Douloti,* but since the two motifs discussed above have taken us into its form, there is perhaps no harm in noting that in its superb control of sympathy and distance, in its use of parody, caricature and 'alienation effects', and in its sensational swerves between stylistic registers, the novella is superior to anything in, say, *Midnight's Children.* While it is true that Mahasweta always prioritizes her urgent human themes over form and technique, one ought not to assume that she is indifferent to the latter. For *Douloti* is a highly self-conscious text not only in its subversive parodies, its careful use of motifs such as hands and burdens, and its images of birds and beasts as well as of carts and trucks, but also in its narrational swerves and principled indirection. Reference has been made to how the narrator keeps deferring the arrival of the heroine in the story until her context has been elaborated. Such deferring, it is worth reiterating, is no mere formalism: a whole ideological, epistemological position informs it.

Equally impressive is the narrator's apparently casual but very deliberate, loaded statement at the beginning of Section VII that her story is not really about Bono's and Prasad Mahato's transformation into radical beings or about how Mohan Srivastava would help Prasad and not the police. The novella ends with a shattered Mohan Srivastava facing Douloti's corpse and the national map, and the narrator wondering what he will do now. From this end perspective, though, we realize the significance of the earlier, casually tendered information about Bono, Prasad and Mohan. In that bit of information, the last question stands already answered. There is nothing casual about her casual interventions or flash-forwards. If anything, these are a 'formal' expression of her regard, her *mamatva*, for the redeemable characters: she is not the one to deny them their 'whole' stories, even if the ending cannot quite accommodate them. I am not at all able to do justice to the novella's formal richness—a full-length study is required for that. Enough to say here that if only attended to, Mahasweta is as complex and self-conscious an artist as Faulkner or Garcia Marquez. Only she does not foreground her form and techniques as her prime concern—which is really one way of saying how superior she is to most champions of form, aestheticism and self-reflexivity.

It is not the absence of radical formal experimentation or subtle artistic effects in her fiction but the presence of a disquieting moral-political agenda that accounts for that incredible blindness in some self-styled avatars of Cleanth Brooks here which makes them announce that Mahasweta is 'no writer at all'.[14] So grotesque, if not obscene, is the formalism behind such positions that it makes one wish to throw the baby of formalism only because of the inhuman stink it releases!

Mahasweta's occasional outbursts against this kind of perversion that uses the garb of aestheticism and formalism are well known. She calls it an indicator of the Nero mentality,[15] of playing at borrowed Euro-American formalism while the nation is burning. So exasperated does she get that she refuses to defend herself as an artist, for such 'guardians' of art!

I should like to conclude this essay by referring to the seven insets in *Douloti*, each stylized, formally isolated from the main narrative, each an apparent case of alienation technique. These insets are an index of both her artistic daring and her ability to distinguish between the three distinct kinds of voices in the narrative, namely the exploiters', the victims', and the narrator's. The reason why the narrator decides to foreground her own voice in this way is that *Douloti* as the narrator's performance is acutely concerned with two all-important questions: does a non-dalit writer have the right to tell a dalit story? And if yes, then how does she go about it?[16]

There are two inset speeches allowed to Parmanand Misra and Munavar Chandela. Here is Permanand, the modern Sankatnarayan:

I really dislike bonded labour
I am compassionate, most compassionate. . . .
I free kamiyas
In the present age the brahman is the liberator of the untouchable
I am that brahman, Sankatnarayan. (*Imaginary Maps*, 45-6)

The inset speech of Munavar is long, but here are some representative lines:

. . . God has made my body and mind
With all the world's compassionate and kind cream—double cream and caramel scrapings
Each year on the day of Rama's celebrations
I cannot *help donating* a whole rupee to the poor,
I must, I must, a body made of compassion! (*Imaginary Maps*, 47)

Both these insets are made up of extravagant, brazen rhetoric and reveal the high characters' unscrupulousness and inflated egos. Each marshals gods to their side and harps shamelessly on their innate god-given kindness *(dayaluta* and *daya)*. Parmanand claims to be the Kaliyug reincarnation of Sankatnarayan, i.e. Lord Vishnu, out to liberate the untouchable bonded labour. His rhetoric abounds with references to gods and abstractions. Munavar's longer speech is in a slightly lower key, but it too is obsessed with references to God's special efforts in creating him. Being the kind of person he is, his terms of discourse privilege the divine milk and cream that have gone into his making. Mythology is invoked by him to terrorize Ganori Nagesia: the bonded labour's loans are 'the troops of blood-seeding'; each single rupee multiplies a thousand times. Parmanand's and Munavar's rhetoric is mythical, self-justificatory, and patriarchal, aimed at forcing the victims into abject surrender to their wishes.

In complete contrast to the terms of discourse evident in these two 'high' and pompous speeches, there are three songs, two directly sung by the harijan women, and the third a choral-like song delivered by the narrator to introduce Parmanand's *bandhua randis*. The first two songs are best called *bandhua* songs: they are based on a fine mix of common sense and routine observation. The first of them depicts the procedure followed by Munavar Chandela to turn small farmers into bonded labourers. The question which the winter-night song knowledgeably answers is: What has been the basis of Munavar's successful conversion of men and women into bonded labour? Put more intertextually vis-à-vis the fairy tales dealing with the secret of a monster's invincibility, the question is: Where lies his real strength?

In the loan only, it lies in the loan
that Munavar hands out—
could be two, ten or a hundred rupees
or ten seer wheat or five seer rice
How do we know what we should do—
We are left gaping like idiots all
While his lackeys, taking charge of our arms
and smearing our left thumb with ink,
get impressions taken on white court paper!
That paper is tagged to a thousand others
and kept locked in his big tin trunk.
On the strength of the loans has he become the king
On the strength of the loans has he become the government!
He is himself the *patwari* and forest officer, too,
and the police station, too, and the constable, too,
administration, administrator and the law court, too!
The day he wants to travel down to the city,
even the train takes a pause at the Chowkipura Halt
and when he sends out invitations to them
even Ministers visit the Seora village!
By giving us loans he became the government
and made us all *bandhuas;*
There's just no way we can be free! (my translation, Section I)

Leaving aside its anguish and pathos, the song is made up of hard, stark details and has no room for that supposedly higher Great Indian Meaning that pervades the rhetoric of the upper-caste characters. Everything here is concrete and authentic.

The second inset in the novella is a stanza from a harvest song. This too is sung collectively by female farm labourers reaping the wheat crop in Munavar's farm:

In the wheat farm has landed
a pretty yellow bird
and inside, its beak is so red, so red! (my translation, Section I)

The lines touch us by their delicate lyricism. They are framed between two contextual details. The first relates to the reason why they suddenly start singing: they dare not talk about Bono's flight from bondage but his daring nevertheless occupies their thoughts: 'We could not free ourselves from the landlord's grip. Still, at least one from amongst us has got away all right. Bono has escaped' (my translation). Bono stands for daring as well as freedom. The other detail follows the song and shows the women's young children each 'picking up wheat grains one at a time—quite like the birds' (*Imaginary Maps*, 22). The tenderness for the bird is an extension of the women's tenderness, their *matritva,* for their own brood. Motherhood, maternal solicitude for one's children being extended to free, sweet little birds, memory of Bono the rebel leading to a song about the free bird whose delightful sight seems to get doubled in the children's—all these details interfuse around the stanza, which, in its own right, is an authentic proof of the villagers' culture-making, creative capacity.

The third song is sung at the brothel. It comes in response, and an informed response it is, to Douloti's query regarding the status of the other inmates here. It is addressed as much to the audience/listeners/readers as to Douloti, and is in the form of the narrator's anguished but knowledgeable response to the refrain: 'Whose *maats* [a synonym for *bandhuas*] are all these young girls here?'

Douloti and Revti and Somni—
They're all *bandhuas* of Parmanand!
Working in fields, breaking earth, digging wells
are not for this one, nor that, nor that one—
Their owner has turned them into fields of his own:
their bodies are ploughed, he collects the harvest.
They're all *bandhuas* of Parmanand!

Whose *maats* are all these young girls here?
In the Himalayas' foothills such beauties in bloom
are customarily called not *bandhuas* but *maats.*

Tulsa and Bisia and Kamla and Kolta—
What about these girls? Whose *maats* are they?
Working in fields, breaking earth, digging wells
are not for this one, nor that, nor that one—
Their owner has turned them into fields of his own:
their bodies are ploughed, he collects the harvest.

Whose *maats* are all these young girls here? (my translation, Section IV)

This song has none of the flush supernatural bombast that dominates the brothel-owner's emancipatory rhetoric. It reinforces the exact parallel between Munavar the landlord and Permanand the brothel owner. Munavar would overload Ganori Nagesia and cripple him for ever; Parmanand too keeps loading, exploiting the young girls' bodies until they are wrecks. It is important to note that the song includes details from Himalayan regions where *bandhua randis* are called *maats*. Such an informed perspective is not possible to the girls or even to Rampiari. To them, there is nothing beyond Palamu. The song thus extends the range of reference for the otherwise specific, localized story.

If this song prepares the way for the national allegory, the other intervention by the narrator—in hard, factual prose—makes the reader grasp the logic of the nationwide phenomenon. The kind of perspective and analytic skill seen in it are offered to the reader as a necessary bit of social instruction.

To the reader, I repeat. For the intervention comes in the wake of her fierce rebuttal of what the social scientists dole out as the neat, well-footnoted explanations of the *bandhua* practice. The narrator sums up their whole approach: they come to research the phenomenon and end up laying the blame on the victims themselves. She refers to the hard facts which no sociologist gives: facts relating to the various dalit sections in Palamu and for how little money and food the 'upper-caste people would make these starving masses their slaves'. The part is caustic towards the methodological sleight-of-hand used by social researchers who 'would tour the district for statistics and then conclude that all these sections had become bonded labourers only because of hassles connected with marriage and religious rituals, thus carefully avoiding any mention of the fact that all those whom the landlords made their slaves were invariably small farmers' (my translation, p. 49).

Having countered this motivated social research, the narrator now offers the following inset intervention. Its tone is blistering, dangerous; it remains unfinished in a most ominous way:

All such scholars need Government support and the Government needs the support of landlords! Landowning-moneylenders are a neo-landlord caste—and this caste has been created by the Government of Independent India. This Government needs the support of landowning-moneylenders, for what are Bhilai and Bokaro and Jamshedpur after all? Nothing, their contribution is really nothing to the Government purse. The Government exchequer is sustained by agriculture land, and that land has landlords for its real rulers! These princes and rulers of agriculture and land need free labour and free land, that's why they come out like warriors and turn people into bonded slaves and servants and labourers. But really uncovering and publishing such facts is illegal, because . . . .

(my translation, Part III)

The unfinished passage is a case of Brechtian alienation technique, especially since it supplies a larger structural perspective to the specific patterns of exploitation in evidence in Palamu. It is also the most unambiguous indictment of the government for its complicity with, and encouragement of, the neo-princes and neo-rulers. Finally, the last, unfinished sentence posits a conscientious, truth-telling writer against the entire state apparatus. The abrupt termination of her sentence offers a kind of irony Mahasweta absolutely loves: apparently stopping her radical, subversive outburst because it is illegal, but really stopping not until she has performed a total demystification of the nation-state. By implication, if such seething demystifications strike some critics as unaesthetic, well, the need is to modify our aesthetics rather than to declare her a persona non grata in the republic of letters.

What this hard-hitting inset reveals is a macro-perspective, an understanding of the structural logic, which is not available to the harijan characters for self-evident reasons. For less acceptable reasons, that kind of a perspective is often not available to the literate, supposedly knowledgeable sections of our privileged population, either. The inset is nothing less than a rebuke to them. This perspective is offered in the hope that they would review their location vis-à-vis both the nation and its victims. It is offered in the hope that they will undergo the necessary, humanizing change of heart and develop some ethical responsibility, some love for the victims.[17]

There is, of course, absolutely no suggestion in the novella that there is anything to stop the harijan characters from getting wise to the overall national logic; indeed, it becomes available to Prasad Mahato towards the end and, through him, to Bono. Still, Prasad Mahato obtains it with the help of the Naxalites; Bono with the help of Father Bomfuller and Prasad and the Naxalites. It is, in other words, not by rejecting all outsiders as dangerous or treacherous but by establishing a dialogue with them on honourable terms that perspectives are enlarged and true enemies isolated. Here, there is need to add that Father Bomfuller's facts alone would not allow such a perspective: for he is not at all willing to exceed his brief. His report is perhaps better than the hired sociologists' theses, but it is not sufficient at all. That is how, one may argue, Mahasweta justifies her own position as an interpreter of, a spokesperson for, her *bandhua* friends. The effort is to be of some use to them, not just because it is a good cause, but because this is the only way for her to justify herself. The need is her own even before it is theirs.

* * *

Mahasweta Devi is the most disturbing writer India has ever produced. She is also our most necessary writer, simply because she lashes us out of complacence in the way conscience is supposed to do. It is important to remember that she is not only a writer. In her case there is no division between the artist who creates and the person who suffers, and works for ensuring justice to the sections who have long been victims, among others, of an appalling national ingratitude. What her life and her fiction demonstrate beyond question is the possibility of a non-dalit, middle-class person to earn the right to write the dalit. But there is no easy route to such a right. It is not even claimed as a right; nor is it earned by dissolving one's own identity as a non-dalit or a middle-class person. One remains what one is: and then one acts, in life and through one's writing, to legitimize one's existence as a decent, socially conscientious, thinking being. The rest takes care of itself, for any effort to preserve one's conscience leads one away from one's cosy class, hurries one down to the victims, and pushes one against the numerous structures of torture that are the badges of identity for our nation. To cling to any dehistoricized, universalist formalism while reading Mahasweta is only to highlight one's own Nero-like location rather than to say something sensible about her art.

NOTES

1. Mahasweta Devi, *Gram Bangla*, trans. Dr Maheswari (Hindi) (New Delhi: Radhakrishna, 1985), p. 90. The English translation is mine.
2. *Douloti* is available in both Hindi and English translations. The Hindi translation, by Dilip Kumar Bannerjee, is included in a collection of three of Mahasweta

Devi's Palamu tales entitled *Douloti* (New Delhi: Radhakrishna, 1987), pp. 9-95; the English translation, by Gayatri Chakravorty Spivak, is titled 'Douloti the Bountiful' and is included in Mahasweta Devi, *Imaginary Maps* (Calcutta: Thema, 1993), pp. 19-95. I find the Hindi translation more reliable, but for quotations in this paper I have mostly adapted Spivak's. I have italicized all those words in quotations which I have substituted in place of Spivak's. Among the more important substitutions, I have kept the Tedha Nagesia of the original, instead of Spivak's Crook Nagesia, for Ganori Nagesia after he is rendered misshapen and crook-backed.

3. Cf. Mahasweta Devi: 'The Palamu I have depicted in my stories . . . is a mirror of tribal India', and 'I have named the village Seora. But there are such villages everywhere in Palamu. . . . Douloti is still true, and true for the rest of India. . . . Decolonization has not reached the poor. That is why these things happen. Women are just merchandise, commodities. . . . For the flesh trade all you have to invest is two saris, a bit of food, some trinkets, and a bit of money for the parents. Poverty, poverty, poverty.' *Imaginary Maps,* pp. iv, xiii-xiv.

   Also cf. Palamu: 'Any number of terms exist for the bandhuas—sevakia, kamia, harwaha, charvaha, etc. Such is the custom that they remain in lifelong debt. Of these, the lot of dharmaru bandhuas is the most pitiable. Palamu is a place where anything goes. In itself Palamu is a microcosm of India.' *Douloti* (Hindi), p. 117.

   Also cf. Mahasweta: 'Using Palamu as an example, I have revealed again and again the exact shape of India's landowning system and feudal class divisions.' 'Bhumika', *Rudali* (Bengali) (Calcutta: Dey's Publishing, 1993), p. 5.

4. For factual details relating to Douloti and Ganori Nagesia, see Mahasweta Devi and Nirmal Ghosh, *Bharat Mein Bandhua Mazdoor*, trans. Anandswarup Verma (Hindi) (New Delhi: Radhakrishna, 1981), pp. 121, 90; these details are also available in 'The Author in Conversation' (1991), Mahasweta interviewed by Gayatri C. Spivak, *Imaginary Maps,* pp. xiii-xiv. I reproduce her words:

   [The bonded labour system is] extremely common in the Himalayan district of Uttar Kashi. Women after or before marriage are taken away when husband or father has borrowed money from the money-lending upper caste. They are taken straight to brothels in the big cities to work out that sum. And the sum is never repaid because the account is calculated on compound interest. . . . I saw Crook Nagesia with my own eyes in the month of June, just before the rainy season. Palamu has very little rainfall. Under the burning sun the landlord loads the bullock cart with paddy and tells the man to pull the cart to the local market. He could not do it. He fell under it. He was crushed. He became twisted and crooked for the rest of his life. The landlord offered me a glass of milk with sugar-cane crystals. He was trying to please me. 'You are an upper-caste person,' he said. 'These bullocks are costly. If I send a bullock, it will suffer in the heat and it might collapse. But these bonded labourers do not count for much. A man can be wasted, a bullock cannot.' This was his argument, the perennial argument, after all, for sweating 'cheap labour' rather than use costly machines. (*Imaginary Maps*, p.xiii)

5. The text does not specifically state that Bono becomes a Christian. However, it is probable that both he and his family convert to Christianity. He is subsequently seen in the employ of Father Bomfuller, who is collecting data on bonded labour in India. Also, the very fact that Bono has set up a small shop for his son indicates that he is no longer in fear of being captured by Munavar. In a hair-raising scene, an inmate of the Misra brothel goes mad following the death of her beggar sons, but continues to pine for famine. She had been led to believe that with the arrival of famine her children would be received by the local Christian mission. Apparently, famine struck the area a little too late. The novella also describes the arrival of an educated priest in Seora village to assuage the superstitious fears of Munavar. This priest preaches communalism and exhorts the harijans to oppose cow-slaughter, but endorses the practice of *bandhua* labour. Another priest uses religion and mythology to ensure that the backs of the *bandhuas* are broken for good. In *Douloti* Mahasweta Devi does not contrast the operations of Christian missions and of Hindu fundamentalist organizations, but the Christian mission is seen as one possible refuge for the desperate. In several of her tribal novels, notably in *Aranyer Adhikar*, while the interface of Christian missions and colonial rule is stressed, the tribals' tactical—and temporary—conversion is also recorded with approval. In *Pterodactyl*, which is set in post-Green Revolution Madhya Pradesh, business considerations underlie the Hindutva inspired developmental lure offered to the tribals.
6. At the seminar on 'Black and Dalit Writings—Some Recent Trends' (IIAS, Shimla: 14-17 October 1997), where this paper was presented, one of the participants, Kunwar Prasun, narrated the first-hand details he had gathered about Douloti. He was also witness to her death—in circumstances different from those given in *Douloti*. The original Douloti, he said, had been taken to Meerut for prostitution by her husband himself—this being the only available way for him to escape *bandhua* life. Clearly, some of the details relating to Somni and the novella also belong to Douloti herself.
7. Mahasweta Devi, 'Preface' to *Bashai Tudu, trans.* Samik Bandyopadhyay (Calcutta: Thema, 1990), p. xvi.
8. Fredric Jameson, 'Third World Literature in the Era of Multinational Capitalism'. *Social Text*, 15 (Fall 1986); Aijaz Ahmad, 'Jameson's Rhetoric of Otherness and the "National Allegory" ' (1987) rpt. in Ahmad, *In Theory: Classes, Nations, Literatures* (London: Verso, 1993), pp. 95-122, esp. pp. 102, 107, 110, 112-22; see also Ahmad's remarks in 'Introduction: Literature Among the Signs of Our Time', pp. 11-12.
9. See Edward Said, *Culture and Imperialism* (London: Chatto & Windus, 1992), pp. 256 ff.
10. Cf. Gayatri C. Spivak on 'Standayini': 'Here the representation of India is by

way of the subaltern as metaphor.' ' "Breastgiver": for author, reader, teacher, subaltern, historian. . .' in Mahasweta Devi, *Breast Stories,* trans. Spivak (Calcutta: Seagull, 1997), p. 79. Also cf. Mahasweta Devi: '"Standayini" is a parable of India after decolonisation.' Unpublished intervention, Subaltern Studies Conference, Calcutta, 9 Jan. 1986, quoted in ibid., p. 78.

11. I am indebted to Javed Alam for this insight.
12. Malini Bhattacharya, 'Mahasweta Devi: Activist and Writer', *Economic and Political Weekly,* 10 May 1997, p. 1004.
13. 'Mahasweta Devi: In Conversation with Amar Mitra and Sabyasachi Deb,' *Indian Literature,* No. 179 (May-June 1997), p. 163.
14. N.S. Jagannathan refers to a supercilious anonymous critic being quoted in an article, on Mahasweta published in *Desh* to the effect that 'we don't consider Mahasweta Devi a writer at all'. 'The Chronicler of Suffering', *The Indian Express,* magazine section, 8 June 1997, p. 4. Jagannathan generously, in a gentlemanly fashion, tries to 'invent' some reason for such a perverted judgement. My feeling is that instead of searching for a reason behind this, it is better dismissed as evidence of 'critical' madness unleashed by politically convenient posturing.
15. Cf. Mahasweta Devi: 'While nobody cares to pay heed to [the landless agricultural labourers'] claims to the right to survive, the hired writers pandering to the middle and upper classes content themselves with weaving narcissistic fantasies in the name of literature. When Rome burnt, Nero fiddled. . . . For a long time now, Bengali literature has indulged in a denial of the reality and has been plagued by an atrophy of conscience. . . . At a critical historical point like this, a conscientious writer has to take a firm stand in defence of the exploited. Otherwise there is no way that history would absolve him or her.' Preface to *Bashai Tudu,* pp. xvii-xviii. Also cf. Mahasweta's 'tired' admission: 'To all such people who say that from the literary point of view, my writing has declined in quality, or that in "Operation? *Tudu" [Bashai Tudu]* and "Standayini" [Breast-giver], I am a failure in terms of style and technique—my humble submission is that I am no longer very interested in stylistic virtuosity.' Preface to *Gram Bangla.,* p. 10.
16. These questions trouble a great many concerned non-dalit citizens. Gayatri C. Spivak argues that there is nothing wrong at all in a non-dalit speaking on behalf of the subalterns—since unlike their ontology, which belongs to themselves, their epistemology might often be accessible only to a specialist. I feel ambivalent, indeed quite sceptical, about this otherwise very attractive distinction. See my 'This Fiction is Injurious to Illusions', *Indian Review af Books*, 16 June-15 July 1997, pp. 4 ff.
17. The most poignant expression of this hope is in "Pterodactyl, Puran Sahay and Pirtha'. Cf. Puran: 'To build [the communication-point with the tribals] you must love beyond reason for a long time. For a few thousand years we haven't loved them, respected them. . . . Only love, a tremendous excruciating, explosive

love can still dedicate us to this work when the century's sun is in the Western sky, otherwise this aggressive civilization will have to pay a terrible price, look at history, the aggressive civiliztion has destroyed itself in the name of progress, each time'. *Imaginary Maps*, p. 197. Gayatri C. Spivak's useful term for this love is 'ethical responding—a two-way road', p. 206.

On Intertextuality: I

5 May 1991

Dear Professor Gill

Thanks very much for sending me a copy of your paper on Lorca and G. Marquez. I find it quite convincing—and there seems to me no doubt that G.M. probably was keeping Lorca's play [*Blood Wedding*] as a text for subversion—of course, for his own Latin American purposes. I read the texts quite a while ago, but I remember *Chronicle*, like *No One Writes to the Colonel* before it, had a sort of Faulknerian readiness about the view of society. It looked absurd, wonderfully, operatically formed though it was. The humour of it all was sardonic, wry—for, in spite of everything, the death occurred—so unnecessarily. If I remember correctly at all, the murderers were extremely clumsy, and the way the hero comes with his entrails in his hands was grotesque. The sense of significance was missing—so that formal significance was almost a compensation. Lorca, on the other hand, was all too confident of making it an epic—everything looked sharp-coloured, brilliant, tragic. Perhaps tragedy is what Latin America denies itself, so futile is the society around the hero. This 'renewal' and reworking of the tragic mode has struck me as symptomatic. It is this cultural/political transformation of society (and it is amazing how little people actually *do* in G.M.—though it is explainable in historical terms) that tells us about the difference between Lorca's and G.M.'s texts. Of course, all this you have brought out very well in your paper. I was also reminded of a romantic transformation of Lorca's theme by Tennessee Williams in *The Rose Tattoo*, which of course also has several other texts for its sources, also perhaps *Desire Under the Elms*.

I am sure the term intertextuality has its abuses as well as uses. I do not find every text being an intertext a terribly helpful, practical suggestion. On the other hand, mere source-hunting is not always worthwhile. It is exactly this kind of cultural-social translation that enables us to read a new text purposively. Allow me please to add this, though, that whether a text is an intertext in relation to an oral tale or a written text does not seem to me to matter all that much. Intertexts can form across genres, mediums (drama, cinema↔fiction), translations, etc. Some years ago I published a rather amateurish essay on Intertextuality/ Influence, and my problems were the following:

(1) Intersubjectivity *v.* Intertextuality; or the reader's transference of his or her readings to a text and seeing the latter as an intertext.
(2) A huge number of texts being intertexts to a single text—these texts including political, historical, social, cultural, literary discourses—.
(3) A text claiming somehow the status of an intertext—and asking the reader to treat it as one.

(i) The first situation is inescapable, but may lead towards arbitrary anarchy. Deconstruction will not mind it, but common sense resents it. Your essay is a legitimate exercise because there are any number of factors supporting the comparability of the texts: the same language, religion, culture, political sympathies, etc. But intersubjectivity, if left to itself and with no constraints of boundaries and legitimacy, can turn everything into an intertext with regard to everything else. This caution, I feel, is the casualty in Deconstruction and Difference and Nietzschean eternal returns.

(ii) Intertext can be an excuse for discounting the author himself, for a text writes itself. The writer's (and through him of time, history, ethos, etc.) intervention should not be devalued.

(iii) The critic should be able to suggest how many texts there are behind or under or in a text. Interesting perhaps, I discovered a whole Chinese Box of intertextuality, for the text led to another which led to yet another. It is inter-text but also inter-inter-inter-text—. Again, I think, purposiveness in the critic will justify delimitation—and of course, delimitation is a virtue—for focus and clarity. This is where I find your essay helpful; an essay which just confuses the reader by piling up text after text for merely suggesting the multiplicity of texts loses purpose.

(iv) Finally, the most tricky aspect was: how do we recognize a text for an intertext? To this day, I am not too clear on this. In a clumsy way, I had dared to plead for a radical re-definition of Julia Kristeva's term and suggested that an intertext be regarded as an incomplete/un-independent text—a text whose meaning would not be available in its entirety until and unless it was read together with the other text. You see, I was struggling to differentiate between local matters like allusions or echoes or more extended matters like influence (*à la* Bloom) on the one hand and intertextuality on the other. Intertextuality announces itself—not always overtly, but always in some way to a competent reader—or sends him or her to an/other text/s. There were further problems—for such 'signals' could be mere pretentiousness/name-dropping. But they legitimated the critical search, the test being how and in what fields the text tied itself to another. If I am a bit frustrated in my tone, this is because so often intertextuality and comparative literature have been burdened with discoveries of relations between texts on ridiculous grounds—commonality of wives in five novels, etc. A very narrow reading, a refusal to look for meaningful relations, have led to a situation when any two chapters in a thesis, discussing two individual novels separately, pass for C.L.

But already, I am afraid, I have disgressed too much. It was good reading this paper. I think Lorca and G.M. will deserve even an extended study—for surely Lorca is part of G.M.'s literary and cultural heritage.

With finest regards

Yours sincerely

JAIDEV

On Intertextuality: II

Lorca's Hispanic Motifs in Màrquez

TEJWANT S. GILL

Intertextuality is a specific mode, particularly in the later fiction of García Márquez. As a result, *Chronicle of a Death Foretold* and *Love in the Time of Cholera* seem rich intertexts vis-à-vis *Autumn of the Patriarch* and *One Hundred Years of Solitude* which for that matter are dense texts. Márquez himself vouchsafes this distinction when in various contexts he holds that into his earlier fiction have gone varied elements from oral tales which as a child he heard from the women nurturing him. In the later fiction, as goes his candid confession, have gone elements from the written texts which he studied in the course of his growth as a writer.

His view projects a veritable distinction between the text and the intertext before which what Roland Barthes holds looks rather hypothetical. Contending that 'any text is an intertext', Barthes discounts its reduction to 'sources and influences'. He underlines it as 'a general field of anonymous formulae whose origins can scarcely even be located, of unconscious or automatic quotations, given without quotation-marks'.

After such a view of the intertext, Barthes attempts a purview of it. In this regard he holds: 'The concept of the intertext is what brings to the theory of the text the volume of sociality: the whole of language, anterior or contemporary, comes to the text, not following the path of a discoverable filiation or a willed imitation but that of dissemination—an image which makes sure the text has the status not of a reproduction but of a productivity'.[1]

As Barthes' definition proceeds, the text replaces/displaces the intertext, showing thereby that what is valid for one cannot be invalid

*Excerpts from the paper published in *Estudios de Hispanismo Contemporaneo* (New Delhi, 1990).

for the other. For him the production of a volume of sociality through language of dissemination is as much the forte of the text as of the intertext. Both get identical because the single perspective exercised on the one does not get double when shifted to the other. The double perspective on the other hand is likely to show that oral or pheno texts do get into the text but it is in fact the intertext that becomes a field for written or geno texts.

The later fiction of García Márquez forwards such a field of intertextuality. It is a different matter though that the attention awarded so far to its textuality has tended to obscure its veracity. Even so remarkable a critic of literature as Edward Said is disposed to confine his attention to textuality when in a passing comment he notes that in story-telling, Márquez is concerned not with a story but with the telling of it. Thus goes Said's actual comment: 'To write a novel or a story thus as in the case of fabulists like Borges, Pynchon and García Márquez, is a desire to *tell* a story much more than it is one for telling a *story*.'[2] While underlining the novelty of Márquez's narrative technique, Edward Said is at the same time disposed to overlook the veracity of his intertextual practice with which otherwise it is vitally interrelated. Only a recognition of this interrelation is likely to bring home the fact that Márquez's narrative technique is a complex not of formal but formative devices.

To get on with all this, García Márquez reverses and renews motifs from the continental writers in general and the Hispanic writers in particular. This becomes evident from the reversal-cum-renewal in *Chronicle of a Death Foretold* of motifs drawn from García Lorca's poetic play *Blood Wedding*. Though an integral aspect of his technique, reversal is not a deconstruction of the sort that marginalizes the central motif, i.e. the leitmotif, and centralizes the subsidiary motifs lurking at the margins, or renders the present motifs as absent and the absent motifs as present. Rather than observe Derrida's paradigm of deconstruction that seeks to perform this dual function, Márquez attempts a spatial displacement that, for the reversal aspect of his technique, is formal and not formative. Likewise, renewal as an integral aspect of his technique is not bound to observe decline of the historicity as its essential paradigm. In this regard it marks a departure from the paradigm so assiduously worked out in *Anti-Oedipus* by Deleuxe, for example. Inclusion or exclusion of the formal type, advocated so vigorously by Foucault as directive principle for discourse-formation, is not acceptable to its formative nature either.

The closest Márquez's category gets in orientation is what Antonio Gramsci has termed 'elaboration' seeking to explain 'how it happens that in all periods there co-exist many systems and currents of thought, how these currents are born, how they are diffused and why in the process of diffusion they fracture along certain lines and in certain directions'.[3] Thus reversal-cum-renewal tends to recognize subordinating, fracturing, diffusing and re-producing as much as producing, uniting, gathering and enhancing as the essential aspects of Márquez's mode of intertextuality.

Seen from this perspective, *Chronicle of a Death Foretold* seems to produce all the motifs of (a) marriage, (b) virginity, (c) fidelity, (d) fecundity, (e) murder, and (f) mourning, celebrated with so much of poetic intensity in Lorca's *Blood Wedding*.[4] In the course of this production, he does not resort just to their reproduction because the method he employs is of reversal-cum-renewal along with the varying and varied aspects entailing it. Lorca portrayed marriage as an event deemed for the perpetuation and prosperity of family life. In portraying it so, he associated with marriage all the residual feelings nurtured for it in the Spanish ethos and culture.

* * *

From Lorca's *Blood Wedding* Márquez produces marriage as a leitmotif in *Chronicle of a Death Foretold*.[5] Of course he reorientates its norms so as to award it the horizontal dimension of Latin American ethos and culture. Unlike Spain, the enclosed country of self-enclosed people, Latin America is a vast land of natural diversity. Upon its terrain have settled people of ethnic variety, cultural heterogeneity, linguistic plurality and religious multiplicity . . . without national unity of the comparable sort.

* * *

Both these marriages [in *Chronicle of a Death Foretold*], one that materializes only to get dissolved immediately after [Bayardo San Romáhas and Angela Vicario] and the other that does not materialize at all [Santiago Nasar and Flora Miguel], are in impulsion unlike the marriage that in Lorca's *Blood Wedding* is not consummated on account of Bride's elopement.

This unlikeness is significative of the difference between the self-enclosed national culture and ethos of Spain and the dismembered and heterogeneous life of Latin America regarded as cultural diversity without national unity. The likeness they reflect is in respect of murders marking their denouements. The ways of their execution are, with multiple associations, reflective of their chronoscopes—Mikhail Bakhtin's term for 'the intrinsic connectedness of temporal and spatial relationships that are artistically expressed in literature'.[6]

In Lorca's *Blooding Wedding,* the murder of Bridegroom and Leonardo by each other comes as a cataclysmic ending. Apart from the fact that Leonardo belongs to a family of murderers, he is the sort of man whom the murderous instinct impels on to terminate only with his own death.

* * *

As a result of bequeathing possible absurdity, Nasar's murder occasions a lot of shock amongst the people. Such is the paradoxical nature of this shock that there is no mourning, not even by his mother, to which may accrue natural or cosmic proportions. Its remnants lurk in the memory of the people even two decades after its occurrence. But to recall it in all its exactness is 'to put the broken mirror of memory back together from so many scattered shards' (*Chronicle of a Death Foretold,* p. 5). Shades of vagueness and confusion have overlaid the memory even of his mother for whom he, according to her confession, was the man in her life. Such is the trajectory that human memory is likely to cover in general but particularly so in the life and culture of Latin America where cultural diversity is yet to cultivate national unity of the comparable sort.

What Márquez seeks to achieve through this intertextual practice seems fair enough. It is to project against universal background of the formative and not the formal sort, the Latin American energy capable of encountering the world. What is even more valuable is the enormous cultural heritage, the multi-sided primordial matter penetrating this social reality. It signifies the culture of rebellion that with all its ambivalences, breaks, ruptures and disorientations is presented in *Chronicle of a Death Foretold.* Its purpose is to win not only the present of Latin American ethos but also the past of Spanish tradition which it has to encounter and challenge.

NOTES

1. Roland Barthes, 'Theory of the Text', included in *Untying the Text*, ed. and introduced by Robert Young (London: Routledge and Kegal Paul, 1981), p. 39.
2. Edward Said, *The World, the Text and the Critic* (Cambridge, Mass.: Harvard University Press, 1983), p. 123.
3. Antonio Gramsci, *Selections from Prison Note Books*, trans. and ed. Quinton Hoare and Geoffey Nowell Smith (London: Lawrence and Wishart, 1971), p. 327.
4. Federico García Lorca, *Blood Wedding* (1933), *Three Tragedies*, trans. James Graham-Lujan and Richard L. O'Connell (Harmondsworth: Penguin Books, 1961, rpt. 1984). All textual quotations from *Blood Wedding* are from this book.
5. Gabriel García Márquez, *Chronicle of a Death Foretold* (1954), trans. Gregory Rabasse (London: Pan Books, 1983). All textual quotations are taken from this edition.
6. Mikhail Bakhtin, *The Dialogic Imagination*, trans. Caryl Emerson and Michael Holquist (Austin: Univ. of Texas Press, 1981), p. 84.

The paper that couldn't be written:

Mamatva Motifs in *Douloti* and *Balchanma*[1]

JAIDEV

Indianness is not treated as something eternal, changeless, or essentialistic. Nor is *mamatva* projected as something uniquely Indian and (therefore) an eternal Indian value in Indian fiction. *Mamatva* is a pervasive motif both in Indian life and Indian fiction. The motif constantly looks out towards life practices, including those relating to culture, politics, caste, community, class and gender.

The motif invariably operates both as a characterizational strategy and as a means of 'controlling' the reader's sympathy and judgement.

The paper will isolate the *mamatva* (and lack of *mamatva*) motifs in two texts, Mahasweta Devi's *Douloti* (1985) and Nagarjuna's *Balchanma* (1952), and then proceed to see them vis-à-vis the narrator's tone (particularly in *Balchanma*, in which the first-person narrator directly addresses the reader some 260 times), irony, satire, judgement, and the use of mythic and other frames. Of these latter, the narrator's tone will be taken up for detailed examination. The remarkable range of tonal variations in the narratives aims at (1) conveying moral distinctions between various characters, (2) implicitly suggesting a 'familial' model for society, particularly by rendering each major character through his or her relatively 'long' familial, caste and social line, and thus (3) inviting the reader to rethink his/her lifestyle and value-system vis-à-vis the less privileged Indians who deserve not only the narrator's *mamatva* but also the reader's, particularly at the praxis level. Characters in the two novels are never treated as lonely, isolated island-like individuals but in larger, familial and social terms. The tonal variations are thus part of a larger 'pedagogical' intent seeking to disturb the reader so as to force him/her to rethink his/her location in the heavily 'flawed' nation, which allows so much of barbaric exploitation, often by invoking mythology or *karma* theories.

The two texts are chosen because of certain conspicuous differences: one is in Bangla, the other in Hindi; one uses the omniscient narrative voice, the other is a first person narrative; one is woman-centred, the other man-centred; one is by a woman, the other by a man. However both the authors are socially committed, and Mahasweta Devi's life as much reinforces her *mamatva* in her fiction as did Nagarjuna's. *Mamatva* rules our excessive egotism, solipsism, narcissism; it attempts at sharing, community and communication, and involves reaching out to others, usually the less lucky ones, and rising above one's private self. *Mamatva* becomes a major means of intervention in culture as an all-embracing bundle of actual sociopolitical processes and procedures. After all, the Naxalities who leave their cosy bourgeois homes and live dangerously for the sake of the brutalized masses are also motivated by *mamatva* only.

NOTE

1. An abstract of the paper Jaidev wished to present at the International Seminar on 'The Indian Character of Indian Literature', 9-11 March 2000, Leiden, The Netherlands.

A Revolution in Translation

JAIDEV

Last month, a popular news weekly made news of sorts when it featured the current, exciting translation scene in India as its cover story. Translation was brought centrestage. It was considered as worthy of attention as, say, the parliamentary elections or the East Timor referendum.

This was not a random event. Just the other day, a young English teacher had a long meeting with an elderly Hindi professor. A Hindi story by Dudhnath Singh had made such impact on her that she had started translating it into English. Apparently, dictionaries weren't very helpful beyond a point. She had to acquaint herself with its cultural specificities, its subtle nuances of rituals and folklore. Her meeting with the professor turned out to be a wonderful experience for her: she discovered another India breathing in the texture of the story.

India has always had a rich tradition of translation. The Sanskrit word *anuvad* encompasses paraphrase, condensation, adaptation—in fact, repetitions in any form. Translations between Sanskrit and Prakrit, as also between Sanskrit and Tamil, were common in ancient India. During the Mughal period, translation attracted the very best of minds. For example, Dara Shikoh was fully soaked in our composite culture, and spent years translating the Upanishads and the *Gita* into Persian. During the colonial period the Orientalists made many of our ancient texts accessible to the world through translations.

Leaving history aside, it is clear now that with the globe steadily shrinking, there has been a phenomenal rise in our interest in translations. Today, we no longer bring a condescending attitude towards translation. We now regard translation as the best possible kind of literary criticism. It is perceived as a creative activity in its own right. Creative writers have known this all along. Nirala, Premchand, Mahasweta Devi, Mohan

*This is the text of a radio talk given by Jaidev on AIR Shimla, in August 1999.

Rakesh, Bhisham Sahni, Nirmal Verma, Girdhar Rathi—the list is endless. They found no contradiction between translation and creative writing. Classics in translation can inspire and influence any writer. They provide him or her with a wider perspective.

It is clear now that the '*adan-pradan*' involved in the translation between Indian languages is of great cultural value. By getting to know our regional Indian literatures, we get to know our plural, heterogeneous culture better. Blessed are those who have access to many Indian languages. But for those not so lucky, the best thing is to know our literatures through translations. Moreover, Hindi fiction is Hindi fiction, but is also something plus. Every regional fiction in India has this 'plusness' about it which comes from its interrelation with other Indian literary traditions. If we do not grasp this plus, we miss out on what is our particular literature's intrinsic trait. Amiya Dev has described Indian literature as an inter-literary condition. A novel like *Maila Aanchal* means so much more if we can read it alongside Satinath Bhaduri's *Dhoday Charitmanas*. Similarly, Jainendra's *Sunita* derives its plusness from Tagore's *Ghore Bahire*. Indeed, it is not sufficient to know one's own literature only. Indian literature is actually Indian literatures. I cannot be considered sufficiently literate if works of Manto and Mahasweta, M.T. Vasudevan Nair and Gopinath Mohanty do not happen to be within my intellectual reach.

Today, postcolonialism permeates all disciplines, including history and culture, literature and media studies. The recent revolution in translation has coincided with postcolonialism. Today, translation is culture-sensitive and free from the colonial cringe. Our *roti* is not British bread; unlike bread, it is not baked, but cooked, made or prepared. A huge cultural gap exists between our *mama* and the European uncle, the Indian *bahu* and the Western daughter-in-law, the village *baithak* and the Western drawing room. Postcolonialism in translation has made us both self-conscious and self-assertive. We keep our *chacha chacha*, and leave it for the reader to find out what *chacha* means in India. *Haath peele karna*, *sindoor*, *chauka-bartan*, *sadhana*, *vairagya*, and thousand other culture-specific details are no longer refracted through an alien mirror; they are not distorted through clumsy Western equivalents; they are incorporated as such, sometimes with footnotes. Indian postcolonial translation prefers Ram and Allah to a plain God, prefers *sukh* and *dukh* to joy and sorrow. It thus avoids violence to our culture-loaded terms.

Finally, three important features of this revolution in translation. One pertains to the subject I teach. Until some years ago, we English teachers frowned upon literatures that were not from Europe or the United States. We did not mind Plato or Kant, Dostoevsky or Thomas Mann. Our English literature courses went freely beyond English but refused to include any Third World components. Translations weren't taboo; but those from Indian languages were. Fortunately, that snobbery is gone now. We now teach not only Indian novels in English, but also Indian novels in English translation. Himachal Pradesh University now runs a full-fledged course in translation. Also, it is perhaps the first university in India to accept a literary translation in lieu of a conventional Ph.D. thesis.

Of course, this revolution hasn't come about out of nothing. Years of dedicated work by Sahitya Akademi, Bharatiya Jnanpeeth, and National Book Trust have created the necessary ground. More recently, prestigious publishing houses like Macmillan, Orient Longman, East-West Press, Katha, Penguin India, Rajkamal, Radhakrishna have promoted professional translation. Already we have legends like Mini Krishnan and Geetha Dharmarajan, who have worked tirelessly to bring a new prestige to translation. Many translations such as *Tamas* and *Rag Darbari* have sold better than their originals.

Today, the translator's name figures alongside the name of the author. Translators are allowed space in the 'Translator's Note' where they explain their tanslatorial experience and problems vis-à-vis the original texts. A translator is no longer confined to the margin. Indeed, one can take up translation as a full-time job. Translation has become highly professional, competent, and self-conscious, and promises rich rewards and literary recognition to any devoted, committed translator. It sounds incredible but is true that today, whereas many good writers may be in search of publishers for their novels, publishers, authors and readers are alike searching for good translators. This is because a huge pile of our classics still awaits translation. Also, unlike the originals, there do not exist final translations: all translations get superseded by better translations. For example, Sujit Mukherjee's translation of *Gora* has superseded the initial one.

Above all, this revolution has exposed the idiocy of teaching or learning English in what is called the direct way. Not permitting pupils to think and feel in their own tongue while teaching them English—this direct approach is both foolish and unproductive. It is of no use to a future translator. What could be the point behind speaking or writing like an Englishman? At best, this can turn us into brilliant mimics. We now appreciate Indian English instead of finding it funny. Our translations today do not ape English English or American English. They seek to be Indian and in Indian English. That is why, it is good to use both Hindi and English while teaching English, or to advise our students to compose their thoughts in Hindi before writing them in English. This may initially result in some awkward expressions, but soon enough it opens up the door to creativity.

In short, translation requires us to test the strengths and limits both of our own language and of the target language. Its frustrations are many but they are offset by its rewards. It is a skill to be sure, but once the skill is mastered, one finds enough room for innovation, experiment and creativity, too.

Conscience, Activism and Intellect: Jaidev's Location

AMIYA DEV

In Jaidev I saw a Nachiketa ready to walk on the razor's edge. When I first met him he was still primarily an English teacher though given to exploring the new English writing much of which was concerned with the problems of self-reflexivity. It was during a seminar at Berhampur University, courtesy Biyot Tripathy, that our meeting took place. We were sharing a room in the university guesthouse and had long evenings of conversation not untouched by frenzy. He was a cigarette smoker then and an avid tea-drinker which meant, he would every now and then go down to the kitchen to get a pot of tea, even as late as ten, not tea-time by any civilized standards. Biyot Tripathy had known him from Shimla where Biyot Tripathy had taught for a while. For him Jaidev was the best of Shimla, scintillating, full of ideas and unsparing of the midnight oil. What struck *me* most was his sincerity, an intensity of commitment to what he was saying. We talked at random of European literature and Indian writing in the Indian languages. I could have perhaps been a bit sparing in my insistence on my favourite issues, but his response was so genuine that I couldn't resist myself. And maybe it was because of that, his sincerity and my insistence, that we developed an unusual kind of friendship in which we needed a lot of talking. I remember many walks we took, at Shimla and elsewhere, during which either he or I was talking. I do remember his letters full of thoughts he had been thinking. I also remember the fiction he used to write for the *Express* including a grotesque account once of a national event that concerned college and university teachers—I wish I had preserved everything he had sent me as witness to how a conscientious mind worked. And how can I reproduce those hundreds and thousands of words he spoke! I can only say that I bore testimony to his growth into one of the foremost literary and cultural critics of our time to whom conscience mattered more than intellect. What I mean is not that he only produced polemic—he was getting into areas where pure intellect would not tread. And conscience for him was not a stance, but a part of his being. In dedicating a novella to him, as he lay dying, Mahasweta Devi said how his fingers offering water to the thirsty at the Sabar mela he had attended, looked as though they were seeking forgiveness of everyone. She couldn't be truer.

In his last letter to me written in December 1999 Jaidev spoke of an essay he was going to write for a Leiden seminar on what he meant by authentic Indianness, no sham or slogan shouting, no fetish, but a sense of sharing. This was going to be a follow-up of his *Pastiche* book. 'That book', he wrote,

> did manage to get misread by one scholar in Delhi who included a section from it in his volume on Nativism. I am not interested in Nativism as such, but feel that the narrator in several of our self-evidently Indian (as distinguished from India-shouting) narratives builds a *rapport* with the reader, this *rapport* including feelings of *apanatva* and *mamatva*. The narrator can chide the reader, educate him/her, laugh with him/her, arouse his/her conscience. There is no question of compromise in view of the reader's preferences, but always there is a 'shary' feel about the tone.

Jaidev was planning to discuss two novellas for evidence, Mahasweta Devi's *Douloti* and Nagarjuna's *Balchanma*. 'Of course', he added,

> no writer might think of any individual reader; still, there is, in novels of Verma and Vaid, some kind of sharing between the narrator and characters, not between the narrator and the reader. This 'sharing' tone can be misused, but by dropping it for the sake of modernism or whatever, the novelist really leaves so much communicative space to anyone interested in using it. To that extent, fiction's surrender of such spaces might mean even the media and politicians occupying that space. Somewhere even the concept of reader is complex enough. If this concept is realistic at all, it may not allow the narrator to cultivate ambiguities and obscurities of formal kind.

He went on speaking further of how Western scholars tend to prefer an essentialist kind of Indian fiction to anything that is crowded and complicated. 'Even when this "preferred" fiction is in a socio-cultural vacuum, they force interpretations on it so as to prove it authentically Indian. Lack of details becomes the Indian way towards *sadharanikarana*.'

I don't know if this essay got written, but it is clear that by positing this author-reader *rapport* as opposed to an author-character *rapport*, Jaidev was arriving at a sense of location and history. His critique of Nirmal Verma and Krishna Baldev Vaid and their like was motivated by their lack of location and historicity, their shying away from the enormity and the irreducibility of the world around them and casting, instead, an absolute interior where class and caste are superfluous, gender the other name of sexuality, material inequality an unfortunate given, and so on. The fact of such writing being hailed as authentic Indian is unfortunate but not unusual. However, Indianness cannot be a ready signifier, bells ringing out as the slightest breeze blows. Indianness is to be sought inside, in the spaces and the times that are being dealt with. Indianness is in the authenticity of these spaces and times. In other words, there is no Indianness as such, nothing that exists *sui generis*, irrespective of the spaces and the times that surround us. But not having an India fetish is not denying the Indian nation. Again, not denying the Indian nation is not laying down all critique. On the contrary, Jaidev's reading of Mahasweta Devi, for instance, projects a view of the nation as a site for oppression—of class, caste, gender and region—a site for the hegemony of the powerful over the powerless. To deny nation is to deny history and the ubiquity of this oppression. The mainstream fiction in contemporary India is the fiction that depicts this history, sure enough in local coordinates but with a clear national implication. To call *Douloti* a 'national allegory' is not to belie Palamou where the novella is situated but to unveil the class, caste, gender and other inequalities of which Palamou provides a case study. And to have a national concern is not to be a nationalist with the perverse rhetoric of the unassailability of the nation. For it is from within the nation that the nation can be set right in terms of class, caste, gender and other inequalities. The bogey that goes by the name of nation cannot be simply wished away, it will have to be contended by turning Palamous into a political discourse. And this is where Jaidev sees a gap between the related ontology and epistemology: Won't our epistemology be partly hollow if we do not approximate the ontology of the place and the people we are writing about? Mahasweta Devi, to Jaidev, is a great writer not only because she is writing Palamou but also because she is approaching its ontology through her long career of activism. And I do seem to see Jaidev too, while speaking of Mahasweta Devi's Palamou text, veering towards that ontology.

Epistemology alone is not enough for him. If he had not been snatched away from us, he might have taken to activism. Conscience was no less his motive force than intellection.

In the recent years, I have been trying to understand location in different ways, one of them being that of the pronouns, *I*, *we* and *you*, both singular and plural. There is a scholarship that tends to ignore the variability of the pronouns, swayed by an objective-cum-universal argument for discourse situations. Once an editor took out a whole paragraph from an essay of mine dealing with the use of pronouns involved in its live presentation. One may make a distinction between an audience and a readership, the former being specific and cognizable, the latter indeterminate. Yet even in writing an author may not be utterly abstracted from his/her readership. At least he/she may have a specific readership in mind at the time of writing. An example I have been giving repeatedly and shall perhaps never tire of giving is that of Umberto Eco on the semiotics of blue jeans which came to this country as a syndicated article, but which was certainly not addressed to us, for what Eco had said about the blue jeans being an emblem of freedom from sartorial and thus perhaps cultural constraints, did not apply to us at the time. The blue jeans came here as high fashion available only to the wealthy youth. If I remember right, there was only one shop in Kolkata where Levis pants were sold at an exorbitant price. Obviously Umberto Eco had nothing to do with that absence of relevance, for he had written the piece for a first world readership; it was foolish on our part to be oblivious of our third world location and believe that since we had access to English it might also have been meant for us. What we could have written at the time was how a sartorial aping of that order fetched a high price—the economics rather than the politics of blue jeans in the third world. And no one can deny that built into our English studies as such is a similar problem of location. To begin with, Macaulay's purpose in thrusting English on us was our dislocation. That dislocation still continues exemplified by our inadvertent lapping up of English studies pursued in England. Obviously the only answer to that dislocation is not a total abolition of English, but finding a location for it here and now. And that has indeed begun. Our English syllabus is changing, first with the recognition of an anglophone world as opposed to the pure English, and then with an inclusion of some Indian writing in English or even, in one or two cases, of a few Indian language classics in English translation; above all, with a conscious reflection of the Indian response to English in the choice of authors and texts. Our predilection, for instance, for the romantics is not as such an extension of the recent re-reading of them in England and America, but in part a continuation of our nineteenth century admiration for them, motivated no less by a surge for freedom that we have had on a national level than by purely poetic considerations. Examples can be multiplied and we can think of our stress on Scott whose historical fiction did provide us with a model in the second half of the nineteenth century in our pursuit of past glory. As to T.S. Eliot, his eminence in our syllabus is explained by the fact that in many Indian languages modernism began with a reception to him.

There are other ways we are trying to register our location with regard to English. Of course there is the Indian English vocabulary recognized by the English dictionaries, but I am not primarily thinking of that. I am thinking of our growing need for using our own cultural vocabulary, whether in the matter of kinship or food and dress or festivities, in the English we are writing. And this applies to our own English translation of our works as well. For one thing, we have come to realize that our target audience for the English we are writing is not the English-speaking world overseas alone, but our own other Indian language speakers as well, maybe the latter more than the former. In fact as a vehicle of intra-Indian communication English is more and more turning out to be a function, not authority. Its official 'link language' status has by and large been a useful piece of pragmatism. Even its being included in the roll of the annual Sahitya Akademi awards, along with the regular Indian languages, has not given it an extra dislocating power. At least the underlying national rhetoric of these awards comes in the way of that. However, the battle of location around our use of English is not fully won. And indeed it cannot be. For as long as English remains a first language elsewhere, a touch of colonial memory added or not, it will be an instrument of dislocation, and we will have to go on relocating ourselves continuously. Our access to the Internet is not going to make the battle any easier.

And this brings me to the realm of theory where too inadvertently, sometimes out of over-enthusiasm, we lend ourselves to occasional dislocation. We import and often lap up an overseas *episteme* that takes our feet off the ground. If Jacques Derrida says the third world is as such a translated text, it pertains to the first world's perception of the third world, not our own perception of our world. And it would indeed be a matter of pity if our perception *per se* of ourselves is a first world construct. We know that we are not a translated text to ourselves. Why should we be so worried if Derrida says so? He is not talking to us! He is talking to his fellow first world audience. It is high time we regained our self-respect. And in order to do that we won't have to conjure up tradition or parade pride for being heir to an old civilization; relating ourselves to our present reality will be enough. Surely this can be a part of our postcolonial agenda.

Of course these are, the issue of English and that of first world theory, only one side of our concern with location. The other and the more important side consists in our understanding of ourselves, in whether we know that we are at the same time many and one, many because of our different linguistic and cultural identities, and one as a nation. I am not raising afresh the old debate of unity and diversity, I am only saying that our immediate location is in our individual languages and cultures, that we do not go from one to many which is tantamount to disintegration, but come from many to one, attaining integration. In other words, one cannot as such be an Indian; in order to be an Indian one has first to be either a Gujarati or an Oriya or a Malayalee or a Santhali or a Banjara—a member of a particular linguistic and cultural community. And it is here that marginal communities are still deprived of their Indian identity. They know what they are with regard to their own community, but they have no idea of a nation around. But that is not to say that there is no nation peeping in their life. It often comes in the form of local administration, or upper class and upper caste oppression, or economic and cultural exploitation. For us to be truly located is to be aware of this inequality and injustice as well, not merely to attain Indianness through a perception of our various communal and linguistic individualities. And that is not an easy task, especially in view of our class moorings. To overcome them mere intellection won't do, conscience too is needed. Whether or not this conscience-driven location leads us to activism, there is no alternative to it. Jaidev will ever be an exemplum for this.

Quite early in his career, as an English teacher he found his location by containing English hegemony with a growing concern with Indian literature, first in English and then in the Indian languages themselves.

And while speaking of Indian literature in the Indian languages he further located himself in the Indian reality, and that to such an extent that he came to disregard much modernist imitation, focusing on the nitty-gritty Indian, mainly represented to him by Premchand, Renu, Nagarjuna and Mahasweta Devi. Even if at any moment of friendship with Jaidev I presumed that I was triggering a few of his interests, it was I who should have sat at his feet the last ten years or so. It is I who now should emulate him in his inculcation of location.

Searching for the Other India in the Other Tongue: Jaidev's Critical Practice

E.V. RAMAKRISHNAN

Jaidev has left behind a valuable body of criticism which is sound in judgement, thorough in scholarship and meticulous in its analytical rigour. As a translator, he has made a mark with just one translation: Bhisham Sahni's *Basanti.* I had known him from the early 1980s but it was during my tenure as a Fellow at the Indian Institute of Advanced Study at Shimla that I had the opportunity to interact with him closely and intimately. His thoughts have influenced me deeply. While I was writing my study of modernism in Indian poetry, I turned to him repeatedly for help and criticism. From my experience, I knew that it was impossible to have honest criticism in India. This was what made my association with Jaidev a highly rewarding experience. In this small piece my purpose is not to evaluate him but to highlight some of his insights and summarize some of his arguments.

His review of *Mauni—A Writer's Writer—Short Stories* shows the courage of his convictions. This review appeared at a time when Salman Rushdie's doubts about the intrinsic worth of Indian literature written in Indian languages had raised a storm of protest. For Jaidev reading Mauni, a reclusive writer who published only about 24 stories in the course of his life, some of which went on to become masterpieces in the genre in Tamil, came as a revelation. He does not hide the excitement of the discovery in his review:

> A banal, non-Maunian thirteenth tale could be built around an Indian like me, a teacher of Anglo-American and European literature who has spent his prime years exploring pre-modernists, modernists and post-modernists elsewhere, although all this while their quintessence was available right at home. Hence the need for a translation renaissance, for letting Indians see the uses of discovering India.[1]

Instead of emotionally reacting to Rushdie's dismissive attitude to 'vernacular literature', Jaidev points out that ignorance is the culprit here. Unless we generate fine translations of our literature, such misconceptions are bound to crystallize into a general opinion. Jaidev took special interest in translation studies and felt that this was one field where English departments in India could make seminal contributions.

His review of *Gora*[2] becomes an occasion for finding out what has gone wrong with our project of nation-building. This review also reveals one of the basic strengths of his writing. The gradual erosion of India's secular democratic framework disturbed him. His moral convictions gave his writing a distinctive force. Jaidev finds that *Gora* anticipates several of our current anxieties about the nation and its meanings. He says:

> Above all the novel asks us to see the other, to learn to see how we appear to others. *Gora* was written in the hope that asking for this much sanity would not be a tall order. From where we are now, it looks as if that hope was either born of wishful thinking or determined by the choice of comic form. A monstrous nation, a violent nation, an insensitive nation—all these look okay so long as we can say we are Hindus—with pride. Things caricatured in *Gora* have become our creed.[3]

It is significant that he praises *Gora* mainly for its sanity. Jaidev knew we were living in irrational times.

One of the signs of this irrationality is modern India's desire to catch up with America. Jaidev lost no opportunity to condemn the gross materialism of our 'modernity'. He strongly believed that something had gone wrong with our project of modernity. In his review of M.T. Vasudevan Nair's fiction he comments: 'Today we are in the grip of a structural logic determined to erase some seventy per cent of our "superfluous" citizens only because they are not consumers. In these hard times, literature is one of the few conscience-keepers we are left with.'[4] The same views are articulated in his review of Srikrishna Alanahally's *Gendethimma*, a Kannada classic which critically comments on the manner in which modernity enters the rural society. In the last few years of his life he extensively reviewed fiction translated from several Indian languages. In his reviews he shares his excitement with the readers with an open mind. While reviewing *Gendethimma* he makes it clear that the book deserves a place alongside books like *The Idiot*. He considers

M.T. Vasudevan Nair's story 'Vanaprastham' one of the most moving love stories in world literature.

There are several classics in Indian literature which remain unknown to the world outside. Jaidev has no hesitation in saying that it was the circumstances of Bibhutibhushan Bandopadhyay—a village schoolteacher most of his life, untranslated during his lifetime, and writing only in Bangla—that prevented him from being considered for the Nobel Prize. In his review of T.W. Clarke's translation of *Pather Panchali* he takes strong exception to Clarke's 'patronizing and self-righteous comments' on the works of Bibhutibhushan. After a detailed and insightful review of both *Pather Panchali* and *Aparajitho*, Jaidev concludes: 'In his fabulous negotiations with Apu's memories and stream of consciousness, Bibhuthibhushan Bandopadhyay compels comparison with Proust or Joyce. And he is easily far superior to either, in his unironic, limitless compassion for the ordinary and the simple.'[5]

The question of compassion bothered him mainly because he knew that the English-educated elite in India could easily be the most selfish and greedy community on the face of the earth. Literary modernism often was an articulation of the world-views of this class. The book-length study Jaidev wrote on contemporary Hindi novel is a scathing attack on the 'culture of pastiche' practised by this class. He uses the word 'pastiche' to denote the mindless use of western codes of experience and expression without the contexts of their production. Pastiche as it manifests in literature refuses to adapt borrowed materials to suit the cultural ambience of native contexts. In the novels of Mridula Garg and Krishna Baldev Vaid, surface brilliance is elevated to an artistic principle. In the age of predatory capitalism it is only natural that acquired markers of global and cosmopolitan culture would carry stamps of western supremacy. He observes that surfaces, presentational methods and technology are crucial factors both in consumerism and pastiche.[6] It is Jaidev's concern for the social and political factors that affect the common man's lot in non-Western countries that gives his book the tone of a crusader.

At the core of Jaidev's book is a plea for cultural care which may sound strange in the age of exotic literary theories. A pastiche culture does not answer to any deep urge in the author or the reader, nor does it engage the total being of the individual. Since it does not emerge from the needs of the people, it contradicts their basic attitudes. In privileging the West, it drains the authenticity of the East and to that extent, misrepresents the reality of countries like India. That this problem is not peculiar to India is obvious from the distinction Seamus Heany makes (following Peter Kavanagh) between 'parochial' and 'provincial' imagination. The 'parochial' imagination finds the local and the indigenous significant in itself while the 'provincial' imagination constantly craves for the endorsement of metropolitan culture. The Hindi novelist's total surrender to the codes of metropolitan culture is symptomatic of a society that is only insufficiently aware of its moorings. As he puts it, 'pastiche occurs when, seduced by alien cultural codes, one sheds one's self-definition, ignores one's legitimate needs and scorns one's culture' (224). The inability of the Hindi writers to synthesize their borrowings results in ruptures and distortions in their fiction that show up as artistic and structural flaws.

Jaidev's analysis of Nirmal Verma's *Ek Chithda Sukh* is instructive. In a close reading of the novel he demonstrates how the novel adopts many motifs from Faulkner, Henry James, Virginia Woolf, Proust, Sartre, Strindberg, and Camus without adapting or assimilating them and burdens the characters with nihilism, pessimism, aestheticism and existentialism without looking deep into their contents or contexts. The surface sparkle of Nirmal Verma's style betrays a deeper intellectual confusion. Following Tony Bennet, Jaidev makes a useful distinction between 'inter-textuality' and 'intertextuality'. The hyphenated term refers to those texts which fail to assimilate what they borrow. The rupture implied by the hyphen corresponds to allusions, echoes, quotations and ideas in a work that become a part of its organic structure. An author who borrows with a purpose and internalizes what he borrows creates an intertext which suffers from no complexes about its bond or bondages to a metropolitan audience. In his review of M.T. Vasudevan Nair's fiction, Jaidev praises him for internalizing and naturalizing influences of authors like Faulkner, Camus, Dostoevsky and Chekhov. What Jaidev strongly disapproves of is the pretentious and meretricious manner in which authors like Krishna Baldev Vaid flaunt their undigested scholarship.

Vaid borrows liberally from Henry Miller, Philip Roth and a host of Western authors. Jaidev painstakingly unearths the originals behind Vaid's fictional situations and characterizations. Vaid's heroes are sexually promiscuous, solitary aesthetes who are deeply impressed by the exotic and the alien. Elaborating on the point that Vaid's alternative discourse lacks conviction and credibility, Jaidev comments: 'Graffiti, mimicry, and candour abound in Vaid's fiction, but they are not accompanied by any involvement in or commitment to India or her culture. Nor do they have any humanity about them. They shock, but they have only a negative function. Vaid's alternative discourse is reductive and dubious' (139).

As opposed to the cultivated postures of Verma, Garg and Vaid, Mohan Rakesh does not chase illusions of grandeur in borrowed costumes. He is able to assimilate and contextualize the received lore of existentialism and modernism. His novel *Andhere Band Kamre* uses doubles as Dostoevsky does and resembles Fitzgerald's *The Great Gatsby* in many respects. But the novel is subtle in its close monitoring of the hero's journey to self-discovery which the novelist intends to be 'a comprehensive statement on the cultural situation in Delhi around 1960' (200). Mohan Rakesh's next novel *Na Aane Waala Kal* is consciously patterned on Camus's *The Outsider*. Manoj Saxena becomes an Indian Meursault who impulsively marries a widow whom he doesn't love and later resigns his Hindi teacher's job to set out on a journey without knowing where he is going. Jaidev comments: 'Manoj is a pastiche. The deeper, more significant, more demanding values of existentialism do not engage him; only its superficial lore does. . . . His quest for authenticity brings him only to a cultureless void, which is absurd in the non-existentialist sense' (221).

My attempt is not to paraphrase Jaidev's book. It has several merits which will be discovered by an attentive reader. Jaidev has done a singular service to the field of culture studies by problematizing the pastiche that is being canonized by our mainstream authors. His criticism is also a search for Indian criteria for evaluating Indian literature in English translation. He was one of the few Indian scholars who was extensively familiar with even the most obscure pieces of fictional works in Anglo-American literature. He used his scholarship to understand the deeper processes that inform the culture of a country. He was convinced that we cannot borrow the social vision necessary for the creation of a just and democratic nation. His function as a critic is a model to emulate for those who are deeply concerned with the directions of our society and literature.

NOTES

1. *Indian Review of Books*, VII, No. 1: 74.
2. *Indian Review of Books*, VII, No. 4: 34-5.
3. Ibid., p. 35.
4. *Indian Review of Books*, VIII, No. 1: 96.
5. *Indian Review of Books*, IX, No. 1: 102.
6. *The Culture of Pastiche* (Shimla: Indian Institute of Advanced Study, 1993), pp. 36, 68-9.

PART II

my humble tribute to Jaidev

MAHASWETA DEVI

Since I have never written literary essays, I will not attempt to write one. Instead, I am sending two of my recent stories, translated by me. Jaidev was the only critic who understood me, and he knew what my beliefs are.

Increasingly my belief becomes more strengthened that in Indian context, it was always politics and class interest. Basically India's land system has remained medieval. And if we go back in history, it was always in support of those in power. No thorough land reform was done after independence, and a feudal land system has nurtured and sustained a feudal value system. I have written 'Daulati', but when were the so-called low caste, later tribal women not purchased, used and thrown out? I was going through Dr Sukumari Bhattacharya's book, and read, even in the Vedic ages, the *munis* often kept the eldest daughters unmarried. They were known as 'BRIDDHAKUMARIS'. What happened to them when they were no longer work-fit?

In India, today, Kolatis and Dombaris, tribal communities still keep the eldest daughter unmarried, used for prostitution to support the family. Read 'Against Many Odds' by Kishore S. Kale. The Dombari community of Telengana in Andhra Pradesh still marry the eldest girl to Venkateswara Shiva, and then initiate her into prostitution.

It is not only politics, but caste and class politics.

And, at the age of 76, it is very clear to me that Educated and Privileged Indians' brain cells remain colonized. This is my realization after a lifetime's experience. 'Kunti and the Nishadin' is not my first story from re-reading the epic from the people's point of view. And 'Mahdu' is too true a story.

I dedicate these two stories to Jaidev. These translations are for this volume alone. These should not be reprinted without my permission. I never translate my stories for publication, always for communication.

It has always been politics in class interest. I have started to write the stories from the epics and hope to write a few more. Researchers and scholars would benefit to read the Bhil tribal version of *Mahabharata* published by Sahitya Akademi. It is bilingual, in Hindi translation and Bhili language in Nagri script. The subalterns have always had their version of our epics in oral traditions. If the tribal versions of the epics are thus translated, we would find the version of the Nishads, Naga-vanshiyas, Kirats and others reaching us from the remote past.

I have not based my story on the 'Bhili-Bharatha'. It is my realization that the more we read through the lines and give voice to the countless infantrymen used to protect the lauded epical heroes, the 'Dasis' (mother of Vidura, mother of Yuyutsu and countless others) and the 'Vratyas' used as cannon fodder during 'Rajavritta' emergency, the more the mythical times come into focus and the eternal game of politics comes into view.

Politics and interest of the exploiters, and the say of the exploited have always been the central point of interest of my writing. I am not sorry to put my thoughts into these stories. I am the writer I know best and I have never been interested in academic discussion of literature. Never studied any theory, only life. Jaidev would understand and I know, his friends will, too.

Kunti and the Nishadin

(In the last phase of their life they had chosen to live in the forests.)

MAHASWETA DEVI

In the 'Ashram Vasik Parva' Kunti has to look after Dhritarashtra and Gandhari every day. Kunti accepts it. Yes, she should attend to her husband's elder brother and his wife Gandhari who chose not to see with her eyes. This is a vanashrama, not a royal palace. She goes to the forest to collect firewood for the daily yagnas. Noon is a magic time. She leaves the ashram, enters the forest. Takes a grass rope, ties the bundles of wood, rests a little and returns dragging the bundles. If only Bhim was here! He would help her.

She sees some middle-aged Nishadins, moving about the forest with their children. Are they past their prime? Their few silver hairs would say so. How strong their arms are, how well-muscled! And their shoulders! They gather wood, tie it into bundles with wild creepers and lift them on their heads at sunset. Rubbing flint stones, they light wooden torches, and follow the jungle track home. They sing songs in chorus. Kunti never tried to learn their language. This forest is full of tall, resinous trees. The Nishadins collect resin, honey, tubers and roots. They are so self-composed, joyous and hardworking! How white their smiles are!

Resin trickles down. The wind is heavy with incense. The soothing breeze caresses Kunti's body and cleanses it of fatigue. She stares at the homegoing Nishadins and it strikes her for the first time, 'Why am I living on rotten leaves and wasting myself? It's not of my own will. Ah, I am just following a predestined path and walking towards death. At the dictate of others. Now she has the time to look back. She never knew that she carried such a burden in her heart. In the 'Rajavritta' her life was so different. Mother of the Pandavas, queen to Pandu, she had so many roles to play! Daughter-in-law, queen, mother! Played too many

*Written in 1999.

roles and never found time to be herself, a woman! And never felt that she had anything that was her own.

Yes, once, only once, in her first youth . . . the very thought burns in her heart like a blazing funeral pyre. It will continue to burn, unabated, till she dies. Now she feels like confessing. If only she could unburden herself to the forest, the rocks, birds, flying insects, the dry leaves! The Nishadins come near her, go away again. But there is no communication between them. Body emaciated with 'tapasya', white-haired, clad in a 'chinangshuka' very threadbare, very pure, very white. Kunti's eyes are still alive with curiosity. She sees the Nishadins all the time, but nothing registers on her mind. There's no point of contact between Kunti and them.

How could there be? In the 'Rajavritta' all she knew was attending to the Brahmins and worshipping the gods. Had she, even once, talked to the Dasis? Was there any human relationship between Kunti and Hidimba? Nothing beyond the 'Rajavritta' was relevant to her.

Why do these Nishadins move about near her? Kunti does not want to know. All she wants is to unburden herself and confess.

Gandhari and her bandaged eyes fill her with awe. How stately she is! How self-contained, even after losing a hundred sons; she knows that she has always been on the right path, and till death she will not waver.

But Kunti has to confess. When shall she find the time: every day she feels weaker. Attending to Dhritarashtra and Gandhari, leaving them at the Ashrama Kutir, she feels even more low, exhausted. It is preferable to tell the forest, the river, the birds, murmuring leaves, the wind and the Nishadins. She will talk in her language and they won't understand, nor will they ask questions. With the sunset, they will go home. She will go back to the ashrama. Arrange for the evening prayer. Sup off rotten leaves, drink some water and would lie on the grassmat.

Did she ever sleep on a sandalwood bed, on milkwhite sheets? Eat off gold plates? Ghee-soaked rice and seven dishes; who arranged the ingredients for the 'Yagnas', kept fast during the Pujas—was it she?

Which Kunti used to worship the rising sun and pray for his blessings? Was she as glowingly beautiful as the crimson rays of the rising sun? Whose wealth of black hair had the dasis dried with incense smoke, who had gone to her husband bedecked with jewellery and draped in Benarasis?

Yes, she nurtured Yudhishthira, Bhima and Arjuna in her womb. But they were not sired by Pandu. Why did she love Nakula and Sahadeva so much? Was it to fulfil what was expected of her? Where lay her courage? Her 'dharma'?

She talked to herself. How would she purge herself of her sins if she did not confess?

O Devi 'Prithvi', Protector of forests, hills, water and live beings, please listen to Kunti, the sinner.

I am not truly 'dharmaprayana' like Gandhari. Dharma did not give me courage. I was overwhelmed to find my sons alive after the 'Dharma-yuddha' was over. But Draupadi and Uttara were griefstricken at the loss of their sons. I could not console them. Gandhari did.

One hundred sons of hers dead. Yet I found her consoling them. Telling them, 'This mass death is preordained and inevitable. Like you, I too have lost my sons. This death-spell is over. Come, we won't let ourselves be destroyed by grief. Strengthen your hearts. Death means grief. But the wives and mothers, daughters and sisters have to learn to survive. In order to carry on, one needs forbearance and courage. One has to learn to live with this grief.'

I do not have her true realization of 'Dharma'.

When she mourned to Krishna, did she mourn for her own sons and grandsons? The countless widows, alone. Abhimanyu on her lap, she bewailing his death made me realize that she was cursing the war on behalf of all the women of the world.

That is why she alone is Gandhari. This was a war for power. To obliterate the opposition and monopolize the power. Was it a victory for 'Dharma'? And defeat for 'Adharma'? The sky-rending cry of the women at the sight of mutilated and bloody corpses was, actually, cursing the word 'war'. And, O mother earth, listen to me. Karna was brighter than flames. He was uncompromising and an archer amongst archers. But in death he looked so full of peace, an unearthly peace. Gandhari's loud lamentation at the sight of a dead Karna whiplashed me.

Why did I not find the courage? Why did I not sit with his head on my lap and scream, 'He is my first born. Dhananjoy, you have killed your eldest brother. He is the son I deserted fearing public scandal. Had I not, people would have called me an unchaste woman.'

Karna is the only son whose father came to me as I wanted him to.

What a laugh, really! None of the five Pandavas were sired by Pandu, yet they are Pandavas, and Karna? Son of a carpenter!

O ancient Mother. Kunti kept mum that day. What can be a greater sin? Gandhari knew she was pure and innocent. This realization gave her courage to speak the truth openly.

Else, could she have cursed Krishna? Say, Krishna could have stopped the war but caused it?

Fearless, self-confident and straightforward, Gandhari cursed Krishna.

I just listened to her voice.

Do not forgive me, O Mother! The brute wealth of the royal palace, the might of the son on the throne, I felt caged and torn to pieces.

Yes, this lonely forest. This closeness to nature, the daily sunsets teach me that human beings are really very ignoble.

No, that futile battle of power, senseless killing has not harmed nature's harmony.

Previously my eyes did not see, mind did not work.

Ah, I lash and lash at my conscience. And now I know, silence would be unpardonable.

Suddenly she lifted her face. The Nishadins were staring at her. Their faces inscrutable. Eyes remote.

Kunti was struck dumb.

The elderly Nishadin said something to the others. They broke into laughter. Kunti shook with fear. Would they come nearer? This pile of faggots would be defiled if their shadows fell over it.

It was near evening. She stood up. With bony fingers, dragged the pile and walked away. No, tomorrow she would go somewhere else. After today's confession she felt at peace. Cleansed, light. Constant worry is both corroding and too heavy a burden to bear.

Yes, the Nishadins heard her. Well, to Kunti they were as dumb as rocks. They did not know her language, nor she theirs.

When Kunti helped her lie down, Gandhari said, 'O mother of the five Pandavas! Everyday your touch is so cold. Today the fingers feel warmer. As if blood circulation is rapid. Your touch is so alive!'

— Respected elder sister! The forest seems to be as loving as a mother.

— Does it give you a little peace?

— Perhaps.

— Liberate your mind from earthly worries.

— I do not have your strength of mind, yet I try.

— With the passing of each second we move towards the end. I await death.

— Yes, elder sister!

Kunti lay down on the grassmat at their feet. No one wanted her to leave. It was alright for Dhritarashtra and Gandhari. Why should Kunti, mother of the emperor of Jambudwipa girdled by seven seas, leave?

Kunti whispered, 'The Life of Rajavritta was suffocating me'. Today Kunti bathed in the stream once again. She turned her back to the sun. Silken white hair covered her back. If Suryadeva stared down, would he know her? A million years of mankind are less than a second for the gods.

Why this tremendous urge to confess it all? No, the Nishadins do not come to this area of the forest. One area is so much like another, that one can easily lose track. But Vidura had taught Kunti the jungle ways. 'On your way, break a branch, place a rock, these signs will help you find your way.'

He said, 'Aranyaka, the forest goodess, avoids human beings. Forest tribes belong there. They never get lost. Aranyaka the sorceress leads the outsiders astray. Do remember the Kingshuka tree on the way to vanashrama. And do not stray far.'

— Anything to be afraid of?
— Fear is just a state of mind.

It is good to be in a forest. No wide roads, rows of shops, march of the cavalry, thundering roar of the wheels of royal chariots!

One can be alone. Can confess in whispers.

'O, Devi Basundhara! Countless pyres were lit after Kurukshetra. Foot soldiers came from faraway places. At Yudhishthira's command Vidura arranged a mass-cremation. The air reeked of burnt flesh, butter and camphor were freely poured to drown the evil smell of putrid flesh. But the death-smell lingered.'

Then I overcame my hesitation. I committed one sin after another. In the first place, I never told my sons about Karna. Then, the day before the war, I went and told Karna to join Yudhishthira, leave Duryodhana.

And he never spoke a rude word.

I said, 'Son! You were born of my womb. Obey me!'

What shamelessness! He could easily have said, 'It is not enough to give birth, you threw me away the moment I was born. You did not do your duty as a mother. How can you ask me to do my duty as a son?'

He did not say that.

No. I did not go to him hungering to hug him in affection. I did not think of him even once. All my concern was for the Pandavas.

But Gandhari lamented for Karna without constraint. She lamented.

'Yudhishthira went without sleep for thirteen years for fear of Karna. Karna was unconquerable like Indra, courageous like Agni, cool and collected like Himalaya!'

Curse me! I just stared at her, speechless.

In the 'Rajavritta' one becomes cunning and treacherous. Love did not drive me to Karna, self-interest did. Today I know, Karna already knew that Krishna would do everything to ensure victory for the Pandavas. Victory is known as Dharmayuddha. The war that the conquered ones fight is not known as Dharmayuddha. That is why Karna said, 'I cannot leave Duryodhana. Of your sons, I'll kill only Arjuna. You will still have five sons alive'.

So he counted himself as one of my sons. And I did not say even once, 'I burn with guilt for abandoning you after your birth'. Because I had no sense of regret. The Pandavas were all I cared for. So I told him, try to help your brothers. O, curse me! Curse the mother of the Pandavas. When the cremations were over, and Yudhishthira went for the 'Tarpana' of the dead, I told him, 'Do it for Karna too. He was my first born, sired by Suryadeva.'

He asked me why I had not said this before the war. And I understood that my sons would never forget it. He further asked me, 'How come he was sired by a god and born in your womb?'

This question to me, Yudhishthira? You, the Pandavas, are not sired by Pandu. I could have told you Karna was born the way you, Bhima and Arjuna were sired by Dharmadeva, Vayudeva and Indradeva. The way the two Ashvinikumars cast their seeds in Madri's womb, Karna was born in just the same way.

Yudhishthira! You ask me 'Why?'

No, I never thought of doing anything on my own. Pandu said that a wife can beget a child by a second person. With permission from him I begot you three. I got Karna, the only time I acted on my own. I was unmarried. Did not need a husband's permission. In today's society, Yudhishthira, when the husband wills so, a wife can beget a child sired by another. But an unmarried girl cannot be a mother even if she wants to. Madhavi, the daughter of a Rishi, bore four sons to four kings because her father asked her to—she was unmarried. But society accepted her as she did it under her father's orders.

I am Pandu's wife. The fathers of my sons are outsiders. Still, you are Pandavas but Karna was a carpenter's son!

Maybe, in a distant future, Karna will receive the honour he so deserves. But I will not!

After confession to the earth, Kunti lifted her face. The elderly Nishadin stood staring at her.

Her eyes were so eloquent! So full of pity!

Pity? The Nishadin was pitying her? She picked up the bundle of firewood and left.

At times the vanashrama seemed so near, today it seemed too far. In a desert one sees mirages. A forest is not a desert! Suddenly she found herself standing near the Kingshuka tree. She half-sobbed with relief.

Gandhari took Kunti's hands and held them in her aged, thin, ivory-coloured fingers. She whispered. 'Calm down, O mother of the Pandavas! Time moves in circles, like the wheels of the chariot. The circle of our lifespan is shrinking. Soon it will be reduced to a dot. That dot too will end in a void.'

— Yes, elder sister!

— Do not condemn yourself too much. See, you cannot bring yesterday back. Today's sunrise was a reality. The sunset too! We will fall asleep but time is always on the move, it will bring tomorrow's sunrise.

She touched Gandhari's feet and lay on the grassmat. She prayed for sleep.

Today at noon Kunti sat on a rock and felt a wave of alarm float through the forest.

She was alerted.

The forest is not silent today. The birds, in flocks, are leaving their nests and flying away. Monkeys, jumping from one tree to another, are vanishing into the forest. How strange, the cheetals too are fleeing in herds. What is wrong? The Nishad families with their hunter dogs and bundles on their heads are leaving the forest.

It's alright. Let them desert the forest. Today Kunti would ask mother earth, where lay her crime? When would she be able to forgive herself?

A shadow.

That elderly Nishadin.

Kunti was astonished. Why is this black statuesque woman standing near her? Why is she bending towards her? Searching for something in her eyes?

— No confessions today?

— You . . . You . . .

— I heard your confessions. Waited to hear if you'd confess the biggest crime you committed!

— Your language . . . like mine?

— Yes! I understand, speak when necessary, though you never thought we too are human! What are we? Dumb rocks, trees, or animals?

— You never spoke a word.

— I was waiting for today. For years I've been trying to trace you. We never go to the cities, you know! And, ultimately, you had to come here. Ah, I've been waiting for years, Kunti!

— Kunti? You know my name?

— It hurts, doesn't it?

She laughed, 'A Nishadin addressing you by name! Yes. You are defenceless in this forest, Kunti! Your sons are in the city. They can't send their soldiers to punish us!'

— Do you know that rishis dwell here!

— Oh, rishis! We see them all the time! We are children of the forest you know! Devi Aranyaka is our mother!

Kunti felt tired, so tired! They came to the vanashrama from Gangadwar. Through 'tapasya' she would starve her body and die! Why, why does it seem great effrontery on the Nishadin's part to address her by name?

— Well Nishadin, what do you want?

— You did not confess your greatest crime.

— Yes, I did. You heard me confess.

— No. Kunti, not that. That belongs to the Rajavritta chapter of your life. Of course your son had not become a king!

— I have confessed about Karna.

— Rajavritta and Lokavritta! Different standards of judgement. If a young Nishadin meets her lover and becomes pregnant, why, we celebrate their marriage!

— By which custom?

— It's nature's law. Nature does not tolerate waste. We honour life. If two human beings unite, they should create new life. You won't understand this.

— What? My confession has no value?

— For you it has. We don't understand it. But to Lokavritta, the most heinous crime is massacre of innocents for self-interest. And you have done just that.

— Me? Towards the Lokavritta?

— Remember Varanavata?

— Yes, I went there many years ago . . .

— Let me remind you. You stayed in the Jotugriha?

— Yes, it was all Duryodhan's . . .

— Remember how it was publicized that you and your five sons had perished by fire?

— But that was . . .

— A heinous conspiracy, was it not? Ah, only the Rajavritta can play such games! For one year you stay there, know fully well the hut will be burnt down and you just have to save your and your sons' lives. So you had to build concrete evidence to prove irrefutably that you six were burnt to death. . . . The Nishads and Nishadins used to come regularly to Varanavata. Am I correct?

— But . . .

— Shut your mouth and listen to me. They came from the forest villages. Sold timber, animal hides, ivory, venison, medicinal herbs, resin, honey. Men and women sold their merchandise and accepted salt, clothes and rice in exchange. Then they drank wine, held each other by the arm, went back singing and playing the flute. Jutogriha was on the fringe of the town. Near the jungle track.

— Yes.

— Tell me, who kept close watch on an elderly Nishadin and her five sons? Who invited them to a feast for the Brahmins? Who saw to it that oceans of wine were served with their food? You have feasted Brahmins many times, Kunti! When did you ever care to invite Nishads, Kirats, Sabars, and Nagvanshi forest tribals? Did you arrange to serve wine each time?

— No.

Nishadin's eyes held a death-sentence for her. But Kunti would not lie.

— Only once, Kunti?

— Only once.

— Only once the Vratyas, the marginalized ones, were invited?

— Yes.

— The mother and her five sons drank too much and slept like logs. When you escaped through the secret tunnel, you knew that, did you not?

— Yes, I knew.

— That Nishadin . . .

— Not you!

— No, she was my mother-in-law. I am the eldest daughter-in-law. My four companions are wives of the other four sons.

— But . . . you are not widows!

The Nishadin proudly said, 'We do not deny the demands of life. We have the right to remarriage. Any widow can remarry if she wants to. Yes, we have husbands . . . children . . . !'

— Will you . . . ?

— No, I won't kill you. A tooth for a tooth, an eye for an eye . . . Rajavritta does this. It was done in Kurukshetra. Our laws are different.

— Tell me, what should I do?

— You committed this crime and entirely forgot about it. Because . . . Kunti . . . to you it was not a crime! Burn six innocent forest tribals to death to serve your self-interest! And it's not a crime! Well, according to our law of justice you, and your sons, your allies, all of you are held guilty in the vicharalaya of Aranyaka. The Nishadin crept nearer, 'Have you really seen this forest? All these are resinous trees. Resin is highly inflammable. Know that?'

— Yes, I know.

— Resin drips down the trees and thickens. The dry fir-cones drop from the trees, roll down the slope of the hill, hit the resin and fire breaks out. Forest-fire!

— Forest-fire!

— Yes! We dwellers of the forest can smell the wind and sense the forest-fire. So the animals and birds are fleeing. We too, are on the move.

— Where to?

— Far away. Beyond the reach of the forest-fire. A place protected by mountains, lakes and winding rivers.

— Forest-fire!

— Yes. Three blind persons cannot go there. One was born blind. One is blind by option. You are the blindest one. You kill innocents and remain complacent about it.

— Nishadin! Is it possible to forgive me?

— Commit a sin and beg forgiveness! Such happenings are beyond our ken! That too, belongs to Rajavritta! When we escaped after Jotugriha, other forest tribes left with us. For decades, this forest has been sustaining us.

— But the forest-fire is coming!

— Fire will rage. Then rains will quench the fire. The scalded earth will grow green again. The law of nature!

The Nishadin fled.

Kunti sat like a zombie. Her mind was devoid of all human sense and will. She stood up. Now is the time to return to vanashrama. We have to await the forest-fire. Dhritarashtra and Gandhari have lost a hundred sons and are awaiting death calmly.

In the "Rajavritta" does one kill the innocent first and then beg forgiveness? Kunti does not know.

Mahdu: A Fairy Tale

MAHASWETA DEVI

1

'I shall deal not only with total hunger, the complete debilitation resulting from lack of food which is called starvation, and which is generally limited to extremely depressed areas or to exceptional situations, but also with the much more common and more numerically lethal hidden hunger which for lack of certain indisposable nutritive elements, condemns whole population groups slowly to die of hunger although they eat everyday' (From *Geography of Hunger* by Josua de Castro, 1952). Mahdu never knew that he had already been referred to in some book written in 1952, long before his birth.

The Korjus are mostly illiterate. Mahdu was born in 1984. The old ones in the settlement used to refer to the year 1984 as the year of some big one being killed in a place called Delhi. 'A rajah died; a rani; no one knew.'

The wooden shack where Mahdu was born had walls of wood planks, thatched with wild grass. The Korjus crept in after sunset, clasped each other and slept. They entered the hut only to sleep.

2

That particular shack had already declared that it was old, and wanted to die. The death signs were clear. The rat snake, the oldest resident of the hut, had one day left its hole in the corner, dragging its tired body as it crawled out. It was so old that the tail end was blunt, rounded and obscene.

Even the Korjus knew that snakes and human beings should coexist in harmony. Their knowledge, or wisdom, or experience, stopped

*Written in 2000.

advancing with the times about a hundred or so years ago. When the Sagwana, or the saga forests, were felled, the Korjus, who were food gatherers, became a condemned people. Their staple food was a gruel made from seeds of the reori grass growing in the saga forest. The green sentinels of the sagwana protected so many plants and herbs on the forest floor. The Korjus ate reori seeds, tuber, roots, fruits, nuts, deer, birds, hares and monitor lizards. Their brains ceased to function when the forest died. Like all Korjus, Mahdu too knows, that if you lift the eyelids of a dead Korju you will find the imprint of the old saga forest on his or her eyeballs. After death, the forest reclaims the Korju. Forests, human beings, and huts die. The rat snake was followed by ants, centipedes and ants. The hut had made its intent known. It wanted to be burnt to ashes.

Mahdu was born in such a hut. His mother had severed the umbilical cord with a rusty blade, tied her son's navel with twine and crawled out clutching the infant. Perhaps Baban's or Kallu's mother had given her a jean-skirt, a gift from the organization DEDICATION. A skirt is so useful! Rip off the waist-band, and you get quite a length of cloth to wrap around your body. Mother and the son were bathed with water drawn from the tube-well once sunk by the Jan Seva people. Mother was given a glass of tea. Tea dust, brewed with salt, chilli powder and wild garlic.

And the hut was set ablaze. The forest guards had once left a notice: 'To start a fire in the forest area is a cognizable offence.'

As long as the notice board hung from the two hooks, birds, perched on it. Now it hangs on one hook. Birds have stopped coming.

Of course the forest guards did not come to see and report the fire. A roaring fire reduced the hut to ashes, and died within a few minutes. An ineffective fire. Like the protest once made by the Korjus. It was no threat to the forest as there was no forest. A few amla trees are all that the Korjus have.

The tin hut made by Jan Seva for Korju development is the sole evidence of their Korju-concern. Good, strong tin. The Korju lifespan has reduced to the twenties; when they sense the approach of death, they crawl into the hut, lie down and wait.

The doctor comes, does not come. A death certificate is not issued every time. But a Korju death-register is meticulously maintained. Doctors Chintamoni Narayan and Subhadra Chintamani Joshi had once seen the death register and were curious. They decided to go and visit the settlement some time in the future.

3

Their first efforts came to nothing. The Korju question belonged to the past. A dead question. Years ago the administration tried to solve the food problem of the Korjus and gave up. The Korjus did not open their mouths. They just stared back. Eyes patient and tired, not hostile. Eventually the Sarkar forgot them.

The new eminent nutritionist Dr Deepak Mahadev Apte was the first doctor ever to reach the Korjus. He was with the DEDICATION team in his pre-eminence days. That the Korjus were apathetic to Sarkar-given rice, wheat or jowar interested him.

The District Collector was young. His first posting in a tribal area. He loved to speak.

— What are you up to? Want to write for the media? That Sarkar is starving the Korjus?

— I'm not from the media.

— They've been refusing food for years.

— But why?

— It's impossible to change the food habits of a primitive tribe. The Jarwas of the Andamans are dying too!

— Why?

— Won't eat anything but pygmy hogs. The Sarkar introduced spotted deer, the cheetal! They refused venison. No tigers there. Deer population increased. Once, say twenty years ago, venison sold for one rupee per kilo! The Korjus are the same. They are supplied with food, but no, they won't eat. It's been going on for a century or so!

— A century?

— Maybe more, maybe less!

Doctor Apte was falling through an abyss. Trapped. Unknown and hostile forces were attacking him.

— What do they die of?

— Malnutrition.

— A primitive tribe dying of malnutrition? In the twenty-first century?

— See the records. We left foodgrains for them. No response. They fell ill when served with cooked food. An in-built resistance. One time Collector Brij Kapur . . . a highly valued officer . . . a Padmashree awardee . . . had really studied them. He said, in-built resistance against progress is killing them. Their mindset controls the body. So whenever they eat something they're not used to, they become violently ill. Actually his paper was brilliant, brilliant.

— All the Korjus are like this?

— How do I know? I have the oldest settlement under my jurisdiction. And I tell you, they are losing . . . can't survive . . . moving towards extinction.

— Extinction!

4

'This is a slow process death. The process continues through quite a number of generations. Nutrition of the body depended upon the food they were used to. And there was their belief, "nature is the provider of food", so integrated with tribal existence. Their psyche is a protected zone. Impossible to penetrate into . . . they are dying in the last five or ten decades . . . no written report . . . very defeating. . . .'

5

Apte went back defeated, read *Geography of Hunger* all over again and thought about the Korjus. Library hunting did not help him much. Won't eat civilized food. What did they eat?

But one day he was electrified to read a Letter to the Editor by Brij Kapur, retd. IAS, President of Feed the Children or FTC. He managed to reach him.

Kapur belonged to the early batch of the IAS, old, erect and spruce, close-cropped grey hair and cleanshaven cheek. He looked quite fit. The board on the wall said he was the President of the Mumbai Chapter of Feed the Children (FTC).

The flat was sparsely furnished. He gave Apte just half an hour. Surprised at the mention of the Korjus, he asked, 'What? Are they still there?'

Ah, they were very much there. No, they never migrated to the industrial district. A shorter lifespan, death at an early age, birth rate dropping, dropping. Still they existed. Listening to Apte, Brij Kapur shook his head.

— Yes, I saw indications alright. But is it that bad? What a pity! Well, I wrote to different NGOs. DEDICATION sank a few hand pumps, but failed to bring the mothers and children to the nutrition centre. They wouldn't come . . . didn't trust us . . .

— Were they violent?

— Oh no! Highly civilized, quiet, soft spoken. No violence. A silent satyagraha! Yes . . . a satyagraha!

— A great tragedy.

— They court death.

— And what do they eat?

— No one knows . . . must be eating something . . . but the resistance is in the mind . . . it affects the body . . . all due to a century-old grievance . . .

— Grievance? They went to court?

— It really is nothing. You'll get all the information in my report . . . got your telephone . . . got the papers . . . you'll find details in my autobiography.

— Published?

— To be released on Children's Day. An FTC foundation publication. Well, namaste! Time for my walk!

— Namaste and thanks!

— Come to FTC if you feel like it. We really do feed children of the poor.

— If nutrition centres could be run there!

— Couldn't. Globalization has made Korjus of human beings all over the globe! The Korjus won't eat because once a few thousand acres of sagwana/saga/teak trees were felled.

— But when?

— In the nineteenth century. By the British.

6

'Indian Railway started functioning in 1853. Bombay to Thane. By 1867, rail connection between Howrah-Delhi and Howrah-Bombay was a reality. We have to keep in mind that even in the first decade of twentieth century, the BHABAR terai-forests of Himalayan foothills, were regularly felled as engines ran on wood/charcoal. When rail connection began materializing, vast forest tracts were cleared so that tree trunks could be sawed into railway sleepers. So sal, sagwana and mahogany forests were devastated. During a phase of the Howrah-Bombay railway extension, the gorgeous teak forests of Maharashtra and the adjoining Madhya Bharat (the then Central province) were felled. Korjus, hitherto sustained by the forests, first became homeless and then their very existence was devastated. Physically alive, they felt they simply did not exist. They were like drifting, lost kites with their strings cut off. Saga forests provided them with a home. The bride and the groom were first married to saga trees to make the marriage lasting, strong and productive. Saga was the deity they worshipped.

'The mighty trees were first converted to timber, then railway sleepers. When the first train left Nasik and proceeded towards Howrah, the awed spectators bashed a coconut to pay homage to the roaring monster of an engine. Yes, shake with fear and bow your heads to the conquerors. The Korjus remained distant spectators, mute and motionless. The non-existent saga forests found shelter in their heart. That is why, on the eyeballs of a dead Korju the image of a live saga tree is imprinted. Korjus became a collective myth and began to shed their desire to survive.'

7

But Apte continued to be needled by the Korju question.

Shalini Tikekar of DEDICATION said, 'They are hopeless. The government gave them hectares of forest land but they never cultivated it, know that?'

— Perhaps they have never done cultivation. Food gatherers, you know!

— That's no excuse. In Amalner, outsiders have been cultivating Korju land for the last so many years, and have become wealthy farmers. They are dodgers. Could have learnt too.

— Perhaps that too they do not know.

— It's impossible to change the mindset of a primitive tribe!

Narayan Sathe said, 'Why do you say Sarkar gave them land? It was, and still is, Korju land. Trees were felled, but the land belongs to them.'

— Any record?

— Record? In the 1860s who tried to know them? To help them take to agriculture? No Shalini, it's not done even now!

— Really Narain, you've become such a know-all after attending the workshop on the Baigas!

— Everything is wrong with our tribal policy, if there is a policy at all!

— Can't we fight? Go to court for their rights?

Apte said, 'Forget them. Lifespan eighteen to twenty, birth rate almost nil, an adult male weighs 40-50 kilos, forget them!' Shalini shouted, 'Why, it's a case of malnutrition!'

— Perhaps.

Apte went and wrote an article on the Korjus. Eventually, 'Government Policy to Starve a Primitive Tribe to Death?' raised a lot of noise and he had to face the gun later.

He went to the settlement. Each time he would take dried fruit, cashewnuts, dried fish. Soya powder and nutri-nuggets, trinkets and cheap toys.

They never responded to his gifts. Even children stared at him with solemn and ancient gravity. A silent satyagraha.

The last time Apte took the Jan Seva people with him. A new NGO, they went with a package of awareness programmes on pure drinking water, health care, birth control, etc. etc. The silence and desolation of the settlement deflated their enthusiasm. They left in frustration but left behind a well-made tin hut as their chief patron owned, amidst many assets, some tin factories. That hut survived the onslaught of time, relentless summers and punishing rains. Now the roof has countless holes.

This time the Collector asked Apte not to come back ever again. Because the American journal *Hunger,* published by WAH (War Against Hunger) printed an article by an NRI, Mahul Raghav. Raghav plagiarized Apte's article and accused the Government of India of denying food to India's 'VORJU' aboriginals to hasten their extinction. It created a furore.

The Collector made Apte halt for two days and gave him a scalding lecture. Scandal-mongering about the GOI in the name of research would no longer be tolerated. Sarkar would take necessary steps. Apte was an ignorant amateur. In the settlement there were neither famines, nor starvation deaths.

'You people just failed to make any inroads. It's your failure, not Sarkar's', he barked.

Apte left the area. His final departure.

8

The settlement became a forbidden area, a 'nishiddha bhumi'.

The Korjus forgot the outsiders and the outsiders forgot them. The timing was great, as the Pokhran Nuclear Explosion took place. Everything became a non-issue to the media, the nation and the power-barons.

Subhadra and Chintamoni Joshi chose this specific time to investigate into the great Korju extinction mystery in an imported safari-car, complete with a kitchenette, a toilet, folding beds and a mini-TV.

They chose to enter in secrecy.

And Mahdu had already been carried to the tin hut two days earlier. The Korjus came to that hut to die. Mahdu lay staring at the tin roof and saw the sky through the holes. His mother came to feed him gruel. She had to make ropes from sisal. The Sarkar gave them sisal. Rope-making was their sole means of livelihood. The Joshis entered the hut and stared at Mahdu.

Sixteen, the BDO said. Looks shrunken and small. They looked at each other, came out and inspected the surroundings. Desolate. They did not waste time in measuring his height or checking his weight. They just gathered him in Chintamoni's arms, laid him carefully in the car and sped away towards Mumbai.

They were conducting research on nutrition balance in order to unravel the mystery of death due to chronic hunger.

9

'Chronic hunger in India, is without doubt one fundamental cause of the high death rate, which competes with that of China . . . 30 out of 1000 die of hunger . . . more than 10 million people die in India every year', *Geography of Hunger*, 1952.

10

The Joshis worked in the same centre. They were in search of proper material, a chronically starved human body to experiment with. They had to prove that chronically starving persons need a balanced and nutritious diet, meeting the requirements of the body. Then they learnt of the Korjus and Apte. Apte said, 'You are on the right side of the government. With such political support you might do something. To date, nothing concrete was ever done. You have political clout, big funds—you might be able to do something.'

— A totally alien environment wouldn't frighten them?

— They are beyond that.

11

Deep secrecy was maintained about Mahdu.

1. To keep a community starving, is politics. And it is a logical extension of global politics.
2. To enter such a community, and obtain a live human specimen to obtain physical evidence of what such a policy ultimately leads to, is politics too.
3. To write about it is politics.
4. And not to write, too, is politics.
5. Not to do anything about it is the ultimate politics, which is an extension of global . . . etc . . . etc.

12

A soundless and insulated cell. Mahdu on a sanitized bed with shaved head, close shut eyes. Under the cover his body was naked and relaxed. He was being fed intravenously. It was very promising, the way his body absorbed the nutrient fluid.

Urmila Jenny Sahana, an assistant dietotherapist, kept watch over him and reported to the team of experts over intercom.

The Joshis had organized a round-the-clock action team of nutritionists, dieticians, biochemists, vitaminologists, enzymologists and dietotherapists to monitor the nutrients and check the condition of MKM or Male Korju Mahdu.

The speed with which Mahdu's body absorbed the drip surprised Subhadra, who snorted, 'Refused to accept food . . . mindset primitive and resistant . . . hoax! Just see what's happening for a week! MKM is intaking the drip and his kidneys are functioning.'

— Well, he hasn't opened his eyes!
— He will.

MKM became their 'child', a precious body. And by the eighth day Urmila reported that drip-intake was going up in measure. Subhadra laughed, '140 years of starvation! He is making it up'.

Actually Mahdu, just by absorbing the nutrients negated the myth (Korjus are one of the slowly dying tribes), opinions of researchers (the entire tribe has turned away from life and is heading towards extinction) . . . etc. He exploded the carefully built-up Korju myth.

Chintamoni Joshi shook his head in disbelief. 'It was all a fabrication? No one even tried once to do anything? What a collective shame!'

Dr. Irani said, 'Let's talk to Russleigh and Oneishi. They will be thrilled!'

— Secrecy is of first importance!
— Yes, it's a political issue now!

13

'A human body needs all the vitamins and minerals like iron, zinc, copper and cobalt; through vegetables, green edible leaves, fish, meat, grain, fruit, sunflower seed oil, margarine, milk and milk products, nuts and oysters. . . .'

14

On the twelfth day MKM opened his lips and took a sip of water.

'Holy Miracle!' Dr Oneishi said, and Urmila Jenny whispered, 'Just see his teeth!' Gone were the grey and decayed teeth. MKM's teeth were healthy, Colgate-white and strong.

— What's his height?
— Dr Joshi knows.
— Russleigh will reach by the evening flight. Please continue to feed him. Say! More Korjus like him? Because . . .

15

On the night of the fourteenth day Urmila's replacement doubted her eyes and bent down to check. Her charge, the mysterious patient, was trying to wake up and stretch his legs. She covered his feet. He looked so strange! With needles, drips, tubes, catheter and a gigantic screen monitoring him. So weird!

16

Oneishi, the Joshis and Dr Mathai talked in whispers over coffee. Mathai the cynic told the Joshis, 'This boy just might get you internationally famous! He might.'

— He'd gain in weight and height?

Oneishi said, 'It wouldn't be the first case! Castro's mention of the pygmy. . . .'

— Yes, and the Shetland ponies. . . .

Mathai said, 'It's a dangerous game you're playing.'

— But why?

— Once our ancestors were gigantic. Through many geo-ages mankind came down to Norman height. Yes, heights for different races. What if MKM starts. . . .

— What?

— The world will come to know that India works in colonial, then global interest. Makes shrunken pygmies of normal people! Think of the political fracas!

Subhadra tried to say something but suddenly the lights went out, the alarm siren rang once and died. Running feet, glass walls crumbling. 'A bomb blast?' Mathai's voice was drowned by a thunderous roar.

'MALA BHUKH LAGALIYA!'

The ten-storeyed centre shook and crashed down and a tremendous roar rent the sky.

'MALA KHAILA DE!'

17

'I am hungry. Give me food.'

18

Since all the characters mentioned are nowhere, no one knows their immediate reaction.

What happened is a horizontal MAHDU awoke from his coma and felt constrained as he was attaining an unattainable height. He stretched his legs and his feet just crashed through the wall and pushed the team of doctors through the wall. He sat up, stretched his arms, and the building just crashed down. And he roared, 'I AM HUNGRY'.

He never stopped growing, so he straddled Mumbai—greater Mumbai—and told the stars. 'MALA KHAILA DE.'

He was naked, with brown eyes and bronzed skin. Lifting his face in a gut-wrenching, stricken voice he cried, 'MALA BHUKH LAGALIYA'.

He stretched his arms and started eating. He swallowed the Usha Kiron Building, the Tata Memorial and Yashpal hospitals, Nariman Towers, hotels Taj and Centaur, Gateway of India, Boot House, Essel World, Film City, mashed under his teeth the assembly house, cars, palaces, apartments and reaching Chhatrapati Terminus he roared 'SAGA CHE JANGAL?'

He lifted the trains off the tracks and swallowed them, caught the flying planes and ate them, and he said, 'PANI! PANI!'

Then he bent down and drank the Arabian Sea in huge gulps. He never stopped walking. No man-made Korju myths. Over.

Thus the true Korju story began. Mahdu would write it on the sky. He would pluck the stars, arrange them into alphabets and write.

He planted his feet on the bed of the Arabian Sea and lifted one leg to move towards the east.

He raised his eyes towards the sky. The stars so near! His eye balls mirrored a tall saga tree resplendent with leafs and blossoms. Mahdu laughed like a child. Freed.

PART III

Literature and Politics

BHISHAM SAHNI

In our intellectual circles there have been a number of discussions, sometimes even bitter ones, about the question whether literature should become a vehicle of political ideas and activities or avoid them, whether such a thing is desirable, and if so, to what extent.

To my mind, there is hardly any scope for controversy on this issue. If literature is concerned with life, and in the act of writing a writer deals basically with life itself, politics, being part and parcel of life, cannot be totally excluded or left out. Like many other aspects of life, politics affects us and gives our lives a direction, at the personal as well as the collective, social level. There are often political reasons for the barbarity of war. Millions of Jews, we know, were massacred for political reasons. It was the aggressive politics of power that lay at the bottom of the appalling incidents of Hiroshima and Nagasaki. Shall we say, then, that literature concentrating on these occurrences fails to qualify as 'literature'? Similarly, the issues of discrimination on the basis of colour, class or caste, though not directly political, are still related to politics. To what extent is it feasible to draw the dividing line between a 'pure' literature and a politics-related literature? In a way the entire socially oriented literature could be termed political literature.

All the elements affecting life can be the subject of literary creativity. As a matter of fact, politics itself is not an autonomous subject. With it there are inevitably intertwined human concerns, hopes and expectations. That is what makes it suitable for creativity. Was our own struggle for independence merely a political movement? Didn't thinking about that struggle invariably involve a deep concern for the plight of our country, concern over the inhuman exploitation and suppression of our people

*The volume was initially intended to be bilingual, hence Bhisham Sahni had written this article in Hindi which has been translated into English by Dinesh Dadhichi.

carried on systematically by the foreign rulers? It would be wrong to term it 'mere politics' wherever there is transgression of human values and a voice is raised against it. When we dream, we dream not merely at the individual level, and not only about our own hopes and achievements. There are some collective social dreams too; some of our dreams are related to our political system, which, we expect, will make it possible for us to fulfil our individual dreams. From this angle also, politics cannot be placed outside the purview of literature.

Another thing that becomes clear when we take into consideration the types of discussions held in our literary-intellectual circles is the fact that their basis has been more often political than literary. It was the detractors of the leftist ideology who generally termed all socially oriented literature as 'crude propaganda'.

Let us leave aside the issues related to our socio-economic system. Shall we say that writing about communalism is also political? Today Dalit literature is emerging powerfully on the sheer strength of the writers' battered sensibilities. Is that literature also trivial and crudely propagandist? Some time back Roop Kunwar was consigned to flames at the funeral pyre of her husband. Should a poem occasioned by that incident be called propaganda? The 'human' aspect of an occurrence stirs the writer's sensibility much more than the 'political' aspect; that is how the author is impelled to creativity.

However, there is no denying the fact—and perhaps there are no two opinions on this issue—that when an author writes a poem or a short story on a socially oriented subject, we expect the writing to be good literature as well, excellent, effective, and reassuring to the reader as literature. No wonder, therefore, it is generally the writings rich in literary attributes that become popular; half-baked and merely slogan-based writings are soon forgotten. Writings that resort to sloganeering may have some utility as means of propaganda; as literary creations, they get little recognition. Some literary qualities are considered indispensable. Just as mere rhyming does not make a poem, mere sloganeering does not make a literary piece.

What is regrettable, however, is that some of our friends equated social orientation itself with sloganeering to exclude it from the ambit of literature altogether. All writings characterized by social orientation were dubbed as 'crude' and 'backward' or 'inferior'. If a writing focuses on the individual and restricts itself to the internal world and processes, it is in tune with the modern sensibility; if it relates itself to the realities of contemporary life and tends to be realistic, it is declared inferior. Such observations have often been made.

I remember having read long back that the development of the novel as a genre has been from the 'outer' to the 'inner' world. Whereas the earlier novelists wove the structure of their novels mainly around the events and incidents of the external world, the modern ones concentrated more and more on the internal life of characters, on their mental processes. And since things are regarded as progressing from backward to forward, the novels based on incidents were termed backward and those concentrating on the individual self were considered advanced.

It seems futile to discuss whether introspective writing is modern and incident-based writing is backward. Perhaps literary creativity does not progress along such a straight path. Admittedly, however, such an interpretation of the development of novel in Europe has been given. In my opinion, incident-based writing cannot afford to neglect the internal world of its characters. Nor can introspective writing completely exclude the incidents of everyday life.

This bias, however, resulted in incident-based writings being regarded as inferior in quality. Also, it adversely affected their evaluation as literature. Related to this bias was the view often expressed that socially oriented writings should be grouped as mere propaganda, whereas the writings focusing on the internal world belonged to the literature of permanent values.

In our literature, in fact, there has never been such a dividing line. Here even propaganda through literature has not been frowned upon. In the Middle Ages very rich literature based on piety and ethical norms was created. We derive aesthetic pleasure from it both as the utterances of great saints and as great literature. Kabir's poetry has been on the lips of millions of people for about six hundred years. It continues to give us solace and inspiration, on the spiritual and devotional planes, and also delight that sublime poetry gives. The same can be said about the writings of Meera, Surdas and Tulsidas.

Some time back, while reading about the Jataka tales, I noted now Mahatma Buddha envisioned the conscious use of this literary form in order to make his teachings easily comprehensible to the ordinary masses.

Likewise, poets deeply inspired by the freedom struggle in India expressed their feelings in poetry. And Brecht presented the contradictions of the capitalist system in the form of excellent satirical dramas. The works of a number of renowned authors were inspired by a similar purpose. During the final phase of his life Premchand, in a letter to Banarsi Das Chaturvedi, stated explicitly that he intended to devote the remaining years of his life to writing literature—the literature that aimed at independence for India.

Shall we, then, classify Premchand as a writer indulging in political propaganda? Premchand has also stated that a writer is not merely a follower but a torchbearer leading the society.

It was not simply a question of using a particular genre of literature. The sensibility of a writer was stirred by a cause and his literary creations were inspired by that cause. A number of internationally acclaimed books belonged to this group.

This commitment in itself was not wrong; it was natural. But it suffered from a type of narrowness. When the Soviet regime was established in Russia it received not only acceptance but also primacy as the objective of literature. In its extreme form it became a part of the administration, and this impaired the spontaneous creation of literature and threatened to discontinue the tradition of free exchange of ideas. This narrow-mindedness certainly caused damage to the natural development of literature. Pasternak and other writers were treated unjustly. Actually they became scapegoats in the political discord between the two power blocs.

But this kind of narrow-mindedness was no less on the other side also. In capitalist countries the leftist writers came under surveillance, and the capitalist establishment, especially the media, began to boycott the writings that severely criticized the system. Various types of restrictions were imposed on writers with leftist leanings during the McCarthy era. The treatment meted out to Charlie Chaplin, Brecht, Romain Rolland et al. is a matter of common knowledge. The independence movement in our own country was inspired by democratic values and the system remained democratic in character, therefore, there were no such restrictions here. At the most there was talk about the party line, etc., and that also took the form of open discussion. These discussions too were often confined to the authors who had leftist affiliation, for example, Ram Vilas Sharma, Amrit Rai, Shivdan Singh Chauhan et al. or Ali Sardar Jafri, and Sa'adat Hasan Manto.

The erstwhile attitude of rejection of politics has today assumed a different form, and the literature of social orientation is once again being pushed to the periphery and the individual-centred literature is being placed at the centre.

The field of literature is fraught not only with different types of misconceptions but also different types of prejudices. For a long time I have been actively associated with the Pragatisheel Lekhak Sangh. I cannot remember even a single instance of any author being pressurized to write in conformity to the 'party-line', or of an author being criticized for not toeing the 'party-line'. Even the expression 'party-line', which I am using here, was unheard of during that time. The writers who got associated with this movement did not do so under any external pressure, but because their own thinking impelled them in that direction. Leftist ideology has had widespread impact. There is no doubt that the leftists gave priority to politics, and this politics was about the conflict between two types of systems. Their role in this conflict was not that of indifferent spectators. But one never heard of a writer being dictated to write in a particular way.

If a writer is inclined towards social concerns in his act of creation, it is his own conscience, his understanding, his sensibility, and his experience that prompt him to do so. And this is very natural. There is no doubt that such socially oriented writing has been the dominant trend in our literature for a long time, since Premchand's era or even before that. There were historical causes for the emergence of this trend: the inconsistencies and contradictions of our national scene, and the consequent restlessness, different types of struggles, hopes and aspirations, and the conflict between tradition and contemporary pressure, etc. This trend, however, does not regard such commitment as 'crude' or 'backward'. At the same time it does not obstruct the pen of other writers who have a different point of view and possess different types of sensibilities. In spite of disputes, our literary environment has been characterized by openness, which continues to be there. I appreciate and welcome it.

Gender and Nation: Iconography of the Past

MEENAKSHI MUKHERJEE

It would be a truism to state that the dominant ideals and values of a culture can be seen embedded in its stories. But it needs also to be emphasized that the stories in their turn construct and define this culture; that stories and communities are bound together in a symbiotic relationship, defining and interpreting each other. By making the readers (or the audience, if it is orally communicated) perceive that their present flows from a common past, narratives—whether they are epics, heroic legends, novels, films, or television serials—can draw a community together, consolidating its identity. Benedict Anderson's thesis posited seventeen years ago, that any community, be it a tribe or a village, a religious group or the larger collectivity called the nation, has first to be imagined for it to become real, remains valid on the whole although one may not agree with all the ramifications of his argument when we apply the thesis to India.[1]

Thus, the construction of a past has always been an agenda of nationalism and the discursive process through which this is achieved enlists the services of history as much as of literature. Nationalist historiography as it emerged in India in the late nineteenth century was in many ways a reaction to the colonisers' account of India's past that traced a movement from the despotism and anarchy of the pre-British period to the order and justice introduced by the imperial rulers. In order to counter the teleology of this version of history a different emplotting of the past was necessary. The spate of historical novels that appeared at the turn of the nineteenth century in different Indian languages may be seen as part of this process of creating a counter-narrative. As a student of the novel as a genre I am interested in probing the reasons why so many writers in different regions of the country felt the need to go back to the past roughly at the same time—the zenith of the British rule in India—and why so many readers seemed spellbound by this new variety of historical romance.

By constructing a glorious pre-colonial past and imagining or highlighting victories against other and earlier invaders, these novels were indirectly helping to crystallize a sense of nationhood through the valorization of both the physical prowess and the spiritual strength of the community. Historical research of an academic nature (not free of teleology) was going on at the same time, and at least in two languages—Bangla and Marathi—this was being disseminated through journals (for example, *Aitihasik Chitra* started in Bangla in 1898 and *Kavyetihas Sangraha* started in Marathi in 1874), and also through school textbooks. At another level songs, stage performances, oral recitals and novels testify to a widening of awareness—at least among the educated upper class, for whom history had assumed the cultural guise for an act of self-assertion. In 1880, the editor of the Bangla journal *Bangadarshan* exhorted its readers to take up the challenge of writing their own history as a collective enterprise: 'Bengal must have her own history. Otherwise there is no hope for Bengal. Who is to write it? You have to write it. It is not a task that can be performed by one person alone. It has to be done by all of us together.'[2]

Rewriting of history was thus seen almost as a moral act for the retrieval of the self-respect of a subjugated people, and as a pedagogic process by which a community could educate itself about how it should represent itself, because, as Sudipta Kaviraj has argued, 'people can generally become what they believe they are'.[3] In such an ethos history writing becomes complementary with myth-making and the construction of moral paradigms that would provide the nation—be it Bengal, or Maharashtra or the whole of India—with a cultural identity. This is partly the reason why the use of history in writing novels became such an important activity in colonial India, specially at the end of the nineteenth century and the early decades of the twentieth.

My objective in this paper is to explore how women were used/perceived/deployed/represented in this predominantly masculinist project. Were they seen as signs and symbols or as participating subjects? Did the projection of male valour necessitate the re-confirmation of female passivity? Paradoxically, why did women figure so centrally in the imaginative project of constructing the idea of the nation?

II

At the beginning of a discussion of gender in colonial India, it is necessary to remember that the British rulers had done much to propagate the myth of effeminacy as far as Indian men were concerned. I do not know how far back the notion can be traced, but I find the earliest evidence in James Mill's *The History of British India* (1759) which was written without the author ever coming to India or knowing any Indian language. Mill had pronounced: '[Hindus] possessed a certain softness both in their persons and address that distinguish them from the manlier races of Europe.'[4] The absence of manliness among Indian men, more specifically among Hindu men, was a prevalent premise of the colonial rulers. The countries which were not Europe were assumed to be outside the pale of history. Men in Western civilization who knew how to shape their destiny, it was believed, had a natural right to penetrate the pristine blankness of this ahistorical space to stamp their own mark here by virtue of their manliness and superiority. This was the implicit presupposition—which did not always remain implicit. We see it articulated intermittently, as for example in the historian Richard Orme's observation in 1770: 'All natives in India showed an effeminacy of character, but the Bengalis were of still weaker frame and more enervated nature',[5] or in Thomas Babbington Macaulay's statement: 'The Castilians have a proverb that in Valencia the Earth is Water and Men, Women; the description is equally applicable to the vast plains of lower Ganges.'[6]

Another way of feminizing the colony was to emphasize its exoticism and romantic mystery by which it enticed Europe. A quotation from a novel by Maud Diver illustrates this widespread analogy: 'India may truly be said . . . to be a woman country, loved of all the male lands and exercising the same irresistible magnetism, the same domination over the hearts of men. . . . India, even to her inmates seems still a veiled mystery, aloof yet alluring, like one of her purdah princesses.'[7] Quotations of this kind can be endlessly multiplied. Behind all of these there is a desire to prove the masculinity of the ruling race in order to establish their natural superiority and justify their right to rule. The economic need to exploit the colonies is thus camouflaged as either romantic attraction or carnal longing—both impulses legitimate in virile men. In a patriarchal ideology women and land are both seen as natural properties of men, the conquest of land and the possession of women often blending into a composite metaphor.

It must also be noted that the subjugated people themselves seemed to have internalized these assumptions and smarted under a gender-based inferiority. As a reaction against this there emerged by the end of the nineteenth century an aggressively militant nationalism which emphasized the need for physical culture, the development of muscular strength along with spiritual regeneration in order to define the identity of the nation and challenge the coloniser's discourse. This could be one of the reasons why Vivekananda became such a lasting icon in many parts of the country and remained so for a good part of the century. In literature we see its counterpart in the proliferation of historical fiction glorifying Rajput heroism and Maratha valour—particularly the heroism of Shivaji.

In his book *The Intimate Enemy* Ashis Nandy has argued that the British dismissal of the Hindu male as weak and unmanly had resulted in a reflex reaction which invoked *kshatriyahood* as the masculine model. It tended to erase the inclusive androgyny of certain Hindu concepts—for example the idea of *ardhanarishwar* or of non-violence which Mahatma Gandhi highlighted later. This assertion of aggressive patriotism had as its corollary the notion of women as sacred and vulnerable—the metaphoric embodiment of the country to be protected. Let me mention at least one popular novel of the time that has a plot encapsulating this entire symbology: Bankimchandra Chatterjee's *Raj Singha* (Bangla 1881, revd and enlgd edn 1894, subsequently translated into several other Indian languages). The story narrates how the princess of Roopnagar, a small state in Rajasthan, writes a letter to Raj Singha, the brave Rana of Udaipur, for protection against the assault of Aurangzeb who was coming to attack Roopnagar and abduct the princess. The seed of this story was embedded in one brief paragraph in Colonel Tod's two-volume *Annals and Antiquities of Rajasthan* (1829 and 1831), a book whose enormous influence on the popular imagination of the country has not yet been properly analysed. This seed from Tod's book sprouted into three full-length novels in three major languages of India: *Raj Singha* (Bangla), *Roopnagarchi Rajkumari* (1902) in Marathi by Hari Narain Apte and in Hindi a novel by Kishorilal Goswami titled *Tara* and subtitled *Kshatra-kulakamalini* (1901). Thus, a minor incident of Rajput valour gets expanded into a symbolic validation of Hindu potential against Muslim invasion, employing the trope of sexual assault as a metaphor for territorial aggression. The princess of Roopnagar takes on the attributes of motherland, and the noble Raj Singha prevents her violation at the risk of his own life. In this semiotic logic, gender distinction has to be rigidly maintained, because men are called upon to be strong if women are unambiguously defenceless. This premise underlies most heroic narratives and historical fiction depicting the so-called martial races of India.

To digress for a moment and take a look at Colonel Tod's volumes may not be inappropriate here. James Tod spent four years in Rajasthan (1818-22) as the Political Agent after which he was recalled from his services. He published his massive two volume work in England in 1829 and 1831 after collating his extensive field notes and working for some more years in the Royal Asiatic Society of London where he also served as a librarian. His work was an unprecedented blend of genealogical research on certain dynasties of Rajputana, collection of folklore, bardic songs and ballads, documentation of social and religious practices of the people of the region, overlaid by the romantic mindset of a man roughly the contemporary of Byron and Scott and influenced by Henry Hallam's *View of the State of Europe during the Middle Ages* (1818) which attempted to understand the structures of feudalism. Tod's influence travelled to more directions than he could have imagined. His book helped colonial administration by suggesting (see the Dedication to King William the Fourth) that the loyalty of the people of Rajasthan to their local kings could be strategically transferred to the Emperor of England by supporting these feudal chiefs and their martial tendencies could be used to help the empire. It fired the imagination of the colonized people, particularly in Bengal where more than a hundred novels, plays and narrative poems came to be written in the next hundred years about Rajput bravery, which vicariously validated the heroic potential of all Hindus. The raw materials used in these texts were usually derived from Tod. Also it has been argued that the Rajputs' self-perception as hyper-masculine warriors, the brave protectors of their land, women and religion against foreign assault owes a lot to Tod's celebratory work.

It would however be too simplistic to say that the only paradigm put forward by Tod for representing women in these past-based narratives was that of the passive woman in need of protection. Often he presents Rajput women as taking part in the control of the family, sharing with their husbands the dangers of war and sport and being contemptuous of cowardice. This alternative model—that of the *veerangana*—the brave woman—was first imaginatively fictionalized in a long narrative poem in Bangla—*Veerangana Kavya* (1861) by Michael Madhusudan Dutt and later we encounter such figures in the woman warrior in *Anandamath* (1882) and the bandit leader in *Debichaudhurani* (1884). At least in Bengal, in the same chronological period when fragile and vulnerable women were heroines of historical fiction, we also find the courageous, the learned and the competent women finding their way into fiction, poetry, drama and school textbooks. In 1887 a school textbook entitled *Pracheen Arya Ramani-ganer Itibritta* (Accounts of Ancient Aryan Women) is prefaced by the following enthusiastic words from the male editor: 'Today is a happy day for womankind! It is also a joyful day for the advocates of female education! Who will not be happy to hear that women had composed Vedic hymns? Everyone is aware of the happiness expressed when a woman is able to defend herself with her debating prowess in front of learned Brahmans schooled in the Vedas.'[8] Statements like this reconfirm what the historian Uma Chakravarti has described as 'the creation of a persuasive rhetoric, shared by Hindi liberals and conservatives alike, especially in relation to the myth of the golden age of Indian womanhood as located in the Vedic period'.[9] It certainly helped to counter, however indirectly, another imperialist assumption about the abject condition of Indian women who required the protection and intervention of the colonial state. It is well known how in numerous English novels about India written by the British, one comes across a recurrent fictional situation which concretizes this pervasive official attitude: the rescue of a '*suttee*' from her pyre by a British officer—obviously a signifier of the British civilizing mission in India. A novel written as late as M.M. Kaye's *The Far Pavillions* (1978) repeats this trope: a woman about to commit *sati* being rescued by an Englishman. Some stereotypes die hard.

If the Bangla textbook mentioned above glorified the achievements of Arya women, a subsequent school book *Arya Keerti* (1896) fused the notion of Aryahood with that of Kshatriyahood to bring together heterogeneous heroic figures—from different ages and different regions in India—Sanjukta, Padmini, Tarabai, Sultana Razia, and a relatively recent figure—Rani Lakshmibai of Jhansi. The women who commit *johar* or the women who die fighting for their husband's honour make the merger of history and myth possible, conflating the ideal of the *sati* with that of the *veerangana*. Woman's courage and self-sacrifice as demonstrated in self-immolation used to be celebrated in the songs of the bardic singers—the charans and bhats in Rajasthan—and ritualized in the temples that sprang up at these *sati*-sites. Colonel Tod transmitted some of these stories and attitudes to the nineteenth century Indian novelists through his highly influential *Annals and Antiquities*. As an example one can look at Ramesh Chandra Dutt's historical novel in Bangla—*Maharashtra Jeeban Prabhat* (1878)—which ends with the following celebratory account of a woman dying on her husband's funeral pyre. Before quoting the passage in translation let me mention a few points of information about the author. Ramesh Chandra Dutt (1848-1908) was one of the earliest Indian members of the Indian Civil Service who ran away from Calcutta to take this examination in London. He had an excellent career record but decided to take premature retirement because his nationalist commitments clashed with his service conditions. Apart from writing four historical novels, he wrote two novels in the eighteen seventies with contemporary background propagating widow-marriage and inter-caste marriage which reflected his radical and reformist attitudes. It also needs to be mentioned that in the novel which ends with this lyrical and evocative description of *sati*, Lakshmi was married to a mean and revengeful man who had abducted and married her to settle a score with her father. All that is forgotten at this point: 'The fire flared upwards in a blaze of light. The tongues of the flame first gently touched Lakshmi's body and then licked it from all sides. Then it surrounded her to reach her head and proceeded heavenwards to illuminate the night sky in a festival of light and sound. Not a limb of Lakshmi's body trembled, not a single hair on her head moved.'[10] This is not an isolated incident. In another novel by the same author—*Rajput Jeevan Sandhya* (1879)—there is a similar description. When the Bhimgarh fort is surrounded by 2000 Muslim soldiers, the queen gathers together all the women who are in the fort and addresses them with a cheerful serenity:

> Sisters! Today we shall all become *satis*, we shall join our husbands. What greater happiness can a Rajput woman hope for? Let the Turkis see that the Rajput soldiers are valiant and the Rajput women are *sati*. With the early rays of the sun, hundreds of women took their ritual bath, and wearing sacred silk garments collected at the palace door. Joyously, they chanted their prayers together. And

then? Following an old Rajput tradition, the women, resplendent in their jewellery, ascended the pyre.[11]

Which one is the real Ramesh Chandra Dutt? The one who is campaigning for the modernization of the Hindu society and autonomy for the women or the one romanticizing *sati* and *johar*? Such self-contradictions between tradition and modernity were not uncommon among the Indian intellectuals of the nineteenth century. In the context of the present, one opposed social oppression and gender iniquities, but once removed in time, such acts became hallowed, part of our golden, heroic and somewhat de-historicized precolonial past.

This relates to the continuing resistance to seeing women as historicized creatures, subject to pressures of changing times. It was much easier to perceive them as part of a durable myth, embodying the essence of a culture that is by implication eternal, unchanging and defies history. Women were seen as custodians of traditional values, keeping at bay its erosion through contact with the West, which in the case of men was seen as inevitable—and even desirable, enabling them to widen their mental horizon in addition to getting them jobs under the British. Partha Chatterjee has argued this point convincingly in his discussion of inner and outer space.[12]

For middle and upper class women in real life, home was supposed to be the domain within which they had to live by a certain code. But reading the fiction of the period, one finds that the code ceased to operate if the woman was placed on a bigger stage outside the enclosed space of domesticity. Examples of this can be found repeatedly in the novels of Bankimchandra Chatterjee. The eponymous heroine of the novel *Kapalkundala* (1866) is kidnapped and then abandoned on a lonely beach by Portuguese bandits. Thereafter the ordinary rules of respectability do not apply to her. She is allowed by the novelist to walk alone in the forest at night and to make heretical statements like 'If I knew marriage meant slavery, I would not have agreed to get married.' Padmavati in the same novel, through abduction, is removed from the confined brahmanical world of a Bengali middle class household to the allegedly licentious atmosphere of the Nawab's court—after which she has mobility, initiative and agency. Bimala in *Durgeshnandini* (1866) escapes being slotted into a pre-determined role, because her birth is illegitimate, her marriage secret, and her residence in the Muslim royal court frees her from the taboos of a Hindu *antahpur*. The examples of Debi in *Debi Chaudhurani* (1883) who led a rebel army and of Shanti in *Ananadamath* (1882) who fought shoulder to shoulder with men in an armed combat are too well known to need recounting. In *Chandrashekhar* (1875) Shailbalini is abducted by the Englishman Lawrence Foster. Not only is her home destroyed by him figuratively, but the act is accompanied by a literal burning down of her conjugal home. Thereafter her life was lived in riverways, forests, hills and caves. This code distinguishing enclosed space from open space can be seen operative in a historical novel of the same period in Malayalam that I have read in English translation—*Marthanda Varma* (1891) by C.V. Ramana Pillai. It has two heroines, one within the palace, and the other in the world outside. Parukutty is the model of meek submissive femininity—the respectable girl who has been trained to bear her pain silently. This ideal of silence and stillness is pushed to a symbolic extreme when she actually loses speech and movement and becomes literally paralysed. The other woman Subhadra is condemned by society as a whore, but she is bold and free, she has mobility and agency and has the resources to wage a political battle to bring back the just ruler. In the overt design of the plots, the women outside are often seen as deviants, while domesticity is held up as the desired goal, but paradoxically the transgressive women get imbued with so much dynamic charge that the ideals of ordinary wifehood appear pale in comparison.

III

Women as loyal wives upholding traditional values and women as *veeranganas*—empowered creatures who can make things happen—are two opposed symbols in the narration of the nation in the colonial period. But there is yet a third paradigm. In the nationalist agenda, the figure of woman which had the most emotional potency was that of the mother. This resonant image brought together three different discourses: the discourse of the family (the biological mother), the discourse of religion (devi or the goddess) and the discourse of nation (the motherland). If the model of the submissive woman is located within the safe confines of the home and the warrior woman inhabits the expansive world outside, the mother image permeates every sphere of life. Bankimchandra's song *Vande Mataram* which first occurred in his novel *Anandamath* (1882) is the most well known articulation of this sentiment of motherland nationalism. The devi image implicit in this image of the mother is not a very simple one because there are several prototypes of mother goddesses in the Hindu pantheon. As Annapurna or Jagadhatri she is the benign icon of abundance and nurture; as Durga or Mahishasuramardini she has the power of destroying evil and as Kali she is the manifestation of the forces of darkness in creation and evokes terror.

It is obvious that the authors who used these powerful symbolic and mythic motifs in their work and the readers who responded to them either consciously or subliminally, were bound together by a belief that the Hindu upper caste values constituted the nation. Tribal and lower caste people who had a different iconography occasionally appeared on the periphery of these novels—e.g. the Bhils in the Rajput stories—but their value in the narratives lay mainly in their loyalty to their masters or faithfulness to the king. If people from another religion figured in the novels, almost invariably they did so in the role of the enemy, for example as Mughal kings or soldiers in the episodes from Rajput or Maratha history. At the time when these novels were being written, the true adversary in the domain of power were the British who had subjugated the people. But by and large, in the arena of literary representation the Muslims continued for a long time to be the surrogate 'other'. Sometimes this substitution has been explained as a matter of expediency because many of these early novelists in India were government servants by profession and mentioning the British in their novels in any but positive terms might have been harmful in their career. They used the strategy of using an earlier period of history so that another set of rulers could be represented as the oppressors. It is true that a few writers had to suffer professionally for their overt nationalism, but that does not quite explain the recurrent demonization of Islam in these novels.

The entire project of constructing the idea of a nation—at least in Bangla—is riddled by the conceptual indeterminacy of the terms used. Bankim could, for example, use the word *jaati* variously to mean caste (as in *jaati-bhed*), to mean a regional language group (as in Bangali *jaati*), a religious community (Hindu *jaati*) and also to mean the nation (as when nationalism is translated as *jaatiyata-bad*). But in his influential text *Anandamath*, which consolidated a brand of militant motherland patriotism in many parts of the country, Bankim's imagined community that resisted alien power was unequivocally Hindu. A Tamil critic writing as late as the late twentieth century recognizes in this novel 'a national purpose which transcended regional loyalty'.[13] According to him, Bankimchandra Chatterjee was attempting a new kind of idealistic romanticized regeneration of the Hindu ethos. The unspoken assumption in this religious nationalism was essentially masculinist which ascribed centrality to the brave men who would protect the honour of the mother. Incidentally the conflation of *Hindutva* with India continues to be a familiar ideology even at the beginning of the twenty-first century, resurfacing with a greater force after a mid-century abeyance when the idea of a secular nation had gained intellectual currency.

But it would be wrong to suppose that this notion of a nation forged by religion had gone uncontested. Even in the early decades of the twentieth century Rabindranath Tagore had begun critiquing this populist strain not only in his discursive prose, but at least through two novels: *Gora* (1909) and *Ghare Baire* (1916) translated in English as *The Home and the World.* In the latter novel, Sandeep, the flamboyant leader of a religious group spells out the cold-blooded political strategy concealed beneath the cult of motherland nationalism:

> 'True patriotism will never be roused in our countrymen unless they can visualize the motherland. We must make a goddess out of her.' Sandeep's followers saw the point at once. 'Let us devise a suitable image of the goddess to represent the country,' they said. 'It will not do if we devise a new image,' Sandeep said. 'We must appropriate one of the existing images of the goddess and convert it into an icon of our country. The worship of our people will then flow towards it along the deep-cut grooves of custom and tradition.' (my translation)

Sandeep's followers surrender to the mystical exaltation of the nation as mother goddess and go into a collective frenzy. But Nikhilesh, one of the other two central characters of the novel—the liberal humanist landlord—prefers to focus on the material condition of the village, the concrete ground reality, rather than be carried away by symbolic abstractions. He attempts to solve the specific problems of the people (many of whom are Muslims and hence outside the emotional ambit of religious patriotism of Sandeep's group) and redress the different forms of local oppression that divide the people. Refusing to be swayed by the evocative rhetoric of *Vande Mataram*, Nikhilesh concentrates on economic reform at the rural level. But Nikhilesh's wife Bimala is drawn towards Sandeep's magnetic personality and his variety of impassioned nationalism. Invariably the woman becomes the crucial site for working out the contesting ideologies of Sandeep and Nikhilesh. Sandeep turns her into a devi, the spirit of the country, the motivating force behind the movement, thereby erasing her autonomy as an individual. Nikhilesh respects her as a person, and recognizes her freedom to make a choice.

Worshipping the nation as mother and essentialising women as the source of spiritual power are parallel processes—one perpetuates the bondage of women, the other exalts the abstract notion of the country over the people who actually constitute it. Rabindranath Tagore's two novels *Gora*[14] and *The Home and the World* carry out an interrogation of the nationalistic project at three levels: they question the notion that India is exclusively a Hindu nation; they question if an emotional brand of patriotism can take precedence over attempts at economic self-sufficiency and social equality; above all they question the model of masculinity on which this militant variety of *swadeshi* was predicated.

* * *

I began the paper by pointing out how at the end of the nineteenth century gender became an invisible but crucial factor in the battle between colonial historiography and nationalist historiography. I shall end by pointing out that after a century a similar contestation of history has resurfaced, albeit under different banners. The debate about whether India will be defined as a Hindu nation or as a plural nation with a composite culture will be determined by the differential ways of highlighting the events of the past. Narratives imperceptibly consolidate and reconstruct history in the popular imagination. I shall remind you of the telling lines from Amitav Ghosh's novel *The Shadow Lines* (1988): 'Everyone lives in a story, because stories are all there is to live in. It is just a question of which one you choose.'

Whichever one you choose, gender remains at the core of it, because every story at heart is concerned with man-woman relationship, and although history might have preferred to ignore them for a long time, in narrative fiction in India women have always been the essential signifier of national culture.

NOTES

1. Benedict Anderson, *Imagined Communities* (New York: Verso, 1983).
2. 'Bangalar itihas sambandhe kayekti katha', in *Bankim Rachanabali*, vol. II (Calcutta: Sahitya Sansad, 1980), p. 337 (my translation).
3. Sudipta Kaviraj, *The Unhappy Consciousness: Bankimchandra Chattopadhyay and the Formation of Nationalist Discourse in India* (Delhi: Oxford University Press, 1995).
4. James Mill, *The History of British India* (1817), ed. H.H. Wilson, vol. II (London: James Madden, Piper, Stephenson and Spence, 1858), p. 149.
5. Richard Orme, *A History of the Military Transaction of the British Nation in Indostan*, vol. II (Madras, 1861), p. 5.
6. Quoted by Mrinalini Sinha in *Colonial Masculinity* (Manchester: Manchester University Press, 1995), p. 15.
7. Maud Diver, *Desmod's Daughter* (London: Blackwood, 1916).
8. Quoted by Indira Chaudhuri in an unpublished essay titled 'History as Empowering Discourse in Nineteenth Century Bengal' (1992).
9. Uma Chakravarty, 'Whatever Happened to the Vedic Dasi', in *Recasting Women: Essays in Colonial History*, eds Kumkum Sangari and Sudesh Vaid (Delhi: Kali for Women, 1989), p. 28.
10. *Maharashtra Jiban Prabhat*, in *Romesh Rachanabali* (Calcutta: Sahitya Sansad, 1982), p. 249.
11. *Rajput Jiban Sandhya*, ibid, p. 304.
12. Partha Chatterjee, 'The Nationalist Resolution of the Women's Question', *Recasting Women: Essays in Colonial History* eds. Kumkum Sangari and Sudesh Vaid (Delhi: Kali for Women 1989).
13. K. Satyam, 'Three Pioneer Indian Novelists', *Indian Literature*, July-August 1981, p. 79.
14. This novel is not discussed here, but for comments on this aspect of the novel see my Introduction to *Gora*, translated into English by Sujit Mukherjee (New Delhi: Sahitya Akademi, 1997).

Women Authors Write Red: Towards a Feminist Rhetoric of Social and Political Justice

SUZETTE A. HENKE

If American women writers of the nineteenth and twentieth centuries have acquired a reputation for the use of experimental forms and avant-garde innovations, it is nonetheless remarkable that female authors in both North and South America have always maintained a powerful social consciousness and concern for issues of sexual, social, and political justice. The voice of the people has found expression in the passionate polemical fiction, autobiography, and poetry of women authors committed to the cause of equality and cultural transformation. In many cases, it was women who felt angriest and most passionate about issues of racial and gender equality. Denied equal rights as women in a man's world, they fought for full enfranchisement, for acknowledgement as citizens of their country, and reformers of the world.

Nineteenth-century authors witnessed a country torn apart by the conundrum of African-American slavery—a corrupt institution that gave birth to some of the most powerful polemical writing in American literary history. The genre of the ex-slave narrative inflamed a nation to take up arms in a civil upheaval that almost destroyed the country for which they were fighting. If Frederick Douglass became an avid spokesman for the freed American Negro demanding the cessation of slavery in the South, a female author like Harriet Jacobs (Linda Brent) articulated

*This essay is dedicated to three extraordinary individuals who died before their time: Jaidev, of Shimla, India; Constance Coiner, my erstwhile colleague at Binghamton University; and her 12-year-old daughter, Ana Duarte-Coiner. Constance and Ana, en route to Paris in celebration of the publication of *Better Red*, died in the tragic explosion of TWA Flight 800, July 1996.

the plight of women slaves in graphic and shocking detail. Among the rights of the southern white master was the privilege of copulation with the female slaves in his charge. Whether his advances were welcomed or disdained, the helpless Negro woman he chose to attack, rape, or impregnate was utterly powerless to reject such phallic aggression. Like a benevolent patriarch, the master could choose to become an incestuous perpetrator, with few constraints on his lascivious desire. The ex-slave narrative inaugurated a genre of *testimonio* in the American literary tradition that would be expanded politically to indict social and economic injustice in later historical epochs. Fiery females responded with righteous anger in the face of a *laisser-faire* economy swerving out of control and crushing those individuals caught in the maw of poverty, violence, or racial discrimination. The legacies of late capitalism were eventually scrutinized and critiqued by militant feminist authors writing in a long polemical tradition begun by nineteenth century African-American agitators.

In 1861, the ex-slave Harriet Jacobs, writing under the pseudonym of Linda Brent, declared: 'Slavery is terrible for men, but it is far more terrible for women.' If *Incidents in the Life of a Slave Girl* reads like a ghastly tale of patient Griselda, the story is all the more moving for its historical validity. With almost no tutoring and minimal literacy, Brent was able to articulate the miseries of slavery with an ingenuous voice that sometimes rivals the eloquence of Harriet Beecher Stowe. Her narrative deflates, once and for all, the longstanding American myth of the happy slave. In theory, Brent's purpose in writing her autobiography was didactic—to expose the social corruption and moral evils of slavery as an institution. She declares: 'Reader, be assured this narrative is no fiction. I am aware that some of my adventures may seem incredible; but they are nevertheless, strictly true.'[1]

If Brent's announced intention is to kindle the reader's compassion, her unconscious, perhaps inadvertent agenda is more therapeutic than instructional. Having endured a subhuman, almost animal incarceration as a hidden, underground woman, Brent must articulate her sufferings in such a way as to reconstruct her personal identity and define the horror of her experience in terms of heroic narrative. Only by appropriating the language of her oppressor can Brent begin to resurrect her buried humanity. Her constant emphasis on the authenticity of her narrative suggests that she is engaged in a desperate attempt to master the rhetoric of persuasion and to elevate personal humiliation to the level of radical heroism.

Instinctively, Brent realizes that language alone can redeem her inhumane and sadistic treatment at the hands of a demented master. Although Brent had never read Voltaire or Jonathan Swfit, she nevertheless manages to adapt to her own rhetorical purposes a voice of ingenuous naiveté worthy of a latter-day Gulliver. The tone of her narrative is far more incredulous than angry. Sublimating feelings of righteous indignation evinced by a decade of torture and imprisonment, she manages to tell her story in a controlled style that ironically exposes cultural slippage between Christian belief and social practice. 'There is a great difference between Christianity and religion at the south', she declares. 'If a man goes to the communion table, and pays money into the treasury of the church, no matter if it be the price of blood, he is called religious' (77). Commenting acerbically on Dr Flint's hypocritical Episcopalian commitment, she reports that 'the worst persecutions I endured from him were after he was a communicant' (77). Flint's unwelcome sexual advances become all the more passionate once he proclaims his social affiliation with the Episcopal religion. When he advises Linda to join the Church, she brashly observes: 'There are sinners enough in it already' (77). The Christian religion clearly serves as a psychological weapon geared to keep African slaves docile and intimidated by paradigms of white supremacy. After Nat Turner's insurrection, 'the slaveholders came to the conclusion that it would be well to give the slaves enough of religious instruction to keep them from murdering their masters' (69).

Like Richardson's Pamela, the adolescent Linda is intent on preserving her virginity and eluding the all-too-fervid caresses of a master who behaves like a potential rapist. One recalls the incorrigible Mr B. leaping out of closets and pressing his attentions on a lower-class servant girl in the eighteenth century novel. Similarly, Dr Flint promises Linda she will enjoy a life of luxury and the status of a wife should she only yield to his amorous imprecations. As Linda grows in age and grace, her exceptional beauty becomes her 'greatest curse' (27): 'My master met me at every turn, reminding me that I belonged to him, and swearing by heaven and earth that he would compel me to submit to him' (27).

When Brent turns her attentions to a 'respectable colored man,' Flint reacts with all the wrath and vengeance of a spurned lover: 'He sprang upon me like a tiger and gave me a stunning blow' (38). He then reminds his impotent victim that he has a right to treat her as he chooses—even to kill her, should he feel sufficiently displeased. Linda is first courted for her beauty, then threatened with mutilation and death. If flattery fails and promises go unnoticed, Flint's dubious favours degenerate into sadistic threats and monstrous attacks.

In self-defence, Linda rebelliously decides to recuperate her dignity and self-respect by taking a lover of her own choosing—a kind and compassionate white man, Mr Sands. In a triumph of understatement, she observes that 'the condition of a slave confuses all the principles of morality' (55). For the ingenuous adolescent, the ostensible sin of fornication 'does not seem so great with an unmarried man, as with one who has a wife to be made unhappy' (55). In a melodramatic encounter with Dr Flint, who excoriates her for immorality, Linda asserts whatever powers of agency and autonomy she can dare to claim. 'Do you love him?' Flint demands, in a 'hissing tone'. Calmly, Linda replies: 'I am thankful that I do not despise him' (60).

At the hands of the ignominious Flint, Linda endures the kind of ineffable torture one now associates with heroic narratives of Holocaust survival. Like Anne Frank, she takes refuge in a hiding place that is little more than a box or a coffin. Confined in a dark hole above the storage room of her grandmother's cabin, she suffers incarceration without light or air. Finally, she contrives a tiny peep-hole that allows her to breathe fresh air and to see her children at play. 'I had my season of joy and thanksgiving', she observes. 'I tried to be thankful for my little cell, dismal as it was, and even to love it, as part of the price I had paid for the redemption of my children. . . . I asked why the curse of slavery was permitted to exist. . . . These things took the shape of mystery' (26).

And so Linda remains hidden, to ponder the mystery, for seven years of incarceration. 'My friends feared I should become a cripple for life; and I was so weary of my long imprisonment that, had it not been for the hope of serving my children, I should have been thankful to die' (130). Like a contemporary hostage or prisoner of war, Brent survives psychologically by the power of reformulating her unspeakable trauma and telling herself endless stories. She recounts the oral history of old Aunt Nancy, a slave cheated of the few rights promised her. She practices competition in cunning by sending letters to her family circuitously addressed from Boston. And eventually, she prepares for her long-awaited escape to the freedom of the North. By virtue of an ingenious exodus by sea, she finally arrives in the promised land of Philadelphia, where she is happily reunited with her daughter Ellen and later with her son Ben.

Like a latter-day Candide, however, Linda feels astonished to encounter deep-seated colour prejudice lurking in the liberal hearts of Northern whites. Enfranchisement, she realizes, is merely the first step in an ongoing battle for racial equality. Laws may dictate change, but consciousness is slow to alter: 'everywhere I found the same manifestations of that cruel prejudice, which so discourages the feelings, and represses the energies of the colored people' (181).

Brent's narrative concludes with an ostensible apology: 'Reader, my story ends with freedom; not in the usual way, with marriage' (207). Once again, her tale exposes the paradoxical gap between a white world in which the traditional romance narrative concludes with marriage, and the nineteenth century world of African-American culture longing for the perquisites of freedom, civil rights, and political equality. By pointing out the radical difference between her own autobiographical *testimonio* and Anglo-American romantic fictions, she appropriates the model of heroism offered by a white world and reconstructs her own self-image in the mode of confessional revelation. Her heroism resides in the history of suffering and rebellion, of courage and autonomy, that she has so courageously recounted. By daring to articulate the narrative of her own suffering and humiliation, she at once reveals the human horrors of slavery as an institution and reclaims the agency and subject-position so flagrantly denied by the preposterous suppositions of an American slaveholding hegemony. Appropriating the most powerful weapon of the master, she has beaten him at his own rhetorical strategies. With the assistance of Lydia Maria Child, who served as editor and possible collaborator in constructing this autobiographical testimony, Linda Brent/Harriet Jacobs was able to share the poignant story of her own heroic survival with an American public ill-prepared for such candid revelation. Truth, in this case, proved stranger and more unpalatable than Harriet Beecher Stowe's 1852 abolitionist novel, *Uncle Tom's Cabin.* It would take a bloody civil war finally to defeat a corrupt economic institution, though the hearts and minds of a large part of the American nation were literally converted to the abolitionist cause by the power of testimonial ex-slave narratives like that of Linda Brent/Harriet Jacobs.

In 1861, the same year that Jacobs's story was published, Rebecca Harding Davis documented a different kind of slavery in her novella *Life in the Iron Mills*. As a naturalist writer, Davis rebelled against popular romantic, sentimental fiction to offer a searing indictment of the industrial revolution and the effects of late capitalism on the lives of a downtrodden proletariat. For workers in America's coal mines and iron mills, survival meant relentless struggle in a brutal, rapacious, competitive economy. Writing without Marx or Jesus, Rebecca Harding Davis depicts Hugh Wolfe, her protagonist, as a victim of environmental forces, internal psychological stress, and economic conditions beyond his understanding or control.

For Davis, members of the American nineteenth century underclass were truly examples of what Julia Kristeva describes as the abject—outcast and derided subjects stripped of agency and exiled from a hostile community as living symbols of defilement.[2] Hugh Wolfe is a 'furnace-tender in one of Kirby & John's rolling-mills', and his family fortunes are characterized by 'incessant labor, sleeping in kennel-like rooms, eating rank pork and molasses', and drinking to excess, 'with an occasional night in jail' by way of atonement.[3] Hugh and his fellow workers inhabit a 'city of fires, that burned hot and fiercely in the night', in an industrial inferno where great furnaces belch an exhaust of soot-black smoke and monstrous 'engines sob and shriek like "gods in pain"' (19-20).

The hunchbacked female mill-worker, Deborah, is a melodramatic example of the alienated subject—a 'thwarted' form whose 'colorless life' unfolds in a 'waking stupor that smothered pain and hunger', and whose figure connotes the abjection of otherness. She is perceived as little more than a 'wet, faded thing, half-covered with ashes', a piece of social detritus whose buried life secretes the mystery of 'a soul filled with groping passionate love, heroic unselfishness, fierce jealousy', and an abiding loyalty to her cousin Hugh (21). Deb bears a burden of intolerable solitude, harbouring an unrequited but dauntless love for a man who unconsciously 'loathe[s] the sight of her' (22). Herein lie the seeds of unsung heroism: 'If you could go into this mill where Deborah lay, and drag out from the hearts of these men the terrible tragedy of their lives, taking it as a symptom of the disease of their class, no ghost Horror would terrify you more' (23).

And yet, despite their abject melancholic condition, Davis's characters heroically endure. The iron mills become a symbol of the purification of the soul through suffering, and Hugh Wolfe exhibits a unique spirit, purified and smelted like the ore he tends. A gifted sculptor of forms made from pig-iron waste, he fashions a Rodinesque korl figure—monstrous, muscular, and uncannily threatening—to embody the frustrated hopes and stifled aspirations ablaze in his heart: 'There was not one line of beauty or grace in it: a nude woman's form, muscular, grown coarse with labor, the powerful limbs instinct with some one poignant longing. One idea: there it was in . . . the wild, eager face, like that of a starving wolf's' (32). From her korl visage emanates unrequited desire, and her empty arms clutch at the air with 'the peculiar action of a man dying of thirst' or a 'mad, half-despairing gesture of drowning' (32-3). When asked for an artistic interpretation of his work, Hugh utters a cry of inarticulate longing. 'She be hungry', he insists (33). And so, in effect, is the sculptor himself.

If mill-owners like Kirby staunchly defend the 'social ladders' in an American class system which, they believe, 'any man can scale' (34), workers like Hugh can do little more than ponder the mysteries of their economic servitude with scant hope of redemption. Like Pontius Pilate, Kirby abdicates responsibility for the men who mechanically stoke the fires of an industrial revolution gone terribly wrong. 'I wash my hands of all social problems', he announces boldy, even while drawing significant analogies between southern slavery and a northern economic caste system, 'white or black' (35).

Unjustly convicted of grand larceny for stealing a cache of money actually pilfered by the devoted Deborah, a consumptive Wolf is sentenced to 'nineteen years hard labor in penitentiary' (50). Utterly desperate, he confesses: 'I cannot bear to be hurted any more' (57), then commits suicide by slashing his wrists in a dark, dank prison cell. Ironically, the philanthropist Dr May brands Hugh an ingrate and a 'scoundrel' and concludes that the harsh court sentence 'serves him right!' (50). Only the uncanny figure of a 'mill-woman cut in korl' survives as a poignant testimony to the crippling injustice of economic slavery and the 'thwarted life' of her proletarian Pygmalion, with 'its mighty hunger, its unfinished work' (64).

'I first read *Life in the Iron Mills*', Tillie Lerner Olsen recalls, 'in one of three water-stained, coverless, bound volumes of the *Atlantic Monthly*, bought for ten cents each in an Omaha junkshop. I was fifteen.'[4] This chance encounter with Davis's proletarian novel proved serendipitous, since it convinced the young author that 'Literature can be made out of the lives of despised people', and that 'You, too, must write' (117). 'Until *Life in the Iron Mills* appeared in that April 1861 *Atlantic*, there had been no Blakean dark Satanic mills in American literature; outside of slavery, no working people whose lives were "tragedy . . . a reality of soul starvation . . . living death"' (49). Because the *Atlantic* story had been published anonymously, Tillie Olsen had to wait almost thirty years to solve the riddle of its authorship, revealed in a chance allusion found in the collected *Letters of Emily Dickinson*. When the Feminist Press agreed to reprint the work in 1972, Paul Laute and Florence Howe asked Olsen to write an extensive biographical preface, later reprinted in her prose collection *Silences*.

Rebecca Harding Davis had been Olsen's initial inspiration, and *Life in the Iron Mills* fortuitously served as a primary model for Olsen's own ambitious proletarian novel, *Yonnondio: From the Thirties*. The book 'was begun in 1932 in Faribault, Minnesota, when the author was nineteen, and worked on intermittently into 1936 or perhaps 1937 in Omaha, Stockton, Venice (Calif.), Los Angeles and San Francisco'.[5] Put aside in deference to marriage, childrearing, work, and domestic duties, the manuscript languished for thirty years, until Olsen received a MacDowell Colony grant that enabled her to reclaim, reconstruct, and tentatively complete the textual bricolage. In 'arduous partnership' with 'that long ago young writer' she once had been, Olsen infused her passionate political commitments into the salvaging and retrieval of a novel wrought in the shadow of America's 1930s' Depression. The work exposes Olsen's leftist convictions and Communist sentiments without ever pandering to the narrow party line dictated by Russia's skewed interpretation of Marxist aesthetics.[6]

In *Yonnondio*, a title that echoes Walt Whitman's '*Lament for the aborigines*' (7), Olsen imbricates a nascent feminist consciousness into her implicit critique of late capitalism, the futile struggles of a downtrodden proletariat, and a sex/gender system that degrades and brutalizes women of the working class. She makes an ingenious connection between the economic Depression that held the United States in a virtual deathgrip throughout the 1930s, and the inevitable psychological depression evinced by the vicissitudes of alienated labour. The lives of Olsen's protagonists, Anna and Jim Holbrook, explode in violent outburst exacerbated by frustration-aggression displacement. The disenfranchised subject, abject or disempowered, will express his pent-up frustrations either on the self, through physical abuse or suicide, or on family members who cannot escape the brutal effects of patriarchal rage. In Olsen's fiction, men are forced into boring, dead-end jobs simply to survive and to feed their destitute families; and women, more often than not, are forced to suffer corollary indignities of wife battering, marital rape, unwanted pregnancy, and spousal desertion.

In Olsen's *Yonnondio*, Jim Holbrook is a downtrodden labourer who works at a series of menial, degrading, and unsatisfactory jobs: as a coal miner in Wyoming, where he is almost killed in a mine accident; as a tenant farmer in South Dakota, where he discovers that the bankers and landowners take all his profits, then claim that he owes *them* rent on house and machinery; as a sewer-worker in the bowels of Omaha, Nebraska; and finally, as an assembly-line worker in a meatpacking plant whose stench, filth, ordure, and stifling heat create a reeking inferno worse than any imagined by Dante Alighieri. Jim exposes the lie of the vaunted American dream when he sardonically rejects 'the bull about freedomofopportunity and a chancetorise and ifyoureallywanttowork youcanalwaysfindajob and rugged individualism and something about the pursuit of happiness' (77). Worshipping the great God Job, he feels convinced that 'a job was God, and praying wasn't enough, you had to live for It, produce for It, prostrate yourself, take anything from It' (77). And yet, Jim knows instinctively that 'individual revolt was not good' enough, that only communal organization and solidarity with fellow workers might effect true political change. Hence his utopian aspiration that, with 'millions of fists clamped into yours, . . . you could wipe out . . . the whole goddam thing, and a human could be a human for the first time on earth' (79). Such triumphal visions illumine the dark side of Holbrook's consciousness in rare moments of epiphany evinced by the rage of witnessing capitalist greed and unfair managerial practices.

Only the Holbrook daughter Mazie, an autobiographical projection of young Tillie Lerner Olsen, bears enough hope in childhood to foster the awestruck ruminations of a hungry, inquiring mind. With an innate talent for lyrical and metaphorical description, she is able to find wonder in the clutter of a garbage dump or, gazing at the fiery stars, to envision splinters of the moon or flowers in the sky. This talented, imaginative child takes pleasure in the process of acquiring knowledge and in her ever increasing mastery of the world. For such gifted youth, the only hope of escape from poverty lies in the promise provided by education and book learning. As Anna explains to her children, 'An education is what you kids are going to get. It means your hands stay white and you read books and work in an office' (11).

For the labourers in America's coal mines, even Mother Earth has become an implacable monster devouring men as sacrifices to a primitive, savage deity: 'Earth sucks you in, to spew out the coal, to make a few fat bellies fatter. Earth takes your dreams that a few may languidly lie on couches' (14). In Mazie's infantile imagination, the mine is literally transmogrified into a lurid intestinal labyrinth through physiological analogy: 'Bowels is the stummy. Earth is a stummy and mebbe she eats the men that come down' (12). This sensitive child is mystified by her family's degradation and feels pervasive anxiety over the threat of bereavement signified by the whistle that alerts the community to accidents in the mine. In melancholic wonder, Mazie concludes: 'All the world is a-cryen, and I don't know for why. And the ghosts [of the mine] may get daddy' (16). With the acerbity of a Swiftian sociologist, Olsen offers us a modern Gulliver in the persona of an ingenuous young girl who sincerely questions the social inequities perpetrated by capitalism. Why, Mazie wonders, does the boss-man luxuriate in a big house equipped with a white tub and indoor toilet, while the workers make do with well-water and outdoor dunnies? 'How come he aint libin like we do?' she asks naively. Mazie realizes that a vague, intangible 'something' is responsible for class difference; but throughout the novel, she continues to grope toward some kind of political comprehension of an inequitable but unacknowledged caste system that perpetuates economic privilege.

The coalminers live in constant danger of death or physical mutilation. But when the ominous mine whistle startles the community by signalling a fatal explosion, Tillie Olsen freezes her subjects in a classical sculptured pose and challenges our aesthetic sensibilities by addressing her audience directly. 'And could you not make a cameo of this and pin it onto your aesthetic hearts?' she asks, while framing the marmoreal panic of her subjects in a stance sardonically entitled 'the War to Live' (30). As Constance Coiner explains, 'In this cameo, as it parodies Keats's "Ode", Olsen has stripped the narrator of the controlling power of imagination and has severed truth and beauty. In so doing, she has torn the aesthetic heart out of her own cameo. Once again we see Olsen writing, as Trotsky believed necessary, in strategic relation to bourgeois texts, usurping their forms for a discourse of resistance.'[7] And that discourse, Coiner believes, must be analyzed in Bakhtinian terms as dialogic, heteroglossic, centrifugal, and carnivalesque in its fragmentation and disruption of hegemonic monologism. 'The myriad heteroglossic voices of the marginalized' in Olsen's fiction 'constitute a social and political force against the tyranny of dominant discursive [and hegemonic] modes' (194).

In both *Yonnondio* and the short story collection *Tell Me a Riddle*, multiple heteroglossic voices engage in the democratizing enterprise of amplifying dominated and marginalized voices. Everywhere in Olsen's work, 'heteroglossia is unleashed to engage in a powerful, playful satirizing of the dominant culture' (194). Hence Olsen's parody of monstrous gods of the coalmining industry that carve *Yonnondio*'s subjects into motionless, panic-stricken statues for the reader's aesthetic delectation. The author boldly provokes her reader into participatory construction of textual meaning by challenging intellectual complacency. For an author like Tillie Olsen, the stance of aesthetic detachment is simply unacceptable. Her vivid description of the miners' degradation provides an objective correlative meant to evoke such powerful feelings of compassion that the reader will commit him/herself to the ongoing struggle for social and political justice.

When the Holbrook family escapes the mines and moves to a South Dakota farm, the pressure of mortgages, taxes, and unscrupulous landlords convinces Jim that tenant farming is simply another form of wage slavery, the farm a factory for labourers of the soil. Men are bound to the exigencies of backbreaking work whose profits are devoured by the landowner; and in which women are condemned to relentless cycles of breeding and parturition, without benefits of contraception, modern obstetrics, sound nutrition, or adequate health care.

The young Mazie Holbrook must stifle her ears against the sounds of marital rape in her parents' bedroom, as an inebriated Jim intimidates his pregnant wife Anna: 'Cant screw my own wife. Expect me to go to a whore? Hold still' (91). And yet the phallic aggression of this *paterfamilias* is both obdurate and self-defeating. In a fit of male disgust at his wife's burgeoning fertility, Jim screams belligerently: 'Who asked for your goddam brats?' Infuriated by the urgency of his own libidinal needs, he lashes out against the female body and its ever-swelling brood of annoying offspring. His challenge provokes Anna's rebellious cry: 'I'll never have another, to starve to death with you' (54). When Jim's sexual advances precipitate a miscarriage, the pompous physician who attends the suffering Anna chides her for uncontrolled sexual prodigality. Bitterly, he thinks to himself: 'Pigsty, the way these people live', and echoes the most invidious sentiments of popular eugenics: 'Damn fools, they ought to sterilize the whole lot of them after the second kid' (93). Even Anna's nursing child is diagnosed with 'Rickets, thrush, dehydrated; don't blame it trying to die' (93). With little cognizance of his own (and his society's) collusion in social oppression, the self-righteous doctor blames the poor for the effects of their own victimization.

Anna Holbrook struggles to survive and make a better life for her children, even as she battles against her own pain, illness, physical exhaustion, and nervous debilitation. Saddest of all, perhaps, is Olsen's poignant depiction of the claustrophobic environment that limits possibilities for the next generation. Children in this novel seem extraordinarily resilient in their patient endurance of poverty, hunger, bullying, and social opprobrium. Their fertile imaginations can transform a garbage heap into a fairyland, their hungry minds take delight in the narratives engendered by games, library books, occasional films, and perpetual experiments in a fantasy world of their own creation. And yet these resourceful youngsters are stifled by the boundaries of class and social stratification, as they suffocate from the psychological constraints imposed by a climate of lowered expectation. They cannot envisage a viable alternative to the life-world inhabited by their parents. Boys go into the mine pits or are gobbled up by the meatpacking assembly line. Girls get pregnant too early and marry too soon, only to continue the cycles of poverty and indigence bequeathed by earlier generations trapped in the relentless vicissitudes of economic destitution.

Once in Omaha, Jim Holbrook finds work in the city's stench-filled sewers, where he labours in fetid darkness for an hourly wage that can not rescue his family from the threat of starvation. In the dog days of August, he is hired at a meatpacking plant, where the nauseous atmosphere and stifling heat condemn male and female workers to a living inferno. The pressure is further exacerbated by the inhumane 'Beedo system' adopted by plant managers.[8] Forced to work in temperature of 110 degrees Fahrenheit, the labourers feel that 'they are in hell; indeed they are the damned. *Steamed boiled broiled fried cooked. Geared, meshed*' (145). This ghastly environment finally erupts in a literal explosion when a steam pipe bursts, 'hissing live steam in a magnificent plume, in a great boiling roll', and women in the Casings room are scalded (146). Incredibly, the plant manager indicts those injured on charges of carelessness and orders them back to their stations. Little more than cogs in the great machine of American industry, such dehumanized subjects are reduced to a kind of wage slavery that threatens to crush any sense of agency or individual dignity. They resemble *Human Wreckage* cast up on the shore of the great American dream (148). The giant maw of twentieth century industry has suffocated its victims in the blood and stench and detritus of a meatpacking plant, where the hearts and minds of workers are symbolically ground up and split out onto a landscape of economic desolation.

Amid such wreckage, what hope? For Tillie Olsen, promise of a better future resides in the newest members of the human community—the infants and children who have not yet been battered by the demands of alienated labour, and whose fertile imaginations might conjure a better, more equitable social environment. And so Anna's baby, Bess, focuses on her first prehensile tasks with a kind of 'neanderthal concentration' and wonder at the promise of future empowerment: 'Centuries of human drive work in her; human ecstasy of achievement; satisfaction deep and fundamental as sex: *I can do, I use my powers; I! I!*' (153). Olsen implies that this sense of individual agency, this ecstasy of creation, must be joined to a broader human community impelled by a passion for social justice in order for the world to reconfigure its landscape of poverty into new egalitarian forms. American women writers have long envisaged utopian possibilities for an expanding world order. They have dreamt of a climate of equal opportunities, where 'a human could be a human for the first time on earth' (79). For politically committed authors like Harriet Jacobs, Rebecca Harding Davis, and Tillie Olsen, nothing less than total social transformation is acceptable.[9] In the words of Susan B. Anthony, 'Failure is impossible'. But the future of this dream so passionately imagined lies with the next generation that will emerge in a technically charged millennial culture, perched on the brink of global revolution at the dawn of the twenty-first century.

NOTES

1. Harriet Jacobs (a.k.a. Linda Brent), *Incidents in the Life of a Slave Girl*, ed. Lydia Maria Child (1861; rpt. New York: Harcourt Brace, 1973), p. xiii.
2. Julia Kristeva, *Powers of Horror: An Essay on Abjection,* trans. Leos Roudiez (New York: Columbia University Press, 1980).
3. Rebecca Harding Davis, *Life in the Iron* Mills (Old Westbury: The Feminist Press, 1972), pp. 14-15.
4. *Silences* (New York: Delacorte Press, 1978), p. 117.
5. Tillie Olsen, *Yonnondio: From the Thirties* (New York: Dell, 1974), p. 157.
6. For an incisive interpretation of the 'Thirties' Literary Left', as well as 'Women in the Communist Party During the Depression', see Constance Coiner, *Better Red: The Writing and Resistance of Tillie Olsen and Meridel Le Sueur* (1995; rpt. Urbana: University of Illinois Press, 1998), Chapters 1 and 2. Coiner offers a perspicacious account of debates about proletarian art that pitted 'one group of writers, many of them associated with *New Masses*', against another, more sophisticated group of leftist writers who 'clustered around *The Partisan Review*' and 'were variously influenced by Trotsky's argument in *Literature and Revolution* that purely proletarian literature and culture were an impossibility. These people considered it necessary to explore those techniques of bourgeois literature that could most productively be borrowed and adapted to the purposes of a working-class literature' (16-17).
7. *Better Red,* p. 187.
8. For an explanation of Charles F. Bedaux's mechanistic system devised to speed up assembly line production, see Crolyn Rhodes's essay in *American Notes and Queries*, October 1976, pp. 24-5.
9. As Fredric Jameson explains in *The Political Unconscious: Narrative as a Socially Symbolic Act* (Ithaca: Cornell University Press, 1981), for Marxism, 'only the emergence of a post-individualistic social world, only the reinvention of the collective and the associative, can concretely achieve the 'decentering' of the individual subject called for; . . . only a new and original form of collective social life can overcome the isolation and monadic autonomy of the older bourgeois subjects' (125). Such a utopian ideal is predicated on 'the "disaccumulative" moment of late monopoly or consumer or multinational capitalism, what Guy Debord calls the society of the image or of the spectacle' (ii). Marxist analysis, 'in the form of a dialectic, affirms the primacy of theory which is at one and the same time a recognition of the primacy of History itself' (14). According to the Marxist schemata, the 'conception of historical "stages" . . . includes the notion of a cultural dominant or form of ideological coding specific to each mode of production', suggesting that an 'oligarchical slaveholding society' will be followed, in turn, by 'feudalism, capitalism, and communism' (89). Thus the structures of 'personal domination' and 'commodity reification' characteristic of nineteenth and twentieth century American culture would eventually be superseded by more 'fully developed forms of collective or communal association' (90).

The Dalits and the Indian Nation: Om Prakash Valmiki's *Joothan*

HARISH NARANG

In the century just ended one of the major areas of discussion has been the existence of several nations—one could spell each one of them with a small 'n'—within the geopolitical bounds of a Nation—which one could spell with a capital 'N'. These nations with the small 'n' have all the characteristics of the nation with the capital 'N': their own socio-political structures, their own economics, their own sets of beliefs and values, their own culture, their own languages, their own songs and stories. For instance, South Africa comprises, despite the abolition of apartheid, two different nations: the blacks and the whites. In fact, within the category of blacks there are two distinct nations, if not more: Zulus and Xosas. Nearer home, even in a small country like Pakistan, the *Mohajirs* are a nation within a nation and so are *Pashtoons* and the *Balochs*.

Speaking of India, even a cursory glance at any daily 'national' newspaper more than fifty years after political independence, could give anyone a fairly reasonable idea that India comprises several Indias existing simultaneously in the same geopolitico-cultural space. Here are some samples of such a situation as reflected in the news items from a national daily, *The Times of India*, on the very first day of the twenty-first century. The first one, titled 'Stage set for the millennium's baby booms' and originating from Ahmedabad, states that 'a few expecting mothers keen on delivering their very own "millennium baby"', have decided to undergo 'a caesarean section precisely on the first minute of the new year. . . .' The second news item announces the results of an opinion poll conducted by the newspaper through e-mail, stating that 69 per cent of the participants considered Ricky Martin to be a better singer while 31 per cent rooted for Enrique Iglesias. The third news item, datelined Bhubaneswar, reports: 'three more unemployed teachers on Friday attempted self-immolation before Chief Minister Biswal's official residence in protest against the government not meeting their demands . . . .' Finally, another news item, again originating from Bhubaneswar, is titled 'Eight killed in Orissa clash, police firing' and goes on to specify that 'The victims comprised seven tribals of the *Kandh* community and one *dalit*.'

Apparently, the fortunate mothers referred to in the first news item who are able to afford the luxury of planning the birth of their babies to coincide with the birth of the millennium cannot have anything in common with those unfortunate unemployed teachers referred to in the third news item who planned the end of their lives to coincide with the end of the millennium. Similarly, those Indians who can afford to indulge in the luxury of choosing between popular western singers, sitting in cozy comforts before their computers and communicating with the rest of the world through the instant mantra of e-mail—implied in the second news item—do not obviously share the same nation with those poor, illiterate *adivasis* and *dalits* who continue to live below the poverty line after more than half a century of political freedom and 'progress' all around them and whose killings at the hands of either exploiting landlords or law-enforcement agencies like the police have become a daily, dull, routine affair—even on the millennium eve—as referred to in the last news item—when a sizeable section of the Indian society was busy wining, dining and dancing at obscenely expensive private clubs and restaurants.

The divide—economic, political, social, cultural and linguistic—among the various sections—the rich and the poor, the majority and the minority, the upper caste and the lower caste, the urban and the rural, the educated and the uneducated, the male and the female—is agonizingly deep and wide. The divisions in the national fabric have had their echoes in the world of literary discourse where too sub-genres of minority discourse like women's writings, Muslim writings, tribal writings and *dalit* writings have emerged, carving out specific literary constituencies for specific groups or communities in much the same way as feminist writings, Jewish writings and African-American writings emerged in the U.S.A. or native Canadian writings, Francophone writings, South Asian-Canadian writings or Caribbean-Canadian writings emerged in Canada during the post-war years.

I propose to analyse in the following pages, the world and the world-view, portrayed in one of the most powerful *dalit* texts—*Joothan*—written by Om Prakash Valmiki and first published in 1997.[1] By writing his own life story—quite similar in form to a *bildungsroman*—Om Prakash Valmiki has focused on the world of '*ati-shudras*'—the lowliest of the low castes, namely the *Chuhra* or *Bhangi* community of northern India who are treated as absolutely untouchables—in the most literal sense of the term—and whose community name is the most hurtful abuse among the upper caste speakers of Hindi.

II

Let me begin with the title of the book—*Joothan*. This term in Hindi—a collective noun—has actually no equivalent in English, or in any other non-Indian language for that matter, and can at best be explained through a rather longish elaboration. *Joothan*, in Hindi, refers to the remains of food left uneaten in the plate by someone after he/she has finished eating. If such food is left in more than one place, for instance in a public feast, etc., it is lumped together in a container and given to *shudras* and *ati-shudras* to eat, an extremely degrading social practice. The English expression 'left overs' does not at all convey the socio-cultural import of the term *joothan*. The concept of *joothan*, incidentally, has been associated so closely with the social organization of caste hierarchy for so long that many *dalit* groups have internalized it as a part of their very being and assert the receipt of *joothan* as their right and have marked territories or households from where to collect this.

So much for the title of the text by Om Prakash Valmiki. Now a brief comment on the choice of autobiography as a mode of writing for highlighting the *dalit* nation. As Om Prakash Valmiki himself tells us, his friends were quite surprised at his choice of this mode of expression: An autobiography at this stage of your career as a writer—reacted many of them, shocked. Another observed that 'by presenting myself in the naked, I'd only add to the degradation of our society'. Yet another was worried that 'by writing autobiography, I may not lose my prestige'. To all of them the author's single reply was: 'Why hesitate to present before everyone what is true?'[2]

What in fact the author implied in his answer was that deconstructing history—social, economic, political and cultural—on the basis of personal experience has the additional advantage of bringing out reality in a very poignant and powerful way. It was perhaps for this reason that social activist-philosophers like Jyotiba Phule, B.R. Ambedkar and Ramaswami Naickar chose this particular genre of expression. In fact, a number of *dalit* writers including Daya Pawar, Laxman Gaikwad, Laxman Mane, Kishore Shantabai Kale, Sharon Kumar Limbale, and Mohan Das Nemishrai, have written *dalit* discourse through autobiography.

Joothan, located in Barla village lying at a distance of less than a hundred kilometres from the national capital Delhi—a fact which highlights the severe limitations of the Nation with capital N—begins by detailing the geophysical space organization of the village on caste lines—something which is true of almost all villages throughout India since caste is a *sine qua non* of Indian way of life—internet, online banking and e-commerce notwithstanding:

> Our house lay next to the house of Chandrabhan Tagā. After that, there were a few families belonging to the Muslim weaver community. Right in front of the *Gher* of Chandrabhan Tagā, there was a *johadi*—a small pond—which had created a demarcation between the cluster belonging to the *Chuhra* community and the rest of the village. . . .
>
> The houses of *Chuhras* were built around this *johadi*, behind which the womenfolk of the village—young girls, old women, even newly wed brides—came to answer the call of nature . . . . This was also the space for holding round table conferences for discussing all matters relating to the village. There was filth all around. The stench was so strong that one could choke in a minute. Pigs scampering around in narrow lanes, naked children, dogs, daily quarrels—this was the kind of environment in which I spent my childhood. Those who consider caste system to be an ideal social system would change their opinion in no time if they were forced to live in such surroundings for a couple of days. (11)

The last sentence, a muted, persuasive understatement instead of a venomous verbal outpouring which is the signature tune of many a writer of minority discourse, is typical of Om Prakash Valmiki's style throughout the book.

In the next twenty-five odd pages Valmiki describes his childhood, particularly the abject poverty in which his family lived. The menfolk slaved it out in the fields of upper caste Tyagis who forced the members of the *Chuhra* and *Chamaar* communities to do the harvesting of their crops in extremely hot weather conditions but paid them pittance as wages which were less than even a kilo of wheat for a whole day's labour.

The fate of *Chuhra* women was no better. The author gives the details of the daily routine of her mother who undertook the work of cleaning the *Gher*—the place where cattle are tied—of many Tagas. It involved taking out five to six basketfuls of cow dung from each *Gher*. Apart from a measly compensation of a few kilos of wheat at harvest time, she got for all this effort a *roti* and some *joothan* and that too not every day. The role of *joothan* in a *shudra's* life has already been pointed out. Here is what Valmiki has to tell us about the myths created by *Chuhras* about the amount of *joothan* collected on special occasions, marriages for instance:

> On occasions of marriage, while the *baaraatis* feasted, the *Chuhras* sat at the entrance carrying big baskets. After the *baaraat* had finished, the *joothan* was dropped into those baskets which they carried home and they preserved this *joothan*. . . . If the amount of *joothan* collected from a particular marriage feast was comparatively less, it was said that the *baaraat* comprised starving fellows who had never had a full meal in their lives. They had eaten all up. Often, on such occasions, the elders would narrate, in an engaging tone, about the *baaraats*—marriage parties—which had yielded so much *joothan* that they ate to their fill for months together. (19)

The most significant aspect of this part of the book is the ambition of Om Prakash Valmiki's father to educate his son because he considered education to be the panacea for all their ills, particularly for overcoming the sin of being born a low caste. Om Prakash himself was very keen on completing his school education but more than poverty, the prejudice of the upper castes against the *dalits'* education stood in the way. Apparently, the upper castes too realized the significance of education in the lives of the low castes, that is why they used all kinds of strategies to prevent Om Prakash Valmiki from sitting in the classroom.

> The Tyagi children would torment me by calling me (the son) of a *Chuhra*. Sometimes, they'd beat me up for no reason. It was a strange painful life that had made me an introvert, irritable and short-tempered. If I felt thirsty in school, I had to wait near the hand pump for someone to show up. They'd raise a shindy on my touching the pump. . . . All kinds of tactics were used for forcing me to leave school, so that I'd also adopt the work for which I was born. According to them, my joining the school was a transgression. (13)

In fact, one day, as Valmiki narrates, the headmaster forced him out of the class, asking him to sweep the whole school premises. When on the second day, he quietly sneaked back to the classroom, the headmaster hounded him out, using the most foul language (15).

The use of filthy abuses involving obscene sexual terms by the headmaster makes Om Prakash Valmiki join issue with some critics on the language of *dalit* discourse:

> Seeing us cry, the teacher was showering us constantly with most filthy abuses. Abuses, which if put into words, would taint the fair name of the Hindi language. Once when I had put an abuse in the speech of a character in a story of mine, 'The Skin of an Ox,' many leading writers of Hindi raised their eyebrows. Coincidentally, the character using the abuse was a Brahmin. Brahmin—that is one who knows Brahm . . . and then the abuse . . . (14)

Not just the language of literary discourse, Om Prakash Valmiki also questions the upper castes' critique of literary texts. In a very moving description, he tells us how when once he questioned why Vyas, the poet of the epic the *Mahabharata*, who contrived a powerful poetic portrayal of Dronacharya's poverty made no mention of the abject poverty of *dalits* in his epics, the teacher had felt so outraged that he had beaten him black and blue, observing:

> '(Son) of a *Chuhra*, you dare compare yourself with Dronacharya . . . come, I'd write an epic on your back. . . .' He created an epic on my back with the help of his stick—*sataak*! . . . *sataak*! That epic is etched on my back even today. This epic—of the hateful reaction of a feudal mindset on the starving and unbearable life (of a *dalit*)—is etched not only on my back but also all over my mind as well. (35)

Om Prakash Valmiki in his typical objective, persuasive style, then goes on to observe that many a time he, like Ashvatthama of the *Mahabharata*, had felt the flame of revenge scorching him within and that increased his uneasiness many times more.

Om Prakash also questions the romantic portrayal of rural India in Hindi epic poetry which he says is sheer lies: 'In literature, there is only the imagined concept of hell. For us, the rainy days were no less than hellish life. We've suffered it while living. This harrowing tale of country life hasn't even touched the imagination of the Hindi epic poets. How ugly is the face of this terrible truth!' (35)

Recalling a blood-chilling incident of very cruel and sadistic public beating of the *Chuhras* by the police on false complaints filed by the upper caste Tyagis who resented the *Chuhras* demanding wages for the work done in the fields, Om Prakash Valmiki observes that the words of Sumitranandan Pant's poem '*Ah gramya jeevan bhi kya* ...' rang false and hollow in the face of this grim reality of the village life. On that particular day, the seeds of a different discourse—*dalit* poetic discourse—were sown within him which sprouted in course of time, forcing a poem like '*Thakuron ka Kuan*' out of him. Once again, Om Prakash Valmiki's comment is quite controlled, in the form of a question—'Why is it a crime to ask for wages for your labour?' (52).

The second half of the book details the opening of new vistas for Om Prakash Valmiki—of acquiring knowledge, developing a new consciousness and gaining self-confidence through interaction in his professional life, first as an apprentice at Ordnance Factory, Dehradun, later as a trainee at Ordnance Factory, Jabalpur, still later as a trainee draughtsman at Ambernath, Mumbai, and finally as an appointee at Ordnance Factory, Chandrapur. In the free atmosphere of the hostel life, his potential as a writer found a fertile ground for his flowering as a poet and a theatre person:

> There were some boys who believed in the Marxist ideology. After coming in contact with them, I could read Marxist literature. . . . I formed a theatre group with these boys. We rehearsed the plays in the hostel itself. We gave a number of performances in the Institute auditorium. . . .
>
> I had also begun to write poems those days. (103)
>
> I also developed a distinct standpoint towards literature. In place of artistic writings, I was attracted towards people's ideology. (104)

His caste, however, continued to haunt Valmiki through his various sojourns of professional life. Although his father believed that after receiving education, his son had 'escaped' the caste, Valmiki observes that his father remained unaware of the fact that there was no escape from caste until death. For instance, a girl from Kulkarni family—Savita—who had fallen in love with him during his stay in Mumbai, had suddenly withdrawn on being told by Valmiki that he was a Scheduled Caste:

> She started crying. As if my being an S.C. was a crime. She sobbed for a long while. Suddenly the distance between us had increased. Our hearts were filled with the hatred of a thousand years. We had come to believe in a lie, taking it for culture.
>
> On the way back we were almost silent. But within us there was tumultuous noise . . . (119)

Om Prakash Valmiki's newly developed consciousness about his identity took him closer to both the *dalit* movement and the *dalit* literature. The agitation launched by Dalit Panthers for renaming the Marathwada University as Dr Ambedkar University provided Om Prakash Valmiki with an opportunity to examine afresh the charge of casteism levied against the *dalits:*

> The centuries-old hatred had raised its ugly head once again. I had looked at this agitation from very close quarters. Every pore of my body felt the reverberations of the movement. The cruel system of the Indian society was denying the merit of an individual. In their eyes Dr Ambedkar was a Mahar by birth. No matter if his scholastic ability touched the heights of the skies. (129)

While Om Prakash Valmiki holds the upper caste Hindu social set-up squarely responsible for the ills of the *dalit* nation, he does not absolve his own community either and presents a very powerful critique of the *dalits'* narrow, unscientific world-view. He showed a distinct distaste towards the *dalits'* belief in the world of ghosts, djinns and spirits, particularly their assumption that a person who had shown signs of physical illness had actually been possessed by a spirit and that instead of a doctor it needed the intervention of a '*bhagat*' and the appeasement of the '*bhoot*' through the offerings of a pig, chicken, goat and liquor:

> This only reinforced my belief that all this was nothing but a big hoax, where no logic worked in the presence of faith. God knows how many people had these *bhagats* killed. Two of my brothers had died in the absence of proper treatment and medication. . . . Every year saw a couple of similar deaths in the *basti*. Even then the faith in these gods and *bhagats* did not wane.
>
> The sacrificial pig and the liquor were no less than a feast . . . such was our life. Those were, however, crucial days for me. Those days, I wanted to run away from all this. (56)

As for himself, he refused to have a *pooja* done on the occasion of his marriage that involved sacrificing a pig. In fact, by referring to many such incidents, Valmiki condemns the acts of animal sacrifice as inhuman: 'For me, animal sacrifice is truly an abominable inhuman act, denoting a violent tendency' (99).

Om Prakash Valmiki singles out a number of *dalit* social practices that are extremely demeaning. One of these is called '*salaam*' where first a newly wedded bridegroom goes round the upper caste households seeking *bakhsheesh* and later the bride does the same after arriving at her in-laws' place. He told his father: 'For the bridegroom to go from door to door in his own marriage . . . it's very bad . . . the grooms of upper castes do not go anywhere like this . . . and the bride too would go from house to house after reaching Barla . . . .' His father was listening to him quietly.

His father reacted in a very positive way,

> 'Munshiji, my sending you to school has borne fruit . . . I too understand what you've just said . . . now we shall discard this ritual.'
>
> My father had indeed discarded that ritual beginning with his own house. My brother Janesar's *baaraat* had gone to Rajopur near Luxor. My father refused point blank, 'My son won't go for *salaam*.' (44)

Through this narration Valmiki uncovers the caste conspiracy behind this and other similar practices which the *dalit* communities have internalized much in the same way as superiority of lighter pigmentation or straight hair has been internalized by many a black African.

Finally, Om Prakash Valmiki discusses in the last part of his autobiography the significance of using his caste name. He had never tried to hide his caste and had blurted out the same on the first available opportunity to the utter discomfiture of both his own people and of those from the upper castes who had enquired about it:

> The Commandant welcomed me with a lot of warmth. He felt happy to learn that I belonged to Barla. We hadn't even sat down properly when he began—'Barla is the village of Tyagis. To which caste do you belong?' I looked at Qureshi. His face had changed colour. The question however had been asked in a routine manner. The face of the Commandant showed a natural ease. The moment I blurted my caste as *Chuhra*, he became uneasy. Also, the flow of conversation ceased suddenly. As if there was nothing more to talk about. This was a new experience for Qureshi. (139)

However, what shocked Valmiki were the strategies adopted by many *dalits* to hide their castes, which to him is once again an acknowledgement of their self-degradation:

> There has arisen a grave crisis among those *dalits* who have become educated—the crisis of identity, for coming out of which they are looking for immediate and simplistic solutions. Many of them have started adding the name of their *vanshgotra*—subcaste—to their names proper. For instance, '*Chinaliye*' have begun to write '*Chandril*' or '*Chanchal*' after their names; or '*Sauda*' have begun to be known as '*Saudai*' or '*Sood*'.... Behind all this is the longing for 'identity' which

has arisen as a direct outcome of the terrible inhuman treatment meted out by casteism. *Dalits* want to join the mainstream after educating themselves but the *savarnas*—the uppercastes—try to stop them from doing so, discriminate against them, treat them as inferiors. (152)

Valmiki recalls how once Mohandas Nemishrai—himself a well known *dalit* writer—had suggested that he should introduce him only as Om Prakash, that is sans Valmiki, because he wanted to hide his own identity:

Going up the steps of the house, Nemishraiji said, 'What if you are introduced only as Om Prakash. . . .'

Listening to this, I had felt a sense of shock. I asked, 'Why?'

'He does not know much about me . . . . he's a nice person . . . respects me a lot, even then. . . .' Nemishraiji had tried to clarify. (154)

What emerges finally from *Joothan* is that education did empower Om Prakash Valmiki in many ways. Not only did it sensitize him about his own 'caste' environment and fill him with sufficient self-confidence to fight prejudice both within and outside his caste but also helped him develop a scientific temper towards life and above all become a better human being. This latter aspect of his personality comes out very poignantly through two incidents described by him. The first involves a woman being abused sexually by two men simultaneously:

Today, when I think of that woman, I feel like throwing up. What compulsions must have brought her to them? . . . This experience, when I was only twelve or thirteen has been a very painful one. The fleeting image of that woman whom two wolves tore the whole night haunts me time and again. Whether there was anything left in her by morning has remained an unresolved question for me. (70)

The second incident involved a small boy whom his friend Qureshi, a senior police officer, caught walking alone at night when Valmiki had accompanied him on his night patrol:

Stopping Qureshi [from beating the boy] I said, 'In your eyes this boy may be a liar, fraud, thief or a robber . . . anything. But that he has no money in his pocket is true. . . . Even then you are beating him. The hotel owner who did not pay him his wages . . . you dare not look at him with suspicion . . . does your police have any law to help him get his wages? Or, to go on beating him is all that is in the criminal penal code of yours?' (144)

Interestingly, it led to the police officer intervening and helping the boy recover his wages.

III

This then is Om Prakash Valmiki's description of *dalits* as a nation as it exists within the geopolitical bounds of India. I had, in the beginning of my presentation, reproduced some news items which had pointed to the existence of another world, another nation with which Valmiki's world, Valmiki's *dalit* nation, has little in common. Let me end the presentation by reproducing a couple of advertisements from the same source, that is *The Times of India* of the same date:

Pick up price
Regular Margherita Pizza just for
Rs. 45/-
Domino's Pizza

and

Makki di roti,
Sarson da saag and . . .
Jaggi

Savour the authentic flavour of pulsating Panjabi pop. Check out Jasbir Jaggi's *Kudi Kudi*, the latest hit on Times Music.
Obviously, these advertisements could not be meant for members of the *dalit* nation, those surviving on *joothan.* Or could they?

NOTES

1. Om Prakash Valmiki, *Joothan* (New Delhi: Radhakrishan Prakashan, 1997).
2. Ibid., p. 8. My translations throughout.

PART IV

Agenda, Activism and Agency: Mapping the Postcolony

JASBIR JAIN

The subject of the IACLALS annual conference was announced in the *Newsletter* of July 2000 as *Locating/Dislocating the Post-Colony.*[+] Meenakshi Mukherjee explained the theme in her Editorial and described the word postcolony as 'a modest and infrequently used noun' and considered it to have only two axes of connotation: spatial and temporal. True, she elaborated upon this in several ways, but the elaborations did not, in any way alter the initial premise. Mukherjee also referred to a response which Amitav Ghosh had made to a question. Rejecting 'colonialism' as a marker, Ghosh had said 'I grew up in India which was a place—not a pre something or a post something'. Both the above statements deserve some close attention.

Imagine the postcolony. Is it a space? A congregation of freed people living on an island without a past? Or demarcated on a map through unchanging boundaries—a construct of cartography?[1] If we move into the temporal dimension, the spatial one becomes irrelevant. The demarcation between the pre and post is marked by the political act of independence and becomes encapsulated in a moment of history. What about the continuation of the colonial mindset and of the structures imposed by the imperial rulers like the Indian Penal Code, the education system and a whole lot of other systems?[2]

I have yet another problem. How do we interpret the word 'post'—as a continuation, a lingering attachment, like a hangover, or as a severance, a final termination, a transcendence of the past? Is it to be

*An earlier version of this paper was delivered as a plenary lecture in the IACLALS Conference, Jan. 2001, held at Jaipur.

[+]Meenakshi Mukherjee uses the hyphenated form, post-colony. I prefer the unhyphenated one.

viewed as a positive or a negative tie?[3] Postcolony with all its varied implications ceases to look like a modest term (even if in infrequent use), but the moment we begin to look at it a little closely it assumes sinister dimensions. It can be seen as a satellite colony which continues to perpetuate the attitudes of a colonized people.

Amitav Ghosh's statement echoes an opinion expressed by Nayantara Sahgal nearly a decade earlier when at a conference in Hong Kong she asked as to how long we were going to measure our lives by a pre this and post that. When can we begin to be simply ourselves, and look for unanchored beginnings?[4] It would call for a tremendous leap in self-confidence, a tremendous amount of self-critiquing and discrimination, a shaking-off of economic imperialism on the one hand, and narcissitic withdrawal on the other. Is the postcolony the diasporic Indian abroad?[5] Is it the Silicon Valley, or is it to be defined by an interrogation of Western systems of knowledge?

How many of us feel as Ghosh does? Is the fact of having been once colonized a strong determinant of our beings? It appears to me that the history of the last fifty years is a cyclic replay of the second half of the nineteenth century, specially where the question of agency is concerned. The mid-nineteenth century reform movements looked to the state for action; towards the end of the century the initiative was appropriated by the community, and finally in Gandhian ethics it passed on to the individual. Similarly from the Five Year Plans, development projects, and the concept of the welfare state, now there is a shift to community intervention and support and, through activism, to individual participation in people's movements.

Some of the major movements of our times—the Narmada Bachao Andolan (NBA), the Right to Information (led in Rajasthan by the Mazdoor Kisan Shakti Sangthan), Vandana Shiva's work on ecology (specifically *Staying Alive* which posits indigenous theories and perceptions against West-oriented systems of development), and the DNTRAG (Denotified Tribes Rights Action Group)[6]—are movements which seem to converge towards the same goal. They question the developmental agenda and its aggressive base which is anti-nature and consequently anti-human. Development in some ways seeks to rupture the relationship between nature and human life, as it had once done between culture and civilization. By placing Indian civilization in the remote past, the British were able to locate its present within a primitive and barbaric construct legitimizing their intervention. Both Gandhi and Tagore were compelled to define civilization as 'right conduct' as opposed to the capitalistic, industrialized Western civilization.[7] But this rupture between a cultural past and a civilizational present has not been easy to heal. The patterns of governance continue to be colonial and hence the emergence of mafia groups and largescale criminalization of politics. There is a separation between knowledge, the act of knowing, and power, the act of doing. And earlier, in the colonial period, there was perhaps also a deterrence to self-knowledge through the intervention of imperial authority and imposition of normative patterns.

Activism today is a struggle against the existing forms of governance (irrespective of political ideologies), and even as it questions the dominant form of knowledge, it explores the ways that knowledge is constructed. For purposes of illustration, I propose to take up two short narratives of Mahasweta Devi—'The Witch' and 'Pterodactyl, Puran Sahay and Pirtha' and Amitav Ghosh's *The Calcutta Chromosome*.[8]

Mahasweta Devi in her introduction to the collection titled *Bitter Soil* writes: 'I have based my writings on truth, and not on fiction. . . . My experience keeps me perpetually angry and makes me ruthlessly unforgiving towards the exploiters, or the exploiting system. That the mainstream remains totally oblivious of the tribal situation furthers that burning anger' (ix).

Several tribes were notified as criminal tribes by successive notifications of the British government and after the Mutiny of 1857 the situation worsened. The British, 'in a paranoid mood, saw "crime" everywhere. Their inability to understand the lifestyle of the wandering communities, compounded by the suspicion that some members of these communities had aligned with the mutineers, led them to take a very harsh view of these people.'[9]

The British government interpreted crime as a caste-based feature and went on to enact the Criminal Tribes and Castes Act in 1871 (to be followed by harsher versions in 1911 and 1924) which allowed the local administrations to confine them in 'prison-like' settlements, thus simultaneously victimizing them and excluding them from opportunities of employment and education. They were a captive population available for use as bonded labour.

Gayatri Spivak in an interview[10] refers to these tribes ranging between 6 to 8 per cent of the population as the indigenous inhabitants (8) and the Report refers to them as the earliest occupants of the subcontinent (4). Spivak goes on to describe India 'as a pre-capitalist precolonial, non-European settler colony where the postcolonial Hindu-majority Indian is, roughly speaking, the first settler' (8).

These tribes, located within their past marginality, stand today in a very complex relationship to the mainstream Hindu majority which is condescending towards them even as it wishes to assimilate them in religious and legal terms and there is a love-hate relationship underlying the state's affirmative action programme. The situation engenders a psychology of fear and an attitude of dependence on the part of the tribal, while at the same time alienating him further from the mainstream. The state, on its part, has ceased to see and respond, wrapped up as it is in its own illogical conclusions and manipulation of statistics in its primary motivation of capturing votes. There is, in fact no cohesive relationship between development goals and cultural heritage and no meeting point between the tribals' perception of their reality and the government's acknowledgement of it.

'The Witch' is a story about a cluster of tribal settlements where conditions of drought are likely to lead to famine. Government aid in terms of relief is their only hope. The villagers are led to believe that the drought is caused by the witch. The margin between human beings and witches is not definitive, anyone can be inhabited by a *daini*. Thus the evil spirit has to be found and chased away. The story works at several levels, realistic as well as metaphorical—the enclosed space, the denuded forests, and the sense of isolation. The escape routes being closed, terror stalks the community as outside forces conspire against it even as they assume friendly guises. All kinds of relationships come under suspicion and distrust—husband and wife, parents and children, friends and, in the final instance, even the relationship with the self.[11] A great sense of insecurity overpowers the people, and religion, wrapped up in high caste morality, pronounces them sinners. The Brahmin priest, Hanuman Misra, confines the lower castes to the world of sin. In his view 'they are major sinners. Or else why would they die in famines and floods?' (59).

Then there is the figure of Peter Bharati, the white man who is a recurring feature in the Indian past and has been here in several incarnations, attracted by the 'exotic', the 'spiritual' and the 'mystical'. He is a collector of Eastern mysteries and ethnicities and is a prototype of the Western invader. In this incarnation Peter has been initiated into the Holy Orders by Swami Anandabharati and is now comfortably ensconced in the Ashram. He begins to follow the story of the *daini*, is willing to finance research on this, and later publishes the findings under the name of Kurt Muller, thus waiving away all previous commitments to the real researcher Sharan Mathur, and also gaining the freedom to alter the nature of the projection.

Another outside intervention is that of the researcher Sharan Mathur. But Sharan Mathur undergoes a transformation through the course of his involvement with the community. Mathur is not in search of any monetary gain, and as he begins to understand the people and the nature of their problems even the pursuit of the research degree which had initially brought him here becomes secondary (113-14). He transcends his earlier self, in which in retrospect he recognizes the element of greed in his search for knowledge and theoretical formulations (100). But even he can never become an insider.

The local Block Development Officer is another person who feels concerned but remains a helpless observer. If he allows his compassion to be visible in his actions, if he truthfully reports the conditions of famine, he is placed under threat of transfer. Compassion and concern are no part of his job requirements; all that is required of him is to support and justify the official stand that it is only a drought and not a famine.

The people of this community, affected as they are by superstitions engendered by upper caste Hindus and surrounded by priests, observers and an unsympathetic administration, begin to fall easily into the role outlined for them—as less than human, possessed by spirits and destined to die of deprivation, hunger and persecution. The resultant violence is an act of self-preservation. They are required to stone the *daini* and chase her away. Finally when they catch up with her, it is discovered that the *daini* is no other than Somri, the dumb, mentally-retarded daughter of the *pahaan*, the tribal priest of Tura, who had been engaged by the Brahmin priest to help with the cows. The Thakur's son had raped her and spread the news of the *daini*. The girl, naked and hungry, had prowled the forests, was stoned and chased away, and now, at the moment of discovery, delivers a child. Her body thus becomes the site of contestation between power and powerlessness. Further, the fear of the *daini* has been instrumental in disrupting the tribal people's relationship with nature. The realization of the exploitation which has created the *daini* now antagonizes them against the upper castes.

The narrative is set against the failure of development—unkept promises, the misappropriated aid, the much delayed relief works and the administration's non-recognition of the conditions of famine. In fact all efforts move in the direction of isolating, suppressing and separating them from the national culture. The entry of upper caste religion brings with it its own fallacies and impositions, and thrusts a caste system upon them. All outside forces exploit them including the foreigner who writes an article for a foreign magazine, which is finally made into a film. This transformation of a human tragedy into a marketable commodity is described in caustic terms which convey a blatant violation of trust. Having violated the trust of Sharan Mathur, and having changed himself from Peter Bharati to Kurt Muller, the reporter 'achieves the impossible' and in his hands the piece turns into a lurid tale:

> There were many photographs with the article. *Sevika* Aileen Bharati was painted black and dressed up as a *daini* for the photographs. Mathur was wonderstruck at the sight of the *roast* chicken in the hands of the *daini* who was supposedly eating the flesh of the *tatui* bird. At the end of the story, the expression in *close-up* on the *daini's* face is so realistic that, on the strength of that one photograph, Aileen Bharati lands the heroine's role in the film, *The Witch*, which is based on the above article. The film will be shot in Arizona in America. Because the geography of that area is similar to that of Palamau. A special feature of the film is that all *Bharatiya* characters will be played by whites, and all white-skinned characters by *Bharatiyas*. (87)

Underlying the irony and the commentary which has its comic elements, there is also the political discourse of capitalistic manufacturing of narratives and a realization of the cruelty of what the First World does to the Third World under the garb of sympathetic intervention. But, sad to say, the local 'babus' who exploit their skills are no better (83-4). The tribal systems of knowledge are allowed to die, for there is no meeting point between them and the mainstream.

'Pterodactyl, Puran Sahay and Pirtha' is Mahasweta's second story I would like to refer to—a bird (flying animal), a man and a place—nature, human beings and environment, all placed together in a network of relationships.

The story opens with Puran Sahay sitting in the Block Development Office, when he gets to know of the unearthly terror. With this the narrative moves into the past to fill up the reader on Puran Sahay's background and informs the reader of the values he has been nurtured on, the defiance of his father to the male-centred system, and his own distancing from the norm of aggressive masculinity. This, in itself, is a critiquing of the social system which believes in stereotypes and polarities.

Pirtha is a block in Madhya Pradesh and when Puran visits Pirtha in search of a story in his capacity of a journalist, he is quick to sense the hostility of the Sub Divisional Officer. The administration wants to keep prying journalists out, for the government is unwilling to recognize or publicize the conditions of famine in this area, following close on the heels of the Bhopal disaster. The official attitude is 'There's nothing more to be seen in the tribal areas' (98). They are to be a frozen zone. The map of the area looks like an animal, a prehistoric creature. The famine in the area is the failure of the administration—the Irrigation Scheme which exists only on paper, the small dams which have never been built, the successive SDOs whose efforts have been stalled and who have been transferred, the funds which get lost on the way and the Inspection visits which are conveniently scheduled to take place during the monsoon. The authorities have made up their mind not to declare it a famine area. The media is equally guilty. It has no time for truth; all that it wants is some sensational news. In fact, there is a serious communication gap between the different participants of the drama (102). It is against this background that the people of Pirtha see the monstrous shadow of a bird fly over them and consider it an inauspicious omen. This truly was an emergency.

There is no dearth of sympathetic and compassionate men but the system makes them helpless. The SDO's plans to dig wells, to extend the road, to build a primary health centre, all remain unrealized due to the apathy of the administration (104). There is no correspondence between the needs of the area and the facilities provided. They need a health centre to prevent women from dying in childbirth and medicines to control epidemics but all they get are family planning posters which they can use either for patching up their thatched huts or as sheets to sleep on. The abundance of natural resources gets wasted through corruption and lack of imagination. Wherever roads have been built, it is through misappropriation of funds earmarked for tribal welfare.

Therefore, when 'the Adivasis walk along the road to market, they walk on the graves of their education system, their irrigation system, their supply of drinking water, their health centres' (109). They are kept in ignorance and perpetual want and subordination. Their histories are unrecognized, their contributions unacknowledged and their knowledge systems marginalized. And now they in their turn distrust everyone, the administration and the media alike (117).

The gap between the tribal system of values and the so-called civilized world is evidenced in the fact that tribal languages have no words to describe the kinds of experiences they are subjected to. There are no words for 'exploitation' or 'deprivation' in the Ho language (118). Their songs narrate their histories. Civilization for them is one long tale of deprivation. Land, fields, homes and even the graves of their ancestors have all been taken away. They are the dispossessed. The question then is, 'Is it possible to fight aggression, plunder, exploitation . . . with their uncontaminated value-system?' (120).

Facts are fabricated, land is sold, records are manipulated, banks cheat them on loans, employment figures exist only on paper, the legal cells are all a hoax and the honest are punished. To protest is to invite death. Even democratic representation does not lead to acceptance of the tribals as part of society. The tribals 'have not received anything from modern India' (146). They are even deprived of basic needs like clothes and food. The outsider's eye values the exotic element in their background. The places where they live have the potentiality of being attractive picnic spots and tourist attractions. The official advice is 'Dislocate them and plant some more trees' (151). The civilized have no compassion for them though they would like to make a film on them, and frame and exhibit their hunger, but it is anybody's guess whether this representation reflects their deprivation and loss, or is just a glamourous framing of the 'difference', what Spivak refers to as the museumization of the exotic.

It is at such a time as this that Bhikia captures the image of the flying bird as it casts its shadow over the village—the bird which is now extinct. The bird represents the unknown terror which is talked about at the beginning of the story. It is a reminder of the seeds of destruction which lie embedded in the evolutionary processes of the so-called progress. One day this civilization will also be extinct, its extinction caused perhaps by a nuclear explosion, war or the 'aggressive advance of the strong as it obliterates the weak, which finally turns you naked, barbaric, primitive' (157). It is difficult to say whether the denuded forests and extinction of animal species is a move forward or a move backward. Those in power are too intoxicated with power to face the truth which stares them straight in the eye. They are not aware of the march of the forces of destruction.

The two civilizational codes run parallel—never meeting, never crossing each other, because human equality has not been recognized.[12] Two systems and two epistemologies live side by side in silence, fear and hostility.

Amitav Ghosh's *The Calcutta Chromosome* is a very different kind of work, yet some of the questions which the narrative asks bear a curious similarity to the ones which Mahasweta Devi's narratives raise. Subtitled 'A Novel of Fevers, Delirium and Discovery', it is the story of Ronald Ross's discovery of the malarial mosquito.

Both Mahasweta Devi and Amitav Ghosh in their different ways problematize the way knowledge is constructed and question the basis of hierarchical relationships. Both emphasize the importance of man's relationship with nature and move away from the individual to questions of human survival and dignity. Both also foreground indigenous knowledge systems and explore different ways of communicating with others. Mahasweta Devi turns to enclosures, and uses myth and creates metaphors out of the material of everyday suffering. Amitav Ghosh, on the other hand, turns to open spaces and makes use of magic, rebirth and the uncanny which governs human life. Whereas she traces the parallel flow of epistemologies which need to relate, he presents an interaction which subverts and re-appropriates authority. In essence they both continue a tradition of counter modernity.

Within this larger position of initiating an oppositional discourse, there are differences. Mahasweta Devi belongs to a literary tradition which is defined by the non-Brahmanic approach, a tradition which resists categories and hierarchies, and posits the human right to be human. Amongst her predecessors are writers like Shivaram Karanth (*Chomuna Dudi*, 1933), Shivashankar Pillai (*Scavenger's Son*, 1948) and Gopinath Mahanty (*Paraja*, 1945). These writers are not necessarily concerned with encountering or problematizing Western modernity but base their work on value and interrelationships, concern themselves with redistribution of economic resources, questioning of the hold of tradition and superstition, and accountability on the part of the power-wielders. This tradition represents an India which has encountered the colonial intervention perhaps at its harshest and has also been ignored and victimized by the local elements. But it does not look towards the Western structures for enlightenment and help.

The Calcutta Chromosome is not only different from Mahasweta's work, it is also markedly different from Ghosh's other novels even as it shares with them the engagement with history and philosophy. It is heavily loaded with cultural inputs which are not always intelligible to the uninitiated reader. At one level it can be treated as a failed narrative with its dystopian conclusions and questioning of the inroads which technology has made into the personal life of an individual.

Part history, part science fiction and part dystopia, it carries within it the structures of both mystery and fantasy. Two epistemological traditions live side by side—one the rationalist discourse of the Enlightenment and empirical sciences, and the other the mystical one of magic and speculation. But they do not remain parallel, they intersect, impose upon each other, look to each other for support and authority and through these interactions dislocate agencies. Is Ross the real discoverer, or is Mangala Bibi? Linear chronologies are disturbed and time moves back and forth, the narrative acquires a cyclic dimension when lives pass into each other. There is never a termination of a life or an event, all apparent terminations have new beginnings. And the crossings are not only of one epistemology into another, but of one life into another. The narrative is deliberately placed within uncertainties and unreliability. The date of Ross's Nobel Prize Award is changed from 1902 to 1906. Again at another point the month of January is merged into February. A great deal of emphasis is placed on written records, diaries, reports, published gazettes, creative writing. But this is counteracted by an equal degree of emphasis on hearsay, tales, oral accounts and unfinished tales. What is seen or known is not necessarily true. The nature of reality is not verifiable. There is also a repetitive pattern in the events which are narrated. The ghost train at the abandoned Renupur railway station, the signal lamp which finds its way in various places, the unwanted, abandoned beggars at Sealdah railway station, the youth who turns up in various roles with only four fingers and no thumb—as the bearer, as Lutchman, as the boy who sells fish. There are several subnarratives—Antar's, Murugun's, Sonali's, Urmila's, and the diary of Cunningham and a whole lot of others. The protagonist keeps shifting as the narrators change and identities get dislocated. The subtext continues to be the malarial parasite which can be of use in curing syphilis and thus the central metaphor of the novel is one of mutation, fertility and a resulting transformation. This is also a cultural metaphor and in this Ghosh counters two primary formulations of postcoloniality—mimicry and hybridity. The novel creates a world indifferent to both and posits the idea that hybridization is a stage which leads us back to our selfhood, but often rendering us unrecognizable.

For Homi Bhabha hybridity has multiple meanings and several of these are tilted in favour of the colonizer. It provides a base for the production of colonial authority, a strategy through which the colonized are made to internalize the process of colonization by bringing about important changes in their perspective.[13] Further it intervenes in the 'exercise of authority not merely to indicate the impossibility of its identity but to represent the unpredictability of its presence' (114).

As against these problematizations of hybridity by Bhabha, the Foucauldian position about the discourses of knowledge and power makes it abundantly clear that hybridity defines one as produced by the other.[14] Ghosh moves away from these points of view and considers hybridity essential for the purpose of continuity of life. He considers it mutual and reciprocal, for those who refute its presence, falsify their experience. To substantiate this, he does not in anyway concentrate on the act of mimicry, which is limited to the anglicized pronunciation of Indian names. He explores the various dimensions of hybridity as plural forces which are pulling collectively in one direction, and by making connections through spaces as well as time. The narrative begins in New York and this is also where it ends but in between it travels to Egypt, Calcutta, Madras, Renupur and several places in Europe. People of different origins, nationalities and regions are involved—Hungarians, Turks, Egyptians, Indians and so on. No single system is adequate, no individual can create knowledge alone. And thus there is no knowing which is irrelevant. Like Foucault, Ghosh follows an archaeological method which is signified by the explorations being conducted by the Hungarian woman who, in Antar's explanation, is a 'dust counter'. Ghosh confronts rationalist knowledge with the 'subjugated' knowledges of the East.[15] He, like Foucault, is opening up a space in which to think 'difference' or 'otherness'.[16]

The medical metaphor also acquires significance in view of Foucault's

The Birth of the Clinic wherein he traces the development of medical science from a language of fantasy to one of visibility. In his second of the two lectures on Power/Knowledge (14 January 1976), Foucault lists several methodological precautions and writes:

> Power is not to be taken as a phenomenon of one individual's consolidated and homogeneous domination over others, or that of one group or class over others. . . . Power must be analysed as something which circulates, or rather as something which only functions in the form of a chain. . . . Power is employed and exercised through a net like organization . . . individuals are the vehicles of power, not its point of application.[17]

Ghosh uses the individual as a vehicle of knowledge which is passed on from one generation to another like a disease, like the malarial infection. There are recurring references to the time of the crossing (for instance see *The Calcutta Chromosome* 27, 207, 253) as well as to the alternative forms of knowing, interpretation and 'Inner States'. In fact, Murugan's whole life is spent in pursuit of 'An Alternative Interpretation of Late 19th Century Malaria Research: Is there a Secret History?' (31)

Thus when Amitav Ghosh says he grew up in India, and not in a pre or post something, what does he imply? His remark is a statement of self-assertion, a refusal to be confined by boundaries. More recently, through his refusal to be categorized as a Eurasian Regional Winner for the 2001 Commonwealth Writers' Prize, he made a similar assertion. In an interview given to the *Outlook*, 2 April 2001, Ghosh objected to the valorizing of a 'particular view of the past or present, in creating, as it were, a literary "bloc". I believe the idea of the "commonwealth" . . . does represent a certain reading of the past and present . . . .' (63)[18]

Where then is the postcolony—imagined or real? In literary and cultural terms, it is possible to move out of the colonial constructs through recoveries of histories, in social terms through responsive needs, in political terms through questioning of hegemonic strategies. Mahasweta Devi in her postscript to the Pirtha narrative writes:

> In this piece no name—such as Madhya Pradesh or Nagesia—has been used literally. Madhya Pradesh is India, Nagesia village the entire tribal society. I have deliberately conflated the ways, rules, and customs of different Austric tribes and groups, and the idea of the ancestral soul is also my own. I have merely tried to express my estimation, born of experience, of Indian tribal society, through the *myth* of the pterodactyl. (198)[19]

Both Mahasweta Devi and Amitav Ghosh represent an Indianness which even when it doesn't refute the past, seeks to stand outside it and to dislocate the centre of power. Mahasweta is involved in a people's movement, and through this activism posits a counter-discourse to the established channels of power. The subversion is partly brought out through myth (in the literary narrative) and through projection of the stark reality, the conspiratorial nature of power and exploitation (both at the literary level and the activist one). Exploitation is seen in its native manifestations and is not necessarily associated with the foreign ruler though the exploitative structures are similar.

Amitav Ghosh, through his validation of indigenous epistemological structures, questions both the relationship between power and knowledge and the relationship between power and agency. There is in this a rejection of the postcolonial mindset. It remains to be examined whether the term postcolonial can be separated and distinguished from the term postcolony. Postcolonial may be treated as an aftermath, and as a marker in time. Postcolony degenerates, in my view, to a replica of the erstwhile colonizer, the more powerful 'other', and would in a way be a ghetto, isolated from the idea of progress. Taking the cue from Meenakshi Mukherjee, this would represent its spatial dimension. Temporally, as a historical marker, we in India have moved away from being a postcolony in terms of intellectual attitudes, positions of resistance and oppositional discourses. But the question is far more complex than this. Other issues, other foces keep on cropping up to remind us of our past.[20]

For the moment, it needs to be stressed that postcolony carries within it all the histories and implications of postcolonialism. If we need to be free of one, we need to be free of the other in the interest of our self-respect and authenticity.

NOTES

1. This would imply that boundaries remain constant. But since 14 August 1947, the map of India has undergone several changes both in its external boundaries and internal divisions. First the carving out of the two wings of Pakistan, then the merger of the princely states, Junagadh, Goa and later Sikkim, the coming up of LOC in J&K, the creation of linguistic states, Himachal Pradesh and later Haryana and more recently the three new states Uttaranchal, Jharkhand and Chhattisgarh. The above list is not exhaustive but it is indicative of the shifts that have been operative over the last fifty years or so.

2. Many of our laws are outdated and shortsighted. They merely add on to the existing structure. A serious example is the Denotified Tribes Act. The education system also has periodically been given a new face but it has never been totally overhauled or rooted to the Indian realities.
3. While asserting that mindsets do not change so easily, I would also like to point out that every generation looks at the past differently. I will give just two examples. The first is the present generation in India, people who do not have the same memories of the freedom struggle which their parents or grandparents had. The second example is the present generation in Pakistan, which also no longer shares the memories or nostalgia of their elders and for whom the relationship with India is very different from the one of the immediate post 1947 generation. The ambivalence is also marked by the double reference to 15 August 1947 as a date which marks Independence as well as the Partition.
4. See Nayantara Sahgal, 'The Schizophrenic Imagination', *Unbecoming Daughters of the Empire*, ed. Shirley Chew and Anna Rutherford (Sydney: Dangaroo Press, 1993).
5. See *The Present: The New Pelican Guide to English Literature*, vol. 8, ed. Boris Ford (Harmondsworth: Penguin, 1983), which has two essays which relate to India—one by William Walsh, 'India and the Novel', and the other by Gamini Salgado, 'V.S. Naipaul and the Politics of Fiction'. Besides this there are other essays on Nigerian writers. The location of the diasporic writers from the erstwhile colonies constitutes in itself a postcolony—if we really need to identify it. It has shifted 'home' to the colonizers. The self-confidence with which these new settlers have moved from their colonial status as a subject people into their new role as full-fledged citizens is remarkable but political and civil rights do not necessarily eliminate racial and cultural differences (and discriminations).
6. This movement is engaged with improvement in the social and economic status of the tribal people. Some of the leading activists of this movement are Mahasweta Devi, Ganesh Devy and Laxman Gaikwad. Gayatri Spivak also has been working with the training programmes of this movement. Of the others, as is well known Medha Patkar, Sundarlal Bahuguna and now Arundhati Roy are associated with the NBA movement and Aruna Roy, Nikhil Chakravarty, Kavita Srivastava and Renuka Pamecha are associated with the Right to Information Movement. These movements question the Developmental Agenda of the government as well as the methodologies of development. (In this connection it may be useful to see Arundhati Roy's 'The Reincarnation of Rumpelstiltskin', *Outlook* (27 November 2000). They are simultaneously directed at making the illiterate peasant or tribal conscious of his political and human rights and at making democracy meaningful. These movements also throw up an alternative model of leadership which is more decentralized, discourages personality cults and works through collective processes of decision-making.
7. Gandhi has used it in *Hind Swaraj* (1909) and Tagore in his 1941 essay 'Crisis in Civilization'. Ordinarily the level of culture indicates the civilizational

level, but for colonized India its civilizational development was projected as thwarted and stagnant, thus bringing about a rupture between the two terms.

8. 'The Witch', *Bitter Soil* (Calcutta: Seagull Books, 1998). The stories in this volume have been translated from the Bengali original by Ipsita Chanda. The second narrative which I have selected is 'Pterodactyl, Puran Sahay and Pirtha', translated by Gayatri Chakravorty Spivak (Calcutta: Thema, 1993), the third work is *The Calcutta Chromosome* by Amitav Ghosh (Delhi: Ravi Dayal, 1996).
9. Refer to the 'Report to the U.N. Commission on Human Rights, October 1998', published first in *Interventions: International Journal of Postcolonial Studies*, 1, 4 and reproduced in *Budhan*, April-June and July-September 2000. The signatories to the Report are Mahasweta Devi, G.N. Devy and Gayatri Chakravorty Spivak, 2-4. The same issue also carries an interview with Gayatri Spivak by Anupama Rao, pp. 5-10.

   The Report records that the notifications began as early as 1793 and were formally constituted into the Notification of Criminal Tribes and Castes Act in 1871, and renewed in 1910 and 1920.
10. See Anupama Rao, 'Interview with Gayatri Chakravorty Spivak', *Budhan* (April-June and July-September 2000).
11. The presence of the *daini* is a 'nameless horror' unleashed on the people. 'Everyone began to suspect everyone else, to mistrust the behaviour of near and dear ones.' Mothers are suspected by their sons, and sons by mothers (6). 'All husbands—fathers—brothers—sons were compelled to keep watch upon the women. Do they cast shadows on the ground . . . does a crow fly above their heads . . . . It's not easy to hunt *daini*. Everyone, everywhere has to suspect everyone else, all the time' (60-1). The situation comes to resemble the feeling of terror experienced under a totalitarian regime although here it is the world of superstition that is unleashed and not the mastery of technology (as it happens in Orwell's *1984*).
12. Mahasweta Devi had once commented: 'The tribals and the mainstream have always been parallel. There has never been a meeting point. The mainstream simply doesn't understand the parallel.' 'Author in Conversation' with Gayatri Spivak, *Imaginary Maps* (Calcutta: Thema, 1993) p. ii.
13. See Homi Bhabha, *The Location of Culture* (London: Routledge, 1994), p. 112, wherein he analyses the effect of colonial power as reflected in the *production* of hybridization. Authority has at its source an ambivalence which not only enables it but also carries within it a subversive potentiality. He goes on to elaborate upon it and comments, 'Hybridity is a problematic of colonial representation and individuation that reverses the effects of the colonialist disavowal, so that other 'denied' knowledges enter upon the dominant discourse and estrange the basis of its authority' (114).
14. See Lois McNay, *Foucault: A Critical Introduction* (London: Routledge, 1994), pp. 80-4.

15. Refer to Foucault's 'Two Lectures' wherein he not only clarifies his use of Power/Knowledge but also what he means by subjugated knowledges. It would be incorrect to treat Power/Knowledge as a straightforward connection which could read that power leads to knowledge, or conversely that knowledge gives you power, i.e. enables you. The manner in which they are related, through an oblique stroke, defines their interrelationship in a different way and allows a complex relationship to come into being which is neither permanent nor unidirectional. By acknowledging the presence of 'subjugated' knowledges he concedes their validity. He says, 'By subjugated knowledge I mean two things: . . . the historical contents that have been buried and disguised in a functionalist coherence or formal systemisation . . . (and) a whole set of knowledges that have been disqualified as inadequate to their task or insufficiently elaborated. . . .' It is through the reappearances of these knowledges 'that criticism performs its work' (Gordon 81-2). Both archaeology and genealogy are important to enable them to resurface (83). At this stage he does not dwell on the agency which has 'suppressed' them or the agency which will enable them to surface. Immediately Said's *Orientalism* comes to one's mind as an example of the processes which subjugate knowledges or construct them. But he goes on to locate power in the individual, the cessation of which enables political power to come into being and the relation that it plays in economic production and class. Foucault is not fully satisfied by approaching or analyzing power as a controlling or a repressive agency. He relates it to its positive aspects which would logically permit subversion and shift of power centres. Joseph Rouse in 'Power/Knowledge' in his comments on Foucault's concepts also considers them as 'dynamic relationships' *The Cambridge Companion to Foucault*, ed. Gary Gutting (Cambridge: Cambridge University Press, 1994), p. 113. Given this premise the kind of power which ManglaBi exercises over her followers interacts with the kind of legitimate authority conferred upon Ross by his position as a medical man engaged in the pursuit of a specific investigation. The knowledge and power of one interacts with the other, not necessarily to dislocate or subvert it but to collaborate with it. In the process it dislocates both the legitimacy and the agency of the scientific discourse through its own discourse which is based on intuition and speculation but is not entirely without empirical basis.
16. McNay, *Faucoult*, p. 49
17. Michel Foucault, *Power/Knowledge: Selected Interviews and Other Writings 1972-1977*, ed. Colin Gordon (New York: Pantheon Books, 1980), p. 98.
18. Amitav Ghosh's objection is to the homogenizing that is being thrust upon the specificity of Indianness by cloaking it in a blanket term like Commonwealth and the categorization which this implies. At the end of the interview he states that he is happy enough to be identified as an Indian writer in English.
19. The tribals, despite their exploitation and alienation from the mainstream, do not qualify as postcolony. If one goes back to an article by U.R. Ananthamurthy, 'The Search for an Identity: A Kannada Writer's Viewpoint' (included in *Creating*

Theory: Writers on Writing, ed Jasbir Jain. Delhi: Pencraft International, 2000), it is possible to see how they, like the peasant of Ananthamurthy's article, have never been influenced by Western thought. Imperialism in its economic and political impact has passed them by. They have also not been impacted by the education system. Further, I have also quoted this passage to draw attention to the kind of oppositional discourse which is at work between Gayatri Chakravorty Spivak and Mahasweta Devi. While Mahasweta Devi expands Madhya Pradesh and Nagesia to include the whole of Indian and the whole of the tribal society, Spivak narrows down the concept of 'nation' to Bengal ('Translator's Foreword to Draupadi', in *In Other Worlds: Essays in Cultural Politics* [New York: Routledge, 1988]) and also the need Spivak feels to frame Mahasweta's narratives within prefaces and commentaries. In the 'Translator's Preface' to *Imaginary Maps*, Spivak explains this as an obligation she feels to act as a mediator, so that the charges of exoticization cannot be laid at Mahasweta's door. The two cultures of the East and the West are so different from each other. Through this interpretative commentary she is perhaps facilitating the subaltern's speech to enter the 'structure of responsible resistance'. But Mahasweta herself is entirely indifferent to this kind of framing (in an unpublished interview with Jasbir Jain, 22 Feb. 2001 at New Delhi) and expresses both her inability and unwillingness to interact with it. Spivak in another essay 'Discussion: An Afterword on the New Subaltern' comments: 'To suggest that the Subaltern produces high theory in an unmediated way is hopelessly romantic' (318). Activism needs to be supplemented by theory in order to intervene with the mainstream political discourse, hence the validity of the prefaces even if they define the perspectives too rigidly. But I do not necessarily agree with Spivak in this respect. This framing becomes, at times, exclusive and morbid, subtracting from the discourse its primary vitality.

20. There remains another question to be addressed: Does the fact of globalization do away with the need to locate a postcolony or does it, through reinforcing the centre, express differences only in relation to the power of the centre?

Postcolonial Theory, Postcolonial Literatures and the Postcolonial Anxiety

ARUN P. MUKHERJEE

I would like to begin with an anecdote about meeting a graduate student from an Ivy League American University at the 1997 Modern Languages Association Conference in Toronto. When he told me that he was thinking about doing a Ph.D. in postcolonial literature, namely Rushdie and the postcolonial nation, I asked him what other authors he had studied and what kind of courses were being offered at his university in postcolonial literatures. Dissatified as I am with my own Department's allocation of space to postcolonial literatures[1] in the undergraduate English Honours curriculum, which continues to be predominantly British, I am always curious to find out about what other universities are doing, and I was particularly curious about this university since it is home to at least two very well known critics in the field of postcolonial studies. Imagine my surprise when he told me that while one of the two Professors taught a course in postcolonial theory, there were no courses in postcolonial literatures at his university.

While I cannot be certain about the accuracy of my informant's comments, it does not take a rocket scientist to notice that there is a flood of books and journal issues on postcolonial theory. If one were to even cursorily examine the titles being published in the field now getting to be known as 'Postcolonial Studies', one would be justified in concluding that whatever else 'Postcolonial Studies' may be, it is not interested in literature.

Besides the scholarly works on postcolonial theory that continue to be published in remarkable numbers, the popularity of postcolonial theory in the academic publishing market is testified to by the burgeoning number of introductory books aimed at the student market. I came across four books published during 1997 and 1998 that aim at introducing postcolonial theory to a student audience. While Ania Loomba's book is called *Colonialism/Postcolonialism*, the other three are called *Postcolonial Theory*.[2] Slight variations in their titles are achieved by calling one *Postcolonial Theory: A Critical Introduction*, the other *An Introduction to Postcolonial Theory* and the third one *Postcolonial Theory: Contexts, Practices, Politics* (Although Dennis Walder's *Post-Colonial Literatures in English: History, Language, Theory*[3] foregrounds literature in its title, and does devote some space to postcolonial literatures as opposed to the books listed above, it, too, privileges 'theory').

Although I had serious problems with the first book published in this genre, the 1989 *The Empire Writes Back: Theory and Practice in Postcolonial Literatures*, on account of the vast generalizations made therein, at least the book purported to focus on the study of literature. The new crop of postcolonial theory books does not focus on literature. The books I mentioned above devote the main part of the text to explicating the work of Edward Said, Gayatri Spivak, and Homi Bhabha. A few other postcolonial theorists are mentioned in their pages but only as responding to the three greats.

As I read these books, I begin to wonder if it is the same book I am reading over and over again. After conscientiously examining the contents of these books, I can no longer tell Said, Spivak and Bhabha apart as these books seem to have put them all in the blender and churned out a cocktail of 'Postcolonial theory'. The writers of these books speak of a 'Postcolonial theory' which speaks, writes and acts on its own, just like a human subject. One could open the pages of any one of these books at random and come up with examples like the following (from Leela Gandhi):

> As we have seen, the happy conjunction of diasporic thought and the discourse of hybridity assists postcolonialism in its search for evidence regarding the mutual transformation of coloniser and colonised. In recent years, much postcolonial attention has focussed on questions regarding the reconfiguration and unsettling of Western/colonial identity.[4]

Usually, when 'a' assists 'b', one thinks of agents. They could be human, animal, or machine, but not abstractions. In the sentence above, 'the happy conjunction' of two abstractions, namely, 'diasporic thought and the discourse of hybridity', 'assists' another abstraction, i.e. 'postcolonialism'. After reading page after page about abstractions become subjects doing things to other abstractions, I begin to lose my grasp on reality.

Then there are statements about 'the emerging consensus on postcolonial literary practice' or what 'postcolonial theory subscribes wholeheartedly to'. Another favourite sleight of hand is: 'Most postcolonial literary critics refer to . . .'.[5] So it is not the human beings as critics who speak and theorize, and who can be spoken to and argued with. I would like to know the names of critics who have reached a consensus. Similarly, it would help to hear the name of a critic making claims or subscribing wholeheartedly to something so that one could direct one's remarks to them. For how does one conduct an argument with an abstraction?

Gandhi's text is no better or worse than the others explaining postcolonial theory to those who find it hard to understand the originals. The following passage from Peter Childs and Patrick Williams's *An Introduction to Post-Colonial Theory* speaks in a similar vein:

> Colonialism's effects, after-effects and the counter-effects of strategies of resistance have only begun to be widely assessed in the last twenty years. The preoccupations of post-colonial theory: syncretism, displacement, difference, marginality, discourse, alterity, and representation, are increasingly the preoccupations of theory more generally. As communities become more culturally diverse and globally aware, the issues and concerns that affect disparate peoples, in dissimilar and conflicting ways, will more obviously converge and may be described as post-colonial. (218)

I could pile many more examples of such decontextualized, deterritorialized and abstraction-ridden language that goes under the name of postcolonial theory. It seems to fall around me in a non-stop downpour, in the shape of anthologies of 'Postcolonial Studies' and 'Cultural Studies' and umpteen introductory books on 'Postcolonial theory'. That 'Postcolonial theory' has successfully institutionalized itself is also evident from the fact that a chapter is routinely devoted to 'Postcolonial theory' in introductory books on literary theory for undergraduates.

I would like, at this point, to declare the position from which I am observing, and being troubled by, these developments. As an academic, a large part of my work involves teaching the literatures of Africa, South Asia, the Caribbean and Canada, Australia, and Aotearoa/New Zealand.

I and my colleagues in the field teach these literatures to undergraduate and graduate students who often have little or no knowledge of the geographic, historical, social, cultural and political contexts of these literatures and the bulk of whose training is primarily formal. Further, I teach these courses in an academic setting in which the dominant assumption, though unstated, continues to be that 'great works' rise above the local context, and that their meanings and pleasures are universalizable. Although I believe that teaching the texts that I do is itself an important intervention in this Arnoldian paradigm, there is, in my view, a pressing need to explore and examine the issues related to the teaching and reading of postcolonial literatures.

From this vantage point, I believe it is important for me to pay attention to this second level of theoretical discourse vis-à-vis postcolonial theory since that is where my undergraduate students (and non-specialist users of postcolonial theory) get their commonsensical ideas about what 'Postcolonial Literature' is and how it is to be studied. I find out what sort of perceptions and expectations my students hold about a course in 'Postcolonial Literature' by asking them to write a paragraph about 'What do I think Postcolonial literature is' on the very first day of classes. What I have discovered by this exercise is that the views expressed by my students are quite similar to the views expressed in a more sophisticated manner by prominent theorists in the 'field'. The following submission, written in my first class of 'English 2370: Postcolonial Literature', on 8 September 1998, is a good illustration of my point:

> Post-colonial literature is an expression of the effect colonialism/imperialism has upon the people, culture and places it dominates. It can assume many forms. For some it is the expression of colonial domination: simply writing in a language second to your own, foreign to your ears. For others it is an active reclaiming of people's histories, life experiences, stories and lives. It is an empowering medium. It is the assertion of one's self, according to one's self concept and not that which is taught and imposed by a system of social, cultural, political and economic oppression. It can be an expression of anger, sorrow, or strength.
>
> It is people speaking of themselves for themselves rather than being spoken for.

I may seem to be belabouring the point, but I would like to juxtapose my student's comments with those made by Charles E. Bressler in *Literary Criticism: An Introduction to Theory and Practice* about postcolonial writing:

Such an author must ask of himself or herself three questions: Who am I? How did I develop into the person that I am? To what country or countries or to what cultures am I forever linked? In asking the first question, the colonized author is connecting himself or herself to historical roots. By asking the second question, the author is admitting a tension between these historical roots and the new culture or hegemony imposed on the writer by the conquerors. And by asking the third question, the writer confronts the fact that he or she is both an individual and a social construct created and shaped by the dominant culture. And the writing penned by these authors will necessarily be personal and always political and ideological. Furthermore, its creation and its reading may also be painful, disturbing, and enlightening. Whatever the result, the story will certainly be a message sent back to the Empire, telling the imperialists what they did wrong and how their Western hegemony damaged and suppressed the ideologies of those who were conquered.[6]

Whether the prominent critics who have been called the 'Holy Trinity'[7] of postcolonial theorists have expressed such sentiments or not, this is how their message has been received by academics who write introductory books that are not necessarily limited to a readership of undergraduate students. Or the academics who write papers for journals about 'resistance' and 'hybridity', to name only two of the popular concepts current in the 'field'.

So when I teach the courses that my Department[8] calls 'Postcolonial Literature', I face students who have already absorbed the 'jargon' of the 'specialty'. I do not begin on a blank slate, awash as the libraries and the bookstores are with 'Postcolonial theory'. I need to work against and around it since I have profound disagreements with the reductive and homogenizing 'Postcolonial theory' that is being thrown in the market by large British and U.S. publishing houses. I agree with the Indian historian Sumit Sarkar who suggests that 'the exposure of one instance after another of collusion with colonial power-knowledge can soon become predictable and tedious'.[9] Although Sarkar is talking about the work of subaltern historians, his comments are equally applicable to the procedures of postcolonial theory-mill that approvingly quotes subaltern historians selectively, disregarding the critiques of their work in India.

What happens, then, if, instead of resisting the colonizer, I want to resist postcolonial theory when I teach? As I suggested in a paper called 'Ideology in the Classroom',[10] the teacher does not speak to *tabula rasa* students but to students who are interpellated with dominant ideologies of literary criticism. I am not surprised, then, when my second year students, when asked to write a paragraph about what they think 'Postcolonial literature' means, write that it refers to literature written by colonized people, that it is about resisting domination and searching for identity.

I wonder how many of my colleagues have to begin by questioning the categorizations that underpin their courses as I have to do. I began teaching in the field by questioning the 'five regions' approach that prevailed in Canada when I entered the 'field' and which found expression in its quintessential form in Ashcroft, Griffith and Tiffin's *The Empire Writes Back* (1989). I have written at length about my disagreement with the founding assumptions that prevailed in the field (in Canada and Australia) at the time of my entry in it in the mid-eighties: that colonized societies around the globe 'shared' certain common features that then produced literatures that were similar in themes and styles[11] (I still remember a conference in 1991 where I upset some elders of the field in Canada and Australia by denying that there was a common bond unifying postcolonial literatures).

I have written at length about these theoretical issues because they underpinned the development of the discipline in Canada. The postcolonial theorists who are based in the United States and whose work has been so influential over the last fifteen years do not write about them. Reading Gayatri Spivak's new book, *A Critique of Postcolonial Reason*, has helped me understand why I get so little help from the 'Holy Trinity' when preparing for my classes. Her book suggests that the Delphic Oracle of postcolonial theory does not teach what we in Canada call 'Postcolonial literatures'. While the book engages in postcolonial readings of Charlotte Bronte's *Jane Eyre*, Jean Rhys's *Wide Sargasso Sea*, J.M. Coetzee's *Foe,* Hegel's take on the *Bhagavad Gita*, and Baudelaire's sexual interest in women of colour, it does not refer to any other writers from postcolonial societies besides Rhys and Coetzee (both white) except in passing to two short stories by Mahasweta Devi.

Spivak sees Mahasweta Devi's work as responsible in its representation of aboriginals and their oppression by the postcolonial state. Spivak's translations of the author's work have popularized her among Western feminists. Without disputing the value of Mahasweta Devi's work and the value of Spivak's translations and readings, I must say that singling out one author from a country as large as India and as heterogeneous in its literary, linguistic and cultural traditions, can be as reductive as singling out and pedestalising Salman Rushdie. Indeed, Spivak not only does not refer to any other authors from India, except when comparing canonical Bengali writers to Mahasweta Devi, or from other postcolonial societies, she casts doubts on the teaching of such authors, in English translations as well as in English:

> Third World studies, including Third World feminist studies in English, become so diluted that all linguistic specificity or scholarly depth in the study of culture is often ignored. Indeed, works in often indifferent English translation or works written in English or the European languages in the recently decolonized areas of the globe or written by people of so-called ethnic origin in First World space are beginning to constitute something called 'Third World Literature'. Within this arena of tertiary education in literature, the upwardly mobile exmarginal, *justifiably* searching for validation, can help commodify marginality. Sometimes, with the best of intentions and in the name of convenience, an institutionalized double standard tends to get established: one standard of preparation and testing for our own kind and quite another for the rest of the world.[12]

I read these words to mean that Spivak does not think that writings in English from Asia, Africa and the Caribbean are worth teaching or should be taught (further reinforced by my inability to find any references in Spivak's work to such writing). Since a large part of 'Postcolonial literatures' is constituted of such writing in English or in what Spivak calls 'indifferent English translation', we who teach this writing need to debate the conditions of our work and our own sense of its worth. The point for me, however, is that Spivak's theory is produced under the conditions of her work in a U.S. university and it should not become 'the' 'Poscolonial theory' that every one needs to rush to read and cite the moment it is enunciated (I find it ironic that one of the most quoted and invited academics finds herself marginalized: 'Indeed, those of us who ask for these standards are becoming marginalized within mainstream feminism' (168)).

It seems to me that we who work in the 'field' need to produce accounts of our working conditions, our own desires, abilities and handicaps, the institutional pressures that channel our efforts, and, finally, our interactions with our students in the classroom. I, too, am tired of what Spivak daringly calls 'white boys talking postcoloniality' (160). I am exhausted just looking at the flood of journal issues, anthologies, introductory books and celebrity books on 'Postcolonial theory', all reiterating, rather, rehashing, issues of marginality, resistance, subalternity, voice, nation, hybridity, authenticity ad infinitum, without ever referring to literary texts and the problems of hermeneutics involved in teaching and understanding texts that are cross-cultural.

I am not saying that these issues are not important. Indeed, they have forced the study of humanities in Euroamerican universities to go beyond aesthetics defined in a very narrow, depoliticised way. I am saying that we need to do less hagiography and more dialoguing. For instance, why is it that it is always Spivak who is interviewed rather than Spivak also interviewing? We need to produce analyses situated in our institutional place, so we can nudge the institution, at least a bit, and hope that those who come after us will nudge it some more.

And we need to engage with the literatures. 'Postcolonial theory' has not done that, or done very little of it. Indeed, it has become a whole new academic field so that English Departments are now advertising for positions in 'Postcolonial theory'. My own Department is in the process of hiring in the field and we are heatedly debating the language of the advertisement. I would like to quote a passage from the position paper presented to the Department by our English Graduate Students Association to highlight the controversies and how they impact on hiring:

> [W]e would like to call for candidates who are students of regional literature but who also have a strong background in Postcolonial Theory. A Postcolonial theorist would have a scholarly expertise over a wide range of literary debates and would have something to offer a broad spectrum of graduate students. Although we obviously want this appointment to teach in an area of regional literature, we do feel that a candidate with a wide range of theoretical concerns would be a scholarly and professional resource for many of the graduate students in the programme. Indeed, a Postcolonial theorist could offer students who do not specifically study Postcolonial literatures alternative paradigms through which to analyze their own historical or national fields.[13]

I cannot but recall Barbara Christian's 'Race for Theory'[14] here. In the mind of the writers of the position paper, theory is primary and literature secondary, even though it is 'literary debates' that the theorist would have expertise in. Then, 'Postcolonial Theory' is detachable from whatever it is the theory of and applicable to 'historical or national fields' that are not 'specifically . . . Postcolonial literatures', i.e. you don't need to bother reading postcolonial literatures, just get postcolonial theory that you can sprinkle on whatever canonical writers of Euroamerica you happen to be studying.

No doubt, the position paper is quite astute about the state of affairs. Indeed, 'Postcolonial theory' and 'Postcolonial theorists', albeit of a certain type, are quite a rage. 'Theory' is hot, and 'Postcolonial theory' is super hot. And, in order to 'do' 'Postcolonial theory', one does not need to bother with the study of literatures of postcolonial societies.

Although I personally find reading 'pure' theory tiring and not very useful to my own work (an evaluator of my grant application called my work 'anti-theoretical'), I do appreciate the fact that others may find it beneficial. What I am objecting to is the state of affairs where theory produced without any reference to literature (Bhabha's work is remarkably 'pure' in that way) gets applied to literary texts from postcolonial societies. As Spivak herself notes in her book, her work is more concerned with a 'persistent dredging operation' so as to render the 'mainstream' murky.[15] As important as the work of muddying the mainstream is, the work of studying literatures from postcolonial societies requires a different kind of theoretical labour.

Spivak, unlike Said and Bhabha, undertakes that kind of work in her engagement with Mahasweta Devi. Her introductory remarks prefacing her translation of Mahasweta's short story, 'Draupadi', in her first book, *In Other Worlds*,[16] bring out the challenges involved in acquiring what Spivak calls 'transnational literacy' in her new book. Beginning with the very name of the heroine, cultural outsiders need extensive glossing, ranging from Mahasweta's ironic allusions to the epic the *Mahabharata* to the revolutionary political movement called Naxalism. Reading Spivak's commentary, one is made to realize that the literary text cannot be read without knowledge of the cultural text that precedes it. She chides 'postcolonialists' in her new book for their 'lack of respect for the singularity and unverifiability of "literature as such"'.[17]

When 'one of the major architects of the whole post-colonial enterprise in the West' (Eagleton) makes an about-turn and begins to make scathing attacks on 'Northern radical chic—hybridism, post-nationalism',[18] I begin to hope that it will slow down the postcolonial theory-mill and move the discussion, as E. San Juan's title suggests, beyond postcolonial theory (Ironically though, after bitterly critiquing Aijaz Ahmad, Bhabha, Said, and Spivak, San Juan endorses Fredric Jameson's model of third world literatures as national allegory along with an all-male canon made of his favourite authors).

To really go beyond 'Postcolonial theory', we would need to think about, as Heather Murray suggests all teachers of English do, 'taking the discipline itself, past and present, as a subject of scrutiny'.[19] That would require paying attention to 'the intense privatization and isolation of the classroom, and about the lack of written record of its practices' that Murray talks about (161). In order to do that, we would have to turn our attention to our own institutional places and practices, and examine the work of dominant postcolonial theorists in terms of their situatedness in the United States rather than take its universality for granted.

I am indebted to Paulo Freire for making me think from the local to the universal, rather than the other way round. His biographer has written about Freire's hesitation about applying his theories developed in Brazilian situations to Guinea-Bissau where he was invited to carry out a literacy programme: 'It was important to forget what had happened in previous literacy schemes so that this previous work would not be given a universal value which then would be transferred to Guinea-Bissau.'[20]

'Postcolonial theory', then, needs to be tested against our local pedagogical sites, rather than universalized. I would like to move the discussion to the marginal place non-Western literatures occupy in Western universities and the impact this marginality has on the theoretical work produced by academics who teach these literatures. I would like exchanges about pedagogical concerns, about our experiences in the classroom where we face students who know next to nothing about the history, culture, society, etc., of the Third World countries.

In that spirit, I would like to share two illuminatory moments during my teaching of a second year 'Postcolonial literature' course during 1998-9. My first example is based on a student's seminar on Sembene Ousmane's *God's Bits of Wood*. The student had chosen to focus her presentation on a song sung by a blind beggar woman named Maimuna. The narrator informs us that the song is from the legend of Goumba N'Diaye. (Although I made a concerted effort to find information on the legend, unfortunately, there is not much information about Senegalese history and culture in the English language materials. I can speculate, though, based on my cumulative experience of reading literature, that the legend must have an impact on the meaning of the song as a subtext. Curious as I am to find out as to how the song will be read by a culturally informed reader, I must remain satisfied with my informed ignorance, hoping that some day it will be filled when an expert in Senegalese culture and literature glosses it.) Here, then, is the song:

'I have come to take a wife', the stranger said.
'My bridegroom must be stronger than I,
There are my father's fields,
And there are the abandoned scythes',
  Replied Goumba N'Diaye.
And the Stranger took up a scythe.
Two days each week, and still they came not to the end,
But the man could not vanquish the girl.
. . .   .
'Stranger', demanded Goumba N'Diaye,
'From what country do you come?'
And the stranger replied, 'I am from every country.
  I am a man like every man.'
'It is not true', said Goumba N'Diaye
'For many seasons, men have fled from me.
  Men are not alike.'[21]

The student read the song as an allegory of the colonial struggle. 'The girl', she said, was the country of Senegal and the stranger was the French colonizer who was trying to dominate. Goumba's resistance was an allegory of Senegalese people struggling to throw out the colonizer.

I am pretty sure that this second year student has not read Fredric Jameson's article about all Third World literature being national allegory.[22] When I asked the student how this pre-colonial epic about a strong woman could come to stand for the colonial domination of Senegal, she suggested that perhaps it foreshadowed colonialism.

I realized that my lecture about Sembene's desire to move away from the colonizer/colonized binaries had not cut much ice with my student. I had focused on the fact that the novel was published in the year of Senegal's independence and yet, instead of glorifying the leaders of the anti-colonial struggle, Sembene had chosen to glorify the workers who had participated in a six-month long railway strike. I had spoken about Sembene's juxtaposition of French workers who send money from France to help the Senegalese workers in their fight against their French employers with Senegalese collaborators who lecture the strikers about the benevolence and benefits of the colonial rule. And to highlight

Sembene's Marxism, I had drawn my students' attention to an exchange between the union leaders and the employers. While the white men demand to know 'where would you be without France and the French people?' the union leader says, 'This is not a question of France or her people. It is a question of employees and their employer' (182).

The point I had tried to make in my lecture was that the text portrayed colonization as a much more complex affair than the dominator/dominated binary and to suggest that the ideal of class struggle inspired many among the colonizers to side with the Senegalese workers. Then there was the question of patriarchal aspects of Senegalese culture, and Sembene, I said, was showing how these had oppressed women and needed to be worked against with the same energy as the anti-colonial and anti-capitalist struggles.

My student's reading of the text made me conclude that my analysis did not have the same authority for the student as the one she may have come across in some postcolonial theory primer.

I observed that my students were often anxious about pinpointing 'the postcolonial aspects' of the text. Often they would enquire about what was 'postcolonial' about a text. A student who had done consistently good work over the year showed me an article by a well known critic that she had downloaded from the Internet on R.K. Narayan's *Swami and Friends*. The student wanted to be reassured that Swami was just a little boy and not someone who was discovering his 'essential Indian identity' as this article claimed.

My students' anxieties about spotting the 'postcolonial' elements in the text were revealed to me in a telling way when, for an in-class assignment, I gave them a few passages to identify and discuss in terms of their language. I was looking for a reassurance that they could spot things like buried allusions, irony, tone of the narrative voice, etc. As I overheard the group discussions going on in the class, I realized, once again, how theoretical frameworks can often predetermine the way a text will be read. Instead of looking at the language, they were trying to figure out what was 'postcolonial' about the passage! Here is the passage from Khushwant Singh's *Train to Pakistan* that was being discussed: 'Sunder Singh put the revolver to his temple but did not fire. There was no point in killing himself. The train had begun to move. He heaved out the corpses of his wife and children and came along to India. He did not redeem the pledge. Only his family did.'[23] I had chosen this passage to see whether my students would recognize the bitterly satirical allusion to Jawaharlal Nehru's speech about 'tryst with destiny' on the midnight of India's Independence and Partition. I had spent a considerable amount of time in the lecture talking about the speech and how the text mocks it. Imagine my disappointment when I overheard the students trying to figure out the 'postcoloniality' of the passage. One of them had identified the revolver as a colonial import that had corrupted Sunder Singh, the colonized subject. The train, too, was a colonizing presence, a symbol of the evils of industrialization.

I asked the students if they remembered my comments in the lecture about the phrase 'redeem the pledge'. I cannot speculate as to how many students in the other tutorial group would have remembered, but only one student in my group of 20 present that day remembered. I take this in my stride since I have been told that the average attention span of human beings is no longer than 15 minutes.

In *Swami and Friends*, one of the questions in the examination requires Swami to write on the moral of the story, 'The Brahmin and the Tiger'. Swami is unsure about which of the two is the right answer: 'We must never accept a gold bangle when it is offered by a tiger' or 'Love of gold bangle cost one one's life.'[24] Narayan's portrayal of coercive education and a child's inability to guess the 'right' answers according to the teacher teaches me humility and the realization that the text is open to several interpretations, including the one offered by postcolonial theory. I may not like it because it is so reductive but it *is* an interpretation.

In our last class of the year, we discussed what I called 'the postcolonial anxiety' of my students. The students said that the title of the course, 'Postcolonial literature', had made them think of the chosen texts as written in a 'postcolonial' style that they will learn to identify in the course. When I asked them whether they looked for the 'Canadianness' of Canadian texts in their Canadian literature course, they said that they did not; that indeed, texts in other courses were read for their characters or for their narrative or social comment or formal structure, etc. We all agreed that the texts read in our course should get the same kind of attention.

I fully appreciate the causes of my students' 'postcolonial anxiety'. Books introducing undergraduates to literary theory routinely devote separate chapters to 'approaches' such as 'New Criticism', 'Archetypal Criticism', 'Feminism', 'Marxism', 'Psychoanalytic criticism', etc., teaching students how to recognize these in a text. The 'approaches' come to be seen as formal and rigid, a mere matter of competency. Bressler, for example, concludes with a chart which provides an 'overview' of the nine 'schools of literary criticism'. The 'goal' of 'Postcolonialism', predictably, is 'show[ing] oppression of colonized people'.[25]

I ended my course the same way I had begun: why do we call these texts and writers we had studied in the course 'Postcolonial' and why could not there be a better name? I ended the year by reiterating my point that it was not just the name that was the problem. Rather, we needed to change a whole lot of things within the Department and the University: more resources in terms of library acquisitions and the number of faculty and more room for these literatures in the 'core' curriculum.

The categories of 'Postcolonial literatures', 'Postcolonial Studies', and 'Postcolonial theory' are generated by an academic enterprise where the bulk of resources are devoted to teaching and researching on minute compartmentalizations of British literature. In Canada, U.S. and Canadian literature carved a nation-based space in the curriculum during the sixties and seventies. Literatures of Third World countries, however, have not been able to do that. Instead, some writers from former colonies of Britain began to be taught in 'Commonwealth literature' courses. The introduction of 'Commonwealth literature' courses, much opprobrium as they have inspired lately, was, indeed, brought about by radical teachers who were interested in pushing the boundaries of the discipline.[26] Problematic as they were in their universalizing frameworks, we need to respect the fact that they breached the closed citadel of English Departments. The task now is to widen that breach and, perhaps, take the fort.

'Postcolonial theory' that has focused more on colonial discourse, nation and nationalism, mimicry and hybridity, resistance and the subaltern, than on the conditions of studying and teaching non-Western literatures in the Western academy, is not going to help bring about that change. Very important as those discussions have been, it is time now to acknowledge the master-slave relationship that operates between the postcolonial theorists and the teachers of postcolonial literatures so that while the theorists give no indication that they spend any time reading and/or teaching the literatures, the teacher of these literatures like myself cannot afford not to read the latest theory, however inadequate it is when applied to literary texts. We who teach these literatures will need to generate another theoretical discourse that foregrounds the theory and practice of teaching non-Western literatures in the universities of Euroamerica.

NOTES

1. I use the name here as a bureaucratic category, acknowledging the fact that my Department's Course Calendar lists courses at the second, third and fourth year level under that name. Like many other critics and writers, particularly Aijaz Ahmad, Thomas King, Anne McClintock and Ella Shohat, I have written about the problems with the concept. To repeat, among its other sins of homogenization of diverse cultures and their literary productions, it also limits us by totally ignoring the precolonial.
2. Ania Loomba, *Colonialism/Postcolonialism* (New York: Routledge, 1998); Leela Gandhi, *Postcolonial Theory: A Critical Introduction* (New York: Columbia University Press, 1998); Peter Childs and Patrick Williams, *An Introduction to Post-Colonial Theory* (Hertfordshire: Prentice-Hall, 1997); and Bart Moore-Gilbert, *Postcolonial Theory: Contexts, Practices, Politics* (London: Verso, 1997).
3. Dennis Walder, *Post-Colonial Literatures in English: History, Language, Theory* (Malden, Mass: Blackwell Publishers, 1998).
4. Gandhi, *Postcolonial Theory*, p. 132
5. Gandhi, *Postcolonial Theory*, pp. 150-1.
6. Charles E. Bressler, *Literary Criticism: An Introduction to Theory and Practice*, 2nd ed. (Englewood Cliffs, New Jersey: Prentice-Hall, 1998), pp. 267-8.
7. Robert Young, *Colonial Desire: Hybridity in Theory, Culture and Race* (London: Routledge, 1995), p. 163.
8. As I say in my book, *Postcolonialism: My Living* (Toronto: TSAR, 1998), 'The field existed before I secured my teaching position in 1989 and hence, as with everything else in life, I entered a conversation that was already going on. It is in this sense that postcolonialism is my "living" or my bread and butter. It is a professional niche which has its rules and regulations, its protocols of entry and qualifications' (xi). My engagement with the teaching and theorizing of postcolonial literatures, then, is oppositional.
9. Sumit Sarkar, *Writing Social History* (New Delhi: Oxford University Press, 1997), p. 105.
10. Arun Mukherjee, 'Ideology in the Classroom: A Case Study in the Teaching of English Literature in Canadian Universities', *Oppositional Aesthetics: Readings from a Hyphenated Space* (Toronto: TSAR, 1994), pp. 30-8, n. 181.
11. Arun Mukherjee, *Postcolonialism: My Living* (Toronto: TSAR, 1998).
12. Gayatri Chakravorty Spivak, *A Critique of Postcolonial Reason: Towards a History of the Vanishing Present* (Cambridge, Mass.: Harvard University Press, 1999), p. 170.

13. English Graduate Students Association, York University, 'EGSA Steering Committee Statement on Postcolonial Appointments', 6 April 1999.
14. Barbara Christian, 'The Race for Theory', *Cultural Critique* 6 (1987): 51-63.
15. Spivak, *A Critique*, p. 1.
16. Spivak, 'Translator's Foreword', *In Other Words: Essays in Cultural Politics* (New York: Routledge, 1988), pp. 179-87.
17. Spivak, *A Critique*, p. 1.
18. Terry Eagleton, 'In the Gaudy Supermarket', Review of Gayatri Chakravorty Spivak's *A Critique of Postcolonial Reason: Towards a History of the Vansihing Present, London Review of Books* 21.10 (31 May 1999): 375.
19. Heather Murray, *Working in English: History, Institution, Resources* (Toronto: University of Toronto Press, 1996), p. 12.
20. Moacir Gadotti, *Reading Paulo Freire: His Life and Work*, trans. John Milton (Albany: State University of New York, 1994), p. 45.
21. Sembene Ousmane, *God's Bits of Wood* (1962), trans. Francis Price (London: Heinemann, 1985), pp. 21-2.
22. Fredric Jameson, 'Third-World Literature in the Era of Multinational Capitalism', *Social Text* 15 (Fall 1986): 65-88.
23. Khushwant Singh, *Train to Pakistan* (1956; New York: Grove Weidenfeld, 1990), p. 178.
24. R.K. Narayan, *Swami and Friends* (1935; Chicago: The University of Chicago Press, 1980), p. 61.
25. Bressler, *Literary Criticism*, p. 278.
26. See Diana Brydon, 'Introduction: Reading Postcoloniality, Reading Canada', *Essays on Canadian Writing* 56 (Fall 1995): 1-19.

The Nature of Criticism in Our Time

BHIM S. DAHIYA

Reading through the vast variety of contemporary critical theories and textual interpretations under the various brand names, such as structuralism and post-structuralism, deconstruction and new historicism, cultural studies and feminism, minority discourse and post-colonialism, one is left wondering where the discipline of literary criticism has arrived in our time. The alien idioms one encounters, the gigantic critical apparatuses one confronts, the mind-boggling systems one has to comprehend, all quickly combine to create a climate utterly discomforting, making one unstable even for a 'temporary stay against confusion'.[1] Terrorized by the teasing games of the dreadful discourses, the common reader instinctively terminates his journey through the dense forestry and returns to his own common-sense reading of the literary works. Of course, after his abortive journey through the verbal forest he does not return the same man; he comes back sadder but not wiser. What leaves him completely nonplussed are the oracular declarations, such as the 'death of God', the 'death of the author', the 'death of the subject', etc. Mortally afraid of encountering more of such declarations, he decides never to seek any critical company for his future journeys into the 'cities of words'.[2]

In such a situation it has become imperative for all those who value literature and literary criticism as instruments of education, essential for preserving and promoting the humanity of human societies, to understand and analyse the factors responsible for effecting this unprecedented change in the nature of literary criticism in our time. Until the end of the nineteenth century literary criticism had remained committed to elucidating for the common reader the social and moral significance of literary works, and was always written in a literary style as readable as literature itself. Note, for example, the following from S.T. Coleridge:

The characters of the *dramatis personae*, like those in real life, are to be inferred by the reader—they are not told to him. And it is well worth remarking that Shakespeare's characters, like those in real life, are very commonly misunderstood, and almost always understood by different persons in different ways. The causes are the same in either case. If you take only what the friends of the character say, you may be deceived, and still more so, if that which his enemies say; nay, even the character himself sees himself through the medium of his character, and not exactly as he is. Take all together, not omitting a shrewd hint from the clown or the fool, and perhaps your impression will be right; and you may know whether you have in fact discovered the poet's own idea, by all the speeches receiving light from it, and attesting its reality by reflecting it.[3]

The very first thing one notices here is the use of an idiom readily available to the common reader. One also notices that the analogy used for explaining the critical method is taken from everyday human dealings, which implies that literature is a representation of life. One notices, too, how in a very simple manner the issue of the author's intention has been explained, which makes clear that it is available within the text itself, and that one does not need to look for it anywhere else, including the author as a historical personage.

A drastic change in the nature of criticism began to become noticeable in the early years of the twentieth century. Those who brought about this change include I.A. Richards, Ezra Pound, T.S. Eliot, and the New Critics. With them literary criticism changed from art to science. Perhaps it had to change with the increasing influence of science in the modern age. As W.T. Stace has observed, 'The positive stage is the stage of science which, when fully attained, abolishes both metaphysics and theology. In the golden age of the future which the triumph of science is to usher in, nothing will be considered knowledge unless it is science.'[4] Read, for example, the following from Ezra Pound: 'The Proper METHOD for studying poetry and good letters is the method of contemporary biologists, that is, careful first-hand examination of the matter, and continual COMPARISON of one "slide" or specimen with another.'[5] Thus was adopted by Pound, as well as by those 'new' poets and critics who faithfully followed the dictates of this poet's poet and the critic's critic, the method of science in poetry and criticism. A similar thrust in the direction of science was given by I.A. Richards, who in his *Science and Poetry* pleaded, once again, for the scientific method of analysing the working of the poem as well as the poet's mind. Note, for example, the following:

> To understand what an interest is we should picture the mind as a system of very delicately poised balances, a system which so long as we are in health is constantly growing. Every situation we come into disturbs some of these balances to some degree. The ways in which they swing back to a new equipoise are the impulses with which we respond to the situation. And the chief balances in the system are our chief interests.
>
> Suppose that we carry a magnetic compass about in the neighbourhood of powerful magnets . . . . Suppose that instead of a single compass we carry an arrangement of many magnetic needles, large and small, swing so that they influence one another . . . .
>
> The mind is not unlike such a system if we imagine it to be incredibly complex. The needles are our interests . . . .[6]

Thus, from Pound's scientific 'method' we moved to Richard's scientific 'system'. In the convention of criticism from Aristotle to Arnold, there used to be approaches to literature based on the social and ethical goals of human society. They considered literature as an instrument of education. Now with these High Modernists it got reduced to the status of material productions of science and industry. The most influential of these high priests of scientism, T.S. Eliot, carried this task with greater force than even Pound and Richards. Note, for instance, the following:

> There remains to define this process of depersonalization and its relation to the sense of tradition. It is in this depersonalization that art may be said to approach the condition of science. I shall, therefore, invite you to consider, as a suggestive analogy, the action which takes place when a bit of finely filiated platinum is introduced into a chamber containing oxygen and sulphur dioxide.[7]

Here the poet's mind becomes the gas chamber in which various experiences combine like different chemicals to form a new compound. The chemical reaction is used to explain the process of composition of a poem or any other literary text. No doubt, this conversion of literary criticism into a study of systems and structures, principles and processes, involved in the making of literature, is effected under the express influence of science. In the same vein, the New Critics, namely John Crowe Ransom, Cleanth Brooks, W.K. Wimsatt, Monroe Beardsley, and William Empson, viewed a poem as a structure of words, reducing the function of criticism to explicating the functioning of various verbal devices such as metaphor, ambiguity, paradox, irony, image, etc., in the working of the structure called poem. In this New Critical effort, while literature changed from being one of the beautiful arts into one of the functional sciences, literary criticism changed from being an educational source into a scientific method.

In its attempt to introduce scientism in literature and literary criticism, the modernist criticism in the early twentieth century also made the author invisible, for like the filament of platinum he does not go into the compound called poem; he just stays behind. It also made the business of criticism a specialist's job. It became inaccessible to the common reader who would not have the benefit of knowing various sciences and their principles and processes, systems and structures. The very language of literary criticism acquired a special ring, becoming far removed from the language of everyday conversation. The macro commentaries of earlier criticism were replaced by the micro explications of verbal devices used in the making of a poem. The writing called criticism became arduous. W.B. Yeats, who called himself one of 'the last romantics', soon realized this arduousness of modern poetry and modern criticism. In a letter to Dorothy Wellesley, he separated himself from the high modernists:

> The difficult work which is being written everywhere now has the substance of philosophy and is a delight to the poet with his professional pattern; but it is not your road or mine & ours is the main road, the road of naturalness and swiftness and we have thirty centuries upon our side. We alone can think like a wise man, yet express ourselves like the common people. These new men are goldsmiths working with a glass screwed into one eye, whereas we stride ahead of the crowd, its swordsmen, its jugglers, looking to right and left. 'To right and left' by which I mean that we need like Milton, Shakespeare, Shelley, vast sentiments, generalizations supported by tradition.[8]

Yeats is obviously drawing a contrast between the popular literary writers and the writers as specialists. We know how the writings of Eliot and Pound, Joyce and Woolf, became special readings, based as they were on philosophies and theories drawn from extra-literary sources. We also know how the critical writings of the New Critics acquired the nature of scientific investigations, seeking relations between the parts and the whole, the components and the structure, modelled on the functioning of a chemical process or biological system. Thus, literary criticism became one of the specialties in the corporation of knowledge disciplines.

The New Critics also changed the nature of literary criticism from a moral source of life to an amoral tool of investigation. Wimsatt and Beardsley came out with their famous (or notorious?) articles on 'intentional fallacy' and 'affective fallacy', with explicit implication of disinfecting literary criticism of moral as well as social significance. Like any physical or biological phenomenon, like any chemical or industrial process, a literary work came to be viewed as only a product of words. Naturally, then, the nature of literary criticism also became amoral, like any discipline of science, having nothing to do beyond the functions of various parts, or the workings of various structures or systems. While the 'intentional fallacy' took away the living voice of the author, the 'affective fallacy' took away the living response of the reader. Both reiterated the scientific study of literature, restricting its activity to the explication of verbal devices, their interrelational functions, and their functions in relation to the working of the structure of which they are internal components.

The Modernists paved the way for the Post-Modernists, who carried further the activity of making literary criticism a super-specialty, subjecting it to scientific empiricism. While 'invisibility' of the author was pushed further to declare the 'death of the author', the 'intentional fallacy' gave way to the 'reader-oriented theories'. The language of the super-specialty made literary criticism far, far removed from the access of the common reader. Even those in the business of teaching literature were forced to choose their micro areas of specialization, for it was impossible for any individual scholar to keep pace with the fast developing specialties in all the areas. In an era of mass production ushered in by the multinationals, literary theories could not have remained otherwise. There came in the literary market numerous brand products of the Post-Modern multinationals. Read, for example, the following from Roland Barthes to have a feel of the special language evolved by one such brand:

> In an author's lexicon, will there not always be a word-as-mana, a word whose ardent, complex, ineffable, and somehow sacred signification gives the illusion that by this word one might answer for everything? Such a word is neither eccentric nor central; it is motionless and carried, floating, never *pigeonholed*, always atopic (escaping any topic), at once remainder and supplement, a signifier taking up the place of every signified. The word has gradually appeared in his work; at first it was masked by the instance of Truth (that of history), then by that of validity (that of systems and structures); now it blossoms, it flourishes, this word-as-mana is the word 'body'.[9]

One can add to this sample a small list of words to show how in comprehensible the language of criticism has become in our time. We frequently come across today in the writings of the Post-Modernist critics words such as dialogic, discourse, enthymeme, exotopy, heteroglossia; agonaporia, differance, deconstruction, grammatology, logo-centrism, phallogocentrism; genotext, phenotext, multivalent, slippage, dispositif, episteme; androcentric, androgyny, biocriticism, biologism, gynocritic, pornoglossia, sexism; actualization, cratylism, idiolect, langue, parole, paradigm, diaspora; fetishism, flaneur, homology, ideologeme, etc., etc. Specialism forces the scholars to evolve their special languages known only to those who have acquired the required efficiency in the super specialty. The special voices cannot coexist in any common space. They must perforce remain alien to each other, each becoming a code communication, leaving no scope for general conversation.

Another bane of scientific spirit, notwithstanding its various virtues, is that, ultimately, it leads to the dehumanization of the human material. One could trace the course of scientific spirit from its early de-mystification of the universe to later despiritualization of society to further mechanization of human life to, finally, dehumanisation of mankind. Literature and literary criticism have always opposed science on this very ground, fighting all along the fast increasing forces of science and technology, industry and commerce. They have always stood for the preservation and promotion of humanism across national boundaries, racial reservations, or cultural constraints. It is a sad phenomenon today that the Post-Modernist critical approaches have adopted the scientific spirit of enquiry, making a casualty of the human concerns to which literature and literary criticism have always been closely related. The manner in which some of the brand products of Post-Modernism have chosen to champion the cultural, ethnic, or genderic causes, has in fact made the remedy worse than the disease. In the name of voicing the concerns of the hitherto repressed, colonized, marginalized, etc., discourses have been developed based solely on the differentiating features of 'cultural', 'ethnic' or 'genderic' life, promoting a new form of tribalism. In these discourses, mankind is viewed as an aggregation of cultural islands, suspicious of each other, clashing on the 'darkling plain',[10] accusing each other of having encroached upon their special rights. One is reminded of Plato's caves inhabited by tribes with horizons of the mind measuring the narrow holes of their respective caves, utterly unable to comprehend the open universe.

If literature and literary criticism are to perform their destined and true function, then they will have to return to the original path of the humanities, leaving the adopted path of sciences (including social sciences) which have deflected them from their prime duty to mankind. Today, what have become more important for criticism are, not the human concerns, but the purely non-human enquiries into the nature of things—a study of principles and processes, systems and structures. As for human concerns, they are conceived, if at all, only in terms of narrow, sectarian rights of groups divided by all sorts of 'spaces.' If we look at the titles of leading books and articles in the field of criticism today, the nature it has acquired, adopted, and imbibed becomes quite clear. The direction of its drift with the dominant current of science and technology becomes quite apparent. Here is a sample list of some of the titles from the vast verbal forest that has grown over the years: *The Semiotic Challenge* (Roland Barthes), *Of Grammatology* (Jacques Derrida), *Writing and Difference* (Derrida), *The Theory of Semiotics* (Umberto Eco), *The Archaeology of Knowledge* (Michel Foucault), *What is an Author?* (Foucault), *Logic and Conversation* (H.P. Grice), *Closing Statement: Linguistics and Poetics* (Roman Jakobson), *A Theory of Literary Production* (Pierre Macherey), *The System and the Speaking Subject* (Julia Kristeva), *The Theory of Reading* (David Morse), *Objectivity, Relativism and Truth* (Richard Rorty), *The Theory of Reading* (Frank Gloversmity), *Meaning and Truth in the Arts* (John Harpers), etc., etc. This list shows how criticism in our time has turned heavily theoretical and, finally, philosophical, focusing on either theorizing about how meaning is produced, or enquiring into the meaning of meaning, working of language, or the behaviour of words. In sum, the nature of criticism has acquired the character of science in all respects, turning away from the humanities, and has become a philosophico-scientific discipline called theory, which mixes literature with non-literary writings and the pseudo-literary films or journalism, and confines itself to the study of sociological behaviour of literary texts, their political overtones, their psychological suggestions, their anthropological patterns, their historical narrations, their linguistic structures, etc. The Post-Modernist criticism has done to literature what science had done to life; it has demystified its creation, despiritualized its contents, and de-humanized its interpretation.

Criticism today has been taken over by the disciplines of philosophy and psychology, sociology and anthropology, entirely changing the parameters of reading literary works. We no longer look for aesthetic or moral grounds for the appreciation of an art work. We look for the sub-texts and sub-structures, for faultlines and fictographs, using the apparatus borrowed from one of the disciplines just mentioned. The reason why this has happened is convincingly stated by Northrop Frye in the following:

> It is clear that the absence of systematic criticism has created a power vacuum, and all the neighbouring disciplines have moved in. Hence the prominence of the Archimedes fallacy . . . the notion that if we plant our feet solidly enough in Christian or democratic or Marxist values we shall be able to lift the whole of criticism at once with a dialectic crowbar. But if the varied interests of critics could be related to a central expanding pattern of systematic comprehension, this undertow would disappear, and they would be seen as converging on criticism instead of running away from it.[11]

Since Frye made this observation in 1957 much water has flown through the Thames. The critical activity has changed beyond recognition. All aspects of a literary work are talked about in the name of criticism except the aspect of literariness. What we have, in fact, is not literary criticism but only critical attitudes drawn from various disciplines that have claimed the vacancy the failure of criticism had created.

No doubt, the discussion of art, particularly literature, cannot confine itself to the formal aspect of art considered in utter isolation. It must consider as well the participation of the literary work in the human vision of the goal of social effort, 'the idea of complete and classless civilization. This idea of complete civilization is also the implicit moral standard to which ethical criticism always refers, something very different from any system of morals.'[12] Unfortunately, the current craze in criticism for the ideas of 'pluralism' and 'amoralism' has left the critical effort devoid of all moral and humane concerns. Its 'grand flourish of negativised rhetoric', comprising such impressive keywords as 'discontinuity, disruption, dislocation, decentring, indeterminacy, and antitotalization',[13] does hypnotise some intellectuals, but it leaves highly dissatisfied the steady explorer of ultimate meanings in literature as well as life. If pluralism means an assembly of mass individual or group opinions, if questioning means challenging one and all who have attained any respectability in society, then one might compare the Post-Modernist critical effort to a jungle of high pitched voices raised in closed corridors.

The goal of criticism must remain, as Frye insists: '. . . the ability to look at contemporary social values with the detachment of one who is able to compare them in some degree with the infinite vision of possibilities presented by culture. One who possesses such a standard of transvaluation is in a state of intellectual freedom.'[14]

The current critical effort refuses to decide upon any goal of literature or literary criticism beyond the contingent. It is high time that resistance was put up to the confusing critical cries of our time, paving the way for the restoration of the ever-abiding ethical goal of literature and literary criticism.

NOTES

1. The phrase is borrowed from Robert Frost's poem 'Birches'.
2. The phrase is borrowed from Henry James, cited in Tony Tanner's *City of Words* (London: Jonathan Cape, 1971), p. 9.
3. 'Characteristics of Shakespeare's Dramas', *Prose of the Romantic Period*, ed. Carl R. Woodring (Boston: Houghton, Mifflin, 1961), p. 125.
4. *Religion and the Modern Mind* (Philadelphia, 1952), cited in Hyatt H. Waggoner's *American Poets from the Puritans to the Present* (New York: Dell, 1968), p. 397.
5. *ABC of Reading*, cited in Waggoner, *American Poets*, p. 399.
6. 'Science and Poetry', *The Great Critics: An Anthology of Literary Criticism*, eds. Winfield Park and James Harry Smith (New York: Norton, 1951), pp. 740-1.
7. 'Tradition and Individual Talent', *The Great Critics*, p. 717.
8. *Letters on Poetry from W. B. Yeats to Dorothy Wellesley*, ed. Kathleen Raine (London: Oxford University Press, 1964), p. 58.
9. Roland Barthes, *The Pleasure of the Text* (1973), trans. Richard Howard (London: Jonathan Cape, 1976), p. 129.
10. The phrase is borrowed from Matthew Arnold's poem 'Dover Beach'.
11. *Anatomy of Criticism* (Princeton: Princeton University Press, 1957), p. 12.
12. Frye, *Anatomy of Criticism*, p. 348.
13. *Linda Hutcheon, A Poetics of Post-modernism: History, Theory, Fiction* (New York: Routledge, 1988), p. 200.
14. *Anatomy of Criticism*, p. 348.

Indian Literary Theory: Relevance and Retrieval

K. AYYAPPA PANIKER

This investigation into the contemporary relevance of traditional Indian poetics has been undertaken with a view to provide a fresh reading of some of the basic texts on Indian literary theory, on poetics and rhetoric in particular, in ancient Sanskrit and Tamil so as to establish their continued relevance and the need to update the long-established theories in the context of present-day literary perceptions.

The basic assumption here is that literary criticism, like literary creation, also evolves through historical periods and carries the imprint of different historical, social and cultural beliefs and practices that have been in force from time to time. This leads to the conclusion that the ancient theories are in need of fresh interpretation and substantive modification to suit the changing needs of the reading public. In matters of literary appreciation, the reader has a prime role to play. The works of one period will be understood and appreciated differently by different generations of readers. New works require new approaches. It is the view of the present writer that Indian classical theories are not dead entities, but are capable of further evolution and elaboration, and can help us read modern literary works also in the light provided by them.

This implies that both the pandits brought up on the orthodox traditional discipline and the new readers mostly dependent on new-fangled theories imported from the West have to shed their pet prejudices and unfounded preconceptions. Kālidāsa noted long ago that '*purānam ityeva na sādhu sarvam*' (old is not always gold). Along with the evolution of society, its perception of beauty also undergoes change. This necessitates a stock-taking and a reinterpretation of time-honoured literary

*An earlier version of this paper was published in *The Vishva-Bharati Quarterly*, October-December 1999.

theories like *rasa*, *dhvani*, *anumiti*, *vakrokti*, *guna*, *alankāra*, *rīti* and *aucitya* (in the Sanskrit tradition) and *tinai*, *akam*, *puram*, *ullurai*, *iraichi* and *meypadu* (in the Dravidian tradition).

Great thinkers like Swami Vivekananda have underscored the pluralist basis of Indian culture as well as the importance of the changes that have determined the course of its evolution, which ensures its *sanātana* or eternal validity, and preserves it from going moribund or static. Indian cultural ethos has always been dynamic, incorporating new developments from within as well as those stimulated by contact with other cultures. Change with continuity has been its hallmark. Centuries seem to co-exist in India, because of the Indian penchant for absorbing 'the other', and this may be seen most clearly in Indian aesthetics. The old continues to be relevant because of its resilience to adjust itself to new situations.

This means that we cannot and should not think of old theories as sacrosanct and immutable. They have been undergoing meaningful changes in the past. From Bharata to Ānandavardhana to Abhinavagupta to Jagannātha is a long journey. Then there came about some stagnation, but new types of writing then came into being. The taste of the reading public also changed. Appropriate changes are therefore necessary and possible in the modes of literary appreciation also.

The hypothesis explored here is that the hard core of traditional Indian poetics—both Sanskrit and Dravidian—is sound and relevant even today, and is applicable to contemporary literature not only of India, but of any other country. The basic universals of Indian poetics need not be abandoned in the now broadened perspective of world literatures, written in any language, Indian or non-Indian.

The dual aspects of any literary theory reveal that it has a regional origin but a wider application, beyond the bounds of the language or literature or culture which produced it, and that it has a historical period-tie, which can sometimes transcend the period of its origin. Without denying the special relevance of time and place of origin, one may think of the possible universality of the theories.

The updating of ancient theories has to be attempted with great care and circumspection. The purely local or period aspect has to be sidelined in order to explore the universal or all-time significance of aesthetic perceptions. No work of art is *swayambhu* or self-created; no work can be appreciated in total isolation from all other works. While the integrity and individuality of every work is to be honoured, it is sometimes useful to look at a work in the light of new theories not originally based on it.

Rasa (Aesthetic Emotion)

Perhaps the oldest statement about *rasa* is to be found in Chapters 5 and 6 of Bharatamuni's *Nāṭyaśāstra*. He discusses the different aspects of *rasa* here in the sequence of *rasa, bhāva, sangraha, karika* and *nirukta*. He says that several things have been left out which can be surmised. In *karikas* 5 and 6 of Chapter 6, he makes it clear that in no way can we find out the end of *nāṭya*, and this is because of the multiplicity of disciplines and the infinite number of works. He asks how we could understand the essence of all disciplines, when the ocean of even one discipline cannot be explained in full.

This implies that Bharata acknowledges the natural limitations of any theoretical formulation. His comments therefore should be taken as tentative, partial, and suggestive—not categorical and final. What he means by '*anumana prasadhaka*' is that all theories should be understood as a framework for inference. This inference potential should be drawn upon by those who want to expound old theories or construct new ones. The definitions and listings in Bharata should be taken as a basis for the construction of actual theories with a wider application, and not as a theoretical stranglehold.

This can be explained with reference to some of the issues which have given rise to meaningless controversies in the past. The definition of *rasa*, the number of *rasas*, concepts such as *rasābhasa*, the nomenclature of the different *rasas*, the interrelationship of the *rasas*, etc., may have to be treated as open-ended categories, and not as unimaginative mechanical formulae. Evidence for divergent interpretations may be found even in Bharata as well as his successors. Some of them have argued for eight *rasas*, some have conceived of *shānta*, *vātsalya* and *bhakti* as valid *rasas*. What is important is not the number and names of *rasas* or *bhāvas*. The classification into *angarasa* and *angi-rasa*, and the ways in which they can be identified in particular literary works clearly suggest that a critic is free to go to the extent of identifying the specific *rasa* of a particular work coining new names or going beyond Bharata's list. In the past critics have used this kind of freedom of interpretation: so have some argued that there is only one *rasa*, some have identified it as *shringāra*, others as *karuna.* One may even consider all *bhavas* as being capable of becoming *rasas.*

V. Raghavan, in his study of Bhoja's *Śṛṅgaraprakāśa*, for instance, observes:

> In this middle stage, Bhoja would recognize not merely eight Rasas, but as many Rasas as there are Bhavas; for, to him, all the Bhavas, in the middle stage, are equal. There is no distinction among them that eight or more of them are 'permanent' (sthayins), thirty-three are transient (sancarins) and eight are sattvikas. All of them are born of the one Ahamkara; all of them can become sthayins; all of them are according to circumstances, and all of them are sattvikas, because they are all mind-born sattva meaning nothing more than mind.[1]

When there is a need to identify a new *rasa* for the dominant or basic emotion presented in a work, one is free to do so. The pity-fear complex, which underscores the Western notion of tragedy, according to Aristotle, can be discussed under the broader concept of *rasa.* The point is not what we call it, but how we bring out the success or failure of the author in projecting the basic emotion (call it x, y, or z).

Such a broad interpretation of terms like *bhāva, vibhāva, ālambana, uddīpana*, etc., will help clarify this and avoid the obscurantism indulged in by unimaginative pandits for long. Instead of endlessly pursuing the game of classification and categorization and sub categorization, the critic or reader has to examine how successful the author of a work is in projecting the concerned emotion, whatever its name be.

The updating of *rasa* theory requires at least four steps to be taken as preliminary:

(1) Make all ancient theoretical texts available in modern Indian languages.
(2) Fill up omissions, explain deficiencies, add new concepts to those basic texts.
(3) Get comprehensive studies of individual works in the light of the updated *rasa* theory.
(4) Recast the received theory on the basis of practical criticism.

In short, the direction should be from theory to the works and back to the theory.

Dhvani (Suggestiveness)

That poetry makes its impact on the reader by its power of suggestion is perhaps accepted by critics all over the world. Figurative meaning, rather than the literal or dictionary meaning of words, is considered the most important feature of great poetry in all languages. How does it become more than a mere truism in the context of Indian poetics? That it was not considered the most valuable aspect of poetry in India at one time is clear from Anandavardhana's attempt to defend it against its detractors in the opening section of *Dhvanyāloka*.

The way the primacy of *dhvani* is established is perhaps indicated by means of a hierarchic pattern:

(i) *Rasa* depends on *bhāva*.
(ii) *Bhāva* is derived from meaning.
(iii) Meaning may be literal (*vācya*) or figurative (*vyangya*).
(iv) Figurative meaning is superior to the literal.
(v) The former may obliterate the latter.
(vi) That poetry which is realized through *dhvani* is the best.

Twelve types of the operation of *dhvani* are identified by Bhoja on the basis of how this operation takes place:

1. Prohibition from Injunction.
2. Injunction from Prohibition.
3. Injunction from Injunction
4. Prohibition from Prohibition.
5. Injunction from Injunction and Prohibition.
6. Prohibition from Injunction and Prohibition.
7. Injunction from a case of neither Injunction nor Prohibition.
8. Prohibition from a case of neither Injunction nor Prohibition.
9. Neither Injunction nor Prohibition from an Injunction.
10. Neither Injunction nor Prohibition from a Prohibition.
11. Neither Injunction nor Prohibition from a case of Injunction and Prohibition.
12. Neither Injunction nor Prohibition from a case of neither Injunction nor Prohibition.

If *dhvani* is a third meaning realized after the literal and the implied meanings are realized, then it is like an echo, which is outside of the word, and tertiary in derivation. The Dravidian concept of '*ullurai*' is that it is inherent in the word, neither outside nor tertiary. '*Ullurai*' is the inner meaning, and it is to be investigated how it can be related to *dhvani*.

Sometimes *dhvani* is said to be the sentence meaning, which evolves out of the meanings of individual words, just as *rasa* is said to evolve from the concerned *vibhāvas*. Here the ratio seems to be: word meaning:sentence meaning::*vibhāvas:rasa*. The appreciation of poetry thus consists in discovering the sentence meaning, which corresponds to *rasa*.

It is possible to extend the concept of *dhvani* to a whole text or discourse, without limiting it to the word or sentence episode. It is not to be confined to a single word or expression; the cumulative effect of suggested meanings throughout a discourse can be tremendous. For example, in Shakespeare's *Macbeth*, all expressions used by Lady Macbeth (like 'unsex me here') carry the apotheosis of cruelty not just in the character of Lady Macbeth alone, but in the whole play. She too appears to be possessed by the evil that emanates from the witches.

Krishna Rayan has in a series of books dwelt upon the potential of *dhvani* as the ultimate key to poetry. He especially connects this concept to modernist poetry. Suggestion, he finds, is a dominant characteristic of modernist literary practice. In texts like *The Waste Land*, or *Ulysses*, or *Waiting for Godot*, the literal meaning is almost irrelevant and inoperative. The *dhvani* reverberation obliterates the literal altogether. Perhaps the rejection of metrical devices also marks a shift of emphasis from the physical/literal to the implied or metaphoric level.

Dhvani, it appears, is an effective means of bypassing cliché and stereotype. When words lose their semantic richness through over-use or wrong use, *dhvani* functions as a source of enrichment for the meaning, or the 'difference' seems to come close to *dhvani*. In *King Lear*, the word 'nothing' is used to deadly effect. It not only implies that the literal meaning is nothing or just insignificant, but also elevates 'nothing', or absence of any literal sense, to a level of explosive potency. Nothing becomes everything. That is perhaps to say, without *dhvani*, everything is reduced to nothing.

Anumiti (Inference)

While Anandavardhana's school conceived of *dhvani* or suggestion as the soul of poetry, Mahimabhatta's school advocated that what matters in poetry is not any kind of meaning inherent or subsisting in the words of the text. Mahimabhatta's work, *Vyaktiviveka*, is an attempt to refute the position of *dhvani*. He thus rejects the claims of the *dhvani* school. The main point of contention is that the second meaning is not located in the linguistic expression, but in the logical skill of the reader.

Sankuka had found that the signified was the work of the signifier, that the former was understood in the latter. Whether meaning comes from the relationship between words, or the relationship comes from their meaning, was the object of his investigation. Meaning is what the reader infers from the signifier. Fire is inferred from the smoke, which itself may be directly perceived. It is the result of intellection. According to Sankuka, therefore, *rasa* is the indirect inference, since the basic mental state is never presented directly by the *vibhavas*. *Rasa*, therefore, is never directly experienced; it is only the *pratīti* arising from inference.

The *anumiti* school does not accept any power for words other than *abhidhā*. *Laksanā* is included in *vyañjanā*, and both are derived by inference, and therefore not inherent and automatic. Both the *dhvani* school and the *anumiti* school accept the role of *vyañjanā*, but the *anumiti* school maintains that 'the apprehension of the suggested meaning is no other than the activity involved in drawing an inference from the sign'.

The objections of the *anumiti* school are based on certain fundamental concepts such as follows:

1. The primary meaning is always the literal one.
2. This literal meaning is the same as the root meaning.
3. There is no need to distinguish three kinds of meaning.
4. Meaning really operates not in the word or the sentence, but in the mind of the reader.
5. There is no meaning—whether *abhidhā* or *laksanā* or *vyañjanā* in a word or sentence, unless it is felt by the reader.
6. The *roodhi* or *yoga* or *yoga-roodhi* meanings are all inherent in the word or sentence.
7. The classification of meaning into *laksya*, *laksanā* and *vyañjanā* is not correct.
8. *Laksanā* and *vyañjanā* do not really exist. What is important is not varieties of meaning, but varieties of usage. So the meaning that the reader infers is what matters in literature.

Anumiti establishes the centrality of the reader's role. This brings it very close to the current Western notion of reader-response. What Wolfgang Iser calls 'the wandering eye'[2] implies the tentative formulations of meaning or interpretation that a reader goes on making while reading a text. Terry Eagleton is of the view that 'the reader makes implicit connections, fills in gaps, draws inferences, and tests out hunches, and to do this means drawing on a tacit knowledge of the world in general and of literary convention in particular'.[3]

As an alternative or even correction to the *dhvani* theory, the inferential approach makes us realize the importance of the *sahrdaya* or ideal reader. It may be possible to reconcile the two systems, if it can be conceded that there is an element of suggestion in the inference made by the reader. The reader is able to make an inference because there is something in the literal meaning which probably prompts the reader to make the inference. If no such reconciliation is attempted, the two systems may be accepted as parallel to each other.

Modern theories of semiotics also have a lot in common with the *anumiti* theory. The interrelationship of the sign, the signifier and the signified could best be explained or understood in terms of *anumiti*.

The role of the reader as creator of meaning of the work is enhanced by the process of inference. This theory may also help us understand the true nature of creation itself. A work of art is not a finished product when it reaches the reader. It is perpetually in the process of being made. That work which draws the reader into this process, which invites the reader's participation, may appear to be perhaps better composed than the one that tells everything, leaving nothing to the imagination. The notion of the reader as co-creator is a corrective to the idea of the poet as the sole creator (*kavireka prajapati*).

Vakrokti (Deviance)

One of the most misunderstood terms in ancient Sanskrit poetics is often reduced to mere *uktivaicitrya* or strangeness of expression. Although Bhamaha and Dandin had already dealt with this concept, the credit for having raised it to the level of universality goes to Kuntaka. According to Kuntaka, *vakrokti* is the very life of poetry. By *vakrokti* he means what distinguishes poetic expression from non-poetic expression. It is not just round-about-ness in speech or circumlocution.

Vakrokti, conceived not as a particular figure of speech but as a general term for poetic excellence, is more comprehensive than *vyañjanā*. All aspects of *dhvani* and *alankāra* are, according to Kuntaka, implicit in *vakratā*. He has identified an elaborate system of multiple *vakratā*, covering all aspects of poetry. Deviance at all levels—sound, letter, morpheme, word, phrase, sentence, episode, discourse, etc.—was his concern.

Below the sentence level, *vakratā* may appear as operating like a figure of speech. But at the higher levels of episode or discourse—*prakarana* or *prabandha*—it raises questions of fundamental significance. Kalidasa's *Abhijñāśākuntalam* marks a deviance from the *Mahābhārata* story—the role of the *abhijñāna* is crucial not to the original story but to the play. Milton's *Paradise Lost* constitutes a deviation from the *Bible*.

The modern theory of intertextuality may be studied in relation to this notion of *vakratā*. The interconnectedness between Nalopakhyāna in the *Mahābhārata* and Unnayi Varier's *Nalacharitam Altakkatha* throws light not only on the two authors or two periods of history, but on two kinds of texts.

Perhaps the post-modernist view of self-reflexivity, pastiche, parody and textual subversion can also be considered an application of *vakratā*. Contemporary literature the world over has thrown up many works which are actually deviants of earlier writing. Shakespeare in his time had reworked earlier texts without compunction; today many of his own plays have been subverted by playwrights like Stoppard, Bond, and others. Robert Graves once said, 'There is one story, and one story only.' But there are umpteen ways of telling it, and the differences may be explained as *vakrokti* or variation.

Appreciation of literary works manifesting *vakrokti* relationship is facilitated by comparative estimates. Shashi Tharoor's *The Great Indian Novel* may be read as a subversive version of the *Mahābhārta*, as a narrative of the freedom struggle and as a discourse on fictional creativity.

The study of motifs of folklore can also be related to the notion of *vakrokti*. Structuralism as well as post-structuralism provides opportunities for further application of *vakrokti*.

Guna/Dosa (Poetic Virtues and Blemishes)

All criticism involves the identification of good and bad. The classification of works as good or bad is indulged in by ordinary readers as well. But at the more sophisticated level one may prepare a schemata to distinguish and isolate the bad from the good. Most often notions of good and bad—at the popular level at least—are quite misleading. The bestsellers of today are seldom recognized as classics in the long run. It is not possible to evaluate the qualities of a bestseller as positive merits or *gunas*. Indian poetics, with characteristic alacrity, has codified virtues and vices, and the diehards of yesteryears castigated works and authors on the basis of what they called *gunas* or *dosas*.

It may be argued here that merits and blemishes are relative terms: the time of composition, the nature of readership (both intended and actual), the language, the literary context, the genre, the mode of presentation (oral or written or performative)—without taking into account several such relevant parameters, literary evaluation cannot be properly attempted. No quality can *per se* be a merit for all time in all kinds of works. What may be good in a heroic poem may not be so in a lyric or satire. Sweetness may be a good quality in a certain type of work in a certain period, but it can easily cloy, and be quite ridiculous in other types. Absolute good and absolute bad probably have no place in literary discourse. Virtues can become blemishes, and vice versa, depending on several factors.

The *guna* and *dosa* qualifications have been meticulously enumerated and classified in Indian critical texts like the works of Dandin, Bhoja and others. Bhoja identifies 16 blemishes in the use of vocabulary, 10 in the use of sentences, and 16 at the level of sentence meaning.[4]

Just as it is difficult, useless and even dangerous to categorize merits and blemishes for all time and all places, it is necessary to anticipate and eradicate prejudices. These may be identified at the level of vocabulary, sentence structure, the plot, etc. *Rasābhāsa* may be a blemish where it is not purposeful and functional. Rāvana's love for Sitā is an instance of *śrngārābhāsa* not *śrngāra*; but it is perfectly legitimate in the portrayal of Rāvana's character. Such behaviour suits him, but in Rāma's portrayal it will be a blemish.

Rīti (Stylistics)

The propounder of every school in Indian poetics claims his theory to be superior to every other theory. This, as a matter of fact, is something he shares with his Western counterpart. Vāmana identifies *rīti* as the soul of poetry. It has been pointed out that the word *rīti* comes from the root *ri*, which means path or method. Vāmana identified three varieties of style on the basis of the quality of diction and word structure. He chose to call them *vaidarbhi*, *gowdi*, and *pānchāli*. Based on the number of compound words, Rudrata added *latiya* as the fourth. Bhoja added two more: *avanti* and *magadhi*, probably under the influence of the regional variations of *pravritti* in *Nātyaśātra*. Saradatanaya took into account certain other criteria, such as figures of sound like alliteration and rhyme. Simhabhupala then added *āndhri*, *saurāshtri*, etc.

Critics who start from the position of Indian poetics may not find the word 'style' to be as expressive as '*rīti*', while those with roots in the West like V.K. Chari may find that there is no equivalent for style in Sanskrit. The problem here too, as in the case of *rasa*, should not be confined to the number and nomenclature of the different varieties. What the critic then should do is to use this as an effective tool to evaluate and appreciate literary works.

Western stylistics—whether based on classical rhetoric or on modern linguistics—has devised ways of using its findings to promote literary criticism. Once the basic features of diction and syntax are identified, one might proceed to the manner and extent of their impact on the sensibility of the reader. The author makes his choices, the critic can identify them, but the chief beneficiary is the reader.

No theory is for its own sake. The relevance of its application can be proved only in relation to specific texts. When the response of the readers is taken into account, it should become clear that *rīti* by itself cannot explain the greatness of a work. *Rīti* is just one of the means at the disposal of the writer to stimulate experiences in the reader. Hence, *rīti* should be studied in close association with other theories, based on *rasa*, *dhvani*, *alankāra*, etc., and not in isolation from them.

Indian poetics associates certain *rītis* with certain qualities or *gunas* like *prasāda*, *ojas*, etc. Generalizations apart, the effect of a particular *rīti* in a particular context in a particular work is what matters. There are no good styles and bad styles as such: the terms are relative to the contextual use. Once the linguistic features are broadly identified, one has perhaps to move on to rhetoric, or higher stylistics. Thematological stylistics may be more effective in the context of literary study, analysis, and evaluation.

Alankāra (Tropes)

As in the case of *vakrokti*, there has been a deterioration of meaning in the case of *alankāra* too. *Alankāra* may signify individual tropes like simile (*upamā*), hyperbole (*atiśayokti*), etc., which are often conceived as ornaments, hence detachable from the body of poetry and non-essential to its soul.

Here again, the Indian genius for classification and categorization has created havoc. *Alankāra* in its profound or nobler sense refers to metaphor, which is not the mere dress of thought. It is an aspect of thought itself—thought or feeling makes its appeal because of its sweetness or intensity or sincerity, etc. From literal comparison to logical analogy to poetic metaphor, the movement is one of qualitative significance. Thus *alankāra*, in its essence, constitutes the stuff of poetic experience. Whether words such as 'like' are used or not has no effect on the poetry itself. The effect is greater when the metaphor is not explicit and obtrusive.

The names and number of tropes have nothing to do with the effect of metaphor in poetry. The elevation of tropes as the most distinctive feature of poetry is a mark of the decline of poetry and true criticism in India. *Alankāra*, in the larger sense of metaphor, has an important place in literary studies. Not at the word or sentence level, but at the level of episode or *prakarana*, or at the level of whole discourse or *prabandha* can *alankāra* function with force and carry conviction. In this sense, *alankāra* becomes almost synonymous with *dhvani* or *anumiti* or *guna* or *rīti*—where a whole episode or a total work may have the status of a symbol or metaphor.

The cloud in Kālidāsa's *Meghadūta*, the wind in Shelley's 'Ode to the West Wind', the cloth imagery in Shakespeare's *Macbeth*, etc., are examples of *brihad-alankāra* or grand metaphor. Wolfgang Clemen's study of Shakespeare's imagery provides a good testimony to the effectiveness of *alankāra* study. Perhaps more important than the stray or casual *alankāra* is the recurring trope or what may be called the integral *alankāra*, which binds a whole work together.

Tinai (Landscape)

Porulatikaram, the third part of the ancient Tamil text *Tolkappiyam*,[5] is the earliest basic text of Dravidian poetics now available to us. It contains an early model of ecopoetics, insofar as it tries to relate poetry to the time and place of its origin. The first principles or *mutal porul* are the landscape of the region as well as the time of the day and the year under reference. The assumption here is that human emotions are conditioned by environmental factors. Ancient Sangam poetry in Tamil evokes those features.

All poetry is divided into *akam* and *puram* types. *Akam* poems may be said to deal with subjective experiences; they are personal, individual-centred and self-directed. *Puram* poems are generally concerned with outdoor life, with heroic exploits, adventure, etc., and concentrate on impersonal or social experiences and events. Together they may be called poems of love and war, although these are not the only concerns or themes. The classification is not so neat as it might look, for sentiments other than the heroic and the romantic are also expressed in Sangam poetry. There are seven *tinais* or regions identified in *Porulatikaram* for each of these two major divisions. Each *tinai* for the two groups is named after a plant or a flower. The major *akattinais* are *mullai*, *kurinji*, *plalai*, *marutam*, and *neyial*, besides unproductive *tinais* like *kaikkilai* and *perumtinai*. The *tinais* marked out for *puram* poetry are *paadaan*, *vanchi*, *vetchi*, *vakai*, *uzhinai*, *tumpa*, and *kanchi*.

What is important here is, again, not the number or nomenclature of the *tinais*, but the approach to poetry through the time-place complex revealed in the poem. These *tinais* are said to correspond to various human emotions, which in turn are evoked by the flora and fauna of the respective regions. The triadic system of *mulal-karu-uriporul*, i.e. the time/place, the flora/fauna, and the emotions, seem to represent the basic essence of *tinai* poetics.

Tolkappiyar apparently identified only 14 *tinais*, for *akam* and *puram* combined, but one may add many more to his list, if literature other than from south India is taken into account. The sea novels of Joseph Conrad, for instance, would argue for a *katal tinai* (sea-scape); here the *karu porul* will be different from those of the *karai-tinai* (land-scape). The appropriate *uriporul* may also have to be identified. Modern novels located in the metropolitan cities are likely to be concerned with an urban *tinai* or *nagara-tinai*. Even in *Tolkappiyam* there is no rigid mechanical insistence on exclusive concentration on unimportant details pertaining to each *tinai*. In Dostoevski the natural *tinai* may be the Russian or Siberian landscape; in Margaret Laurence it may be the prairie that forms the proper *tinai*.

When one uses the *tinai* approach for the interpretation of poetry, one must first of all ascertain whether a poem belongs to the *akam* or *puram* type or a mixture of both. Then one may proceed to identify the landscape and the season or part of the day that is particularly relevant. The reference to time, it is suggested here, may be taken to indicate perhaps the period of history as well, i.e. a larger unit of time than the day or the year. When one looks at a historical novel from France, for instance, the specifically French location of the events narrated and the specific period of European history may also be found significant. This is to say that both micro-time and macro-time may be taken into account in any total literary evaluation.

The interrelationship of the *tinais* is yet another point of interest in the *tinai* approach. The mixing of *tinais* was sanctioned in *Tolkappiyam* itself—which is a master-stroke of openness and freedom from orthodoxy. There can also be the coexistence of different *tinais* in a work that is either long or complex. Like *tinai mayakkam*, there can be *tinai pinakkam*, which can be used to achieve ironic contrasts, as in Shakespeare's *Macbeth*, where the battlefied, the heath, and the palace appear in quick succession. The sudden shift of contrary environments upsets the emotional equilibrium of the play. And a moving Birnam wood symbolizes the ecological disaster already prefigured by the sight of ghosts and sleepwalking.

Nadodi Siddhantam (*Folk Poetics*)

Folk literature is basically oral. Since it is transmitted orally from one generation to another, and possibly from one place to another, it is prevented from becoming fixed in meaning and form. This ensures the creative flexibility natural to it. Classical literature in this respect appears to offer a sharp contrast to folk literature.

Folk literature does not seem to have anywhere a long tradition of sustained criticism based on constructed theories. It is almost all practice and very little theory. But one may discover in it a poetics different from that of classical literature, although this dichotomy sometimes leads to misunderstanding rather than enlightenment. Ideally, folk poetics is, and will perhaps always remain, uncodified or under-codified. Perpetual flux accounts for its rich variety and vitality.

Folk literature is not the creation of an individual. It is the work of communal authorship. It has therefore no authorized or definitive form. It may not have any preconceived structure or form. This liberates creativity and preserves dynamism. Spontaneity is maintained, because it continues to evolve perpetually. No work of folk literature has a final closure. Most works are open-ended, providing for improvization.

These features are shared by folk literature all over the world; these may therefore be considered universal. The presence of a rhythmic undercurrent, like that of the sequence of day and night or the cycle of seasons, is deeply felt in all folk literature.

The creator-appreciator or performer-spectator dichotomy does not seem to apply to folk literature. Since the work is seldom mediated through print, the auditor-spectator is often a participant in creation.

Folk literature maintains an impersonality different from that of classical Indian literature. The *apaurusheya* or non-personal stance of classical literature is the result of an attempt at conscious extinction of personality. But that of folk literature everywhere is the result of group participation.

The integral unity—not uniformity—of oral folk literature is reinforced by repetitions, which are often incremental in nature, like the half-repeated refrain and the perpetual variation of the order of items. They are half repetitions and half variations.

Local colour is very prominent in folk literature. Such uniformity as the folk literature of one language or country may share with folk literature elsewhere comes from the universality at the grass roots level. Inclusiveness, rather than exclusiveness, is the distinctive feature of folk art and folk culture anywhere in the world.

NOTES

1. V. Raghavan, *Bhoja's Śṛṅgāraprakāśa*, 3rd rev. enl. ed. (Madras: Punarvasu, 1976), pp. 401-2.
2. Wolfgang Iser, *The Act of Reading: A Theory of Aesthetic Response* (Baltimore: John Hopkins Univ., 1978).
3. Terry Eagleton, *Literary Theory: An Introduction* (Oxford: Blackwell, 1983; rpt. 1994), p. 76.
4. Raghavan, *Bhoja's Śṛṅgāraprakāśa*, Chs. XV, XVI.
5. *Tolkappiyam*, ascribed to Tolkappiyar, written in ancient Tamil, available in Malyalam transliteration and translation has been used by the writer.

Notes on Contributors

DINESH DADHICHI, who translated Bhisham Sahni's article into English, is Reader, Department of English, Kurukshetra University, and is a creative writer of Hindi. His two collections of poems are *Ibarat Hashiye Ki* (1983) and *Burj Ke Khilaaf* (1999), and a collection of essays *Neembu-Pani* (1993). He has abridged and translated an Oxford University Press edition of *Godan* (1996).

BHIM S. DAHIYA, former Vice-Chancellor of Kurukshetra University, has taught English and American literatures at various universities in India and abroad. He is known for his critical books and articles on American literature, especially those on Ernest Hemingway. He has also written extensively on higher education. His latest book on education is *The University Autonomy in India: The Idea and the Reality* (IIAS, 2001).

AMIYA DEV, former Vice-Chancellor of Vidyasagar University, taught Comparative Literature at Jadavpur University for nearly four decades. He writes criticism both in Bengali and English. He was editor of the *Jadavpur Journal of Comparative Literature* for more than a decade and was Vice-President of the International Comparative Literature Association for six years. He has recently edited, with Earl Minerva, a volume of essays on the lyric *The Renewal of Song: Renovation in Lyric Conception and Practice* (Seagull Books).

MAHASWETA DEVI is the well known Bengali short story writer, novelist, playwright and social activist whose works have been translated into many Indian and foreign languages. Among the various awards bestowed on her are the Jnanpith award (1996), Padmashree (1986), Sahitya Akademi award (1979) and Magsaysay award (1996). Some of her distinguished works are *Aranyer Adhikar* (1977), *Agnigarbha* (1978), *Hazaar Chaurashir Ma* (1974). Some of the distinguished translations of her works are *Breast Stories* and *Imaginary Maps* (trans. Gayatri Chakravorti Spivak) and *Bitter Soil: Palamu Stories* (trans. Samik Bandopadhyaya).

TEJWANT S. GILL, former Professor of English at GNDU, Amritsar, and Fellow of the Indian Institute of Advanced Study (1999-2001), is currently editor of the Punjabi daily *Desh Sevak*. He writes both in English and Punjabi, and has translated several Punjabi poets, novelists and playwrights into English. Some of his recent publications are *Pash* (1999), *Surjit Patar: Jeevan te Rachana* (2000), *Reckoning with Dark Times* (2000).

SUZETTE A. HENKE is Morton Pofessor of English at the University of Louisville, KY, USA. She is the author of *Joyce's Moraculous Sindbook: A Study of 'Ulysses'*, and *James Joyce and the Politics of Desire* (Routledge, 1990), and co-editor of *Women in Joyce*. She has published numerous articles in the field of Modern Literature and Women's Studies. Her most recent book is *Shattered Subjects: Trauma and Testimony in Women's Life-Writing* (2000).

JAIDEV, born at Jwalapur (Haridwar), brought up at Shamli, had his education at Shamli, Muzaffarnagar and Meerut University. He joined Himachal Pradesh University in 1972 as Lecturer and became Professor in 1991, with a brief tenure as Reader at MDU, Rohtak (1979-81). He was awarded British Council Scholarship for a year in 1977 and went to the University of East Anglia to work on Angus Wilson. He went to York University, Toronto, in 1993 on a Faculty Research Fellowship awarded by Shastri Indo-Canadian Institute. He was a Fellow of the Indian Institute of Advanced Study (1989-92) where he wrote his much acclaimed book *The Culture of Pastiche* (IIAS, 1993). His edited books include *On Literature* (1990), co-edited *Social Awareness in Modern Indian Literature* and *Cultural Reorientation in Modern India* (1996). He translated into English Bhisham Sahni's *Basanti* (1997), and also edited the first number of *Studies in Humanities and Social Sciences* (1994). For past some years he had also started writing with equal felicity in Hindi as well and had been writing for *Samakaaleen Sahitya*.

JASBIR JAIN, former Professor of English at the University of Rajasthan, is currently Director IRIS and K.K. Birla Fellow. She has written extensively on Feminist, Postcolonial and Indian writing. Among her recent publications are *Contextualising Modernism: The Novel in India 1880-1950* (in Punjabi) (Ludhiana, 2001), *Creative Theory: Writers on Writing*, (Delhi, 2000), and (ed.) *Contesting Postcolonialisms* (Jaipur, 2000).

SUKRITA PAUL KUMAR is a poet and critic and teaches English at University of Delhi. A former fellow of the India Institute of Advanced Study, she has three collections of poems and some of her other publications are *The New Story, Ismat: Her Life, Her Times, Conversations on Modernism, Breakthrough: Short Stories of Hindi and Urdu*, and edited *Mapping Memories*. She has also translated an Urdu novel into English, *Sleepwalkers*.

ARUN PRABHA MUKHERJEE is Associate Professor of English at York University, Toronto, Canada. From February to June 2000 she was Vice-President, Shastri Indo-Canadian Institute. She has written extensively in the areas of Postcolonialism and Women's Studies. Among her books are *Postcolonialism: My Living* (TSAR, Toronto, 1998), *Oppositional Aesthetics: Readings from a Hyphenated Space* (TSAR, Toronto, 1995). She has edited with an Introduction *Sharing Our Experience* (Canadian Advisory Council on the Status of Women, Ottawa, 1993). Most recently, she is one of the six members who put together *York Stories: Women in Higher Education* (TSAR, Toronto, 2000).

MEENAKSHI MUKHERJEE, until recently Professor of English at Jawaharlal Nehru University, Delhi, is at present Honorary Professor, University of Hyderabad. Founder-editor of the journal *Vagartha* (1973-9), she writes fiction criticism both in English and Bangla. Her books include *The Twice Born Fiction* (1971), *Realism and Reality: Novel and Society in India* (1985), *Re-reading Jane Austen* (1993) and *The Perishable Empire* (2000).

HARISH NARANG is Professor of English at Jawaharlal Nehru University, Delhi. His areas of specialization are African literature and literary translation. Among his publications are *Politics as Fiction* and an edited volume *Mightier than Matchette*. His translations in Hindi include *Janta ka Adami, Is Sadi ki Prem Kahani, Uhuru Street*. He is currently translating into Hindi *The Book of Secrets* by M.G. Vassanji.

K. AYYAPPA PANIKER is a renowned poet, critic and translator in Malayalam and English. Among the many awards bestowed on him are Sahitya Akademi (1984), Kerala Sahitya Akademi (1974), Kabir Samman (1997), etc. Founder editor of *Kerala Kavita* (1968-) he is the chief editor of *Sahitya Akademi Encylopedia of Indian Literature* (rev. ed. 1999-). He has edited World Classics and Complete Works of Shakespeare in Malayalam translation. A prolific writer, he has 4 volumes of poetry, 10 monographs in English and 10 collections of criticism in Malayalam. He has translated Russian, English and Indian authors into Malayalam.

E.V. RAMAKRISHNAN, is Professor of English, South Gujarat University, Surat, and writes in both English and Malayalam. Some of his English publications are *Making it New: Modernism in Malayalam, Marathi and Hindi Poetry* (IIAS, 1995), and *A Python in a Snake Park* (1994), and he has edited *The Tree of Tongues: An Anthology of Modern Indian Poetry*, and *Indian Short Story 1900-2000*. His Malayalam book *Aksharavum Adhunikathayum* won the Kerala Sahitya Akademi award for criticism in 1995.

VEPA RAO is a poet, short story writer and journalist. A veteran journalist who was the Sunday Editor of *The Hindustan Times* for many years, Vepa Rao is currently Professor of Journalism at Himachal Pradesh University, Shimla. He writes for *The Statesman* regularly. A former fellow of the Indian Institute of Advanced Study, he is the author of *A Curve in the Hills: Communication and Development* (IIAS: 1996) and a collection of poem *Liquid Folds*. Another book of poems *Still Beats* is in the pipeline.

BHISHAM SAHNI is the well known Hindi novelist, short story writer and playwright whose works have been translated into many Indian and foreign languages. Among the many awards bestowed on him are Padma Bhushan (1998) and Sahitya Akademi award (1976) for *Tamas*. His other important novels are *Basanti, Maiya Das ki Mari, Kunto* and more recently *Nilu Neelima Nilofer*. Among his plays are *Hanush, Kabira Khara Bazaar Mein, Madhavi, Muavze*. He has also translated Russian works into Hindi.